Windows 10

ALL-IN-ONE

for
dummies

A Wiley Brand

Windows 10

ALL-IN-ONE

for dummies®

A Wiley Brand

2nd edition

by Woody Leonhard

A Wiley Brand

Windows 10 All-in-One For Dummies®, 2nd Edition

Published by: **John Wiley & Sons, Inc.**, 111 River Street, Hoboken, NJ 07030-5774, www.wiley.com

Copyright © 2016 by John Wiley & Sons, Inc., Hoboken, New Jersey

Published simultaneously in Canada

For general information on our other products and services, please contact our Customer Care Department within the U.S. at 877-762-2974, outside the U.S. at 317-572-3993, or fax 317-572-4002. For technical support, please visit https://hub.wiley.com/community/support/dummies.

Wiley publishes in a variety of print and electronic formats and by print-on-demand. Some material included with standard print versions of this book may not be included in e-books or in print-on-demand. If this book refers to media such as a CD or DVD that is not included in the version you purchased, you may download this material at http://booksupport.wiley.com. For more information about Wiley products, visit www.wiley.com.

Library of Congress Control Number: 2016950189

ISBN 978-1-119-31056-3 (pbk); ISBN 978-1-119-31060-0 (ebk); ISBN 978-1-119-31059-4 (ebk)

Manufactured in the United States of America

10 9 8 7 6 5 4 3 2 1

Contents at a Glance

Table of Contents

Introduction

Think of Windows 8/8.1 as an extended, really bad, no good, horrible nightmare. Microsoft's woken up now. They fired almost everybody who ran the Win8 operation, cleaned out the house, and brought in some truly gifted engineers. Windows 10's a brand new day. Whether it's *your* brand new day is another story.

Windows 10 looks a little bit like Windows 7 and a little bit like Windows 8.1. It doesn't work like either of them, but for the billion-and-a-half Windows users out there, at least it's recognizable as Windows.

If you haven't yet taken the plunge with Windows 10, I advise you to go slowly. Microsoft is furiously working on extending the product and shoring up problems. The Windows 10 you know today will change in a few months, and you may like the new one better. Before installing Windows 10, I would simply . . . count to ten.

For most Windows 8 and 8.1 users, Win10 is a no-brainer. You can kvetch about some problems — the disappearance of Windows Media Center, for example — and Microsoft cloud storage OneDrive users are going to have a hard time adapting to the now-you-see-it-now-you-don't interface (see Book 6, Chapter 1) until Microsoft figures out how to fix it. There are dozens of additional details, but by and large, Windows 10 is what Windows 8.1 should've been.

Windows 7 users, though, don't have as much incentive to move to Windows 10, but there are some good changes. Microsoft effectively ditched Internet Explorer and built a much lighter and more capable browser, called Microsoft Edge. Instead of desktop gadgets, which in Win7 were held together with baling wire and chewing gum, Win10 sports an entire infrastructure for tiled Universal apps. Win10 works with all the new hardware, touch, and pens. There's an improved Task Manager, File Explorer, and a dozen other system utilities.

Is that enough to convince Win7 users to abandon ship in droves? Probably not. The single biggest allure of Windows 10 for the Win7 battle-hardened is that it's clearly the way of the future.

If you want a better Windows, for whatever reason, you'll have to go through Windows 10.

Here's what you should ask yourself before you move from Windows 7 to Windows 10:

>> Are you willing to learn a new operating system, with a number of new features that may or may not appeal to you?

>> Are you willing to let Microsoft snoop on your actions, more than they do with Windows 7? We don't know exactly what's being snooped, but it appears to be roughly on par with Google snooping and arguably less intrusive than Apple snooping.

>> Are you willing to let Microsoft take control of your machine? MS has already shown that it can take Win7 and 8.1 machines to town, with the Get Windows 10 campaign. But in Win10, it's considerably more difficult to keep patches at bay.

This isn't the manual Microsoft forgot. This is the manual Microsoft wouldn't dare print. I won't feed you the Microsoft party line or make excuses for pieces of Windows 10 that just don't work: Some of it's junk, some of it's evolving, and some of it's devolving. My job is to take you through the most important parts of Windows, give you tips that may or may not involve Microsoft products, point out the rough spots, and guide you around the disasters. Frankly, there are some biggies.

I also look at using non-Microsoft products in a Windows way: iPads, Androids, Kindles, Gmail and Google apps, Facebook, Twitter, Dropbox, Firefox, Google Chrome, iCloud, and many more. Even though Microsoft competes with just about every one of those products, each has a place in your computing arsenal and ties into Windows in important ways.

I'll save you more than enough money to pay for the book several times over, keep you from pulling out a whole shock of hair, lead you to dozens if not hundreds of "Aha!" moments, and keep you awake in the process. Guaranteed.

About This Book

Windows 10 All-in-One For Dummies takes you through the Land of the Dummies — with introductory material and stuff your grandmother can (and should!) understand — and then continues the journey into more advanced areas, where you can truly put Windows to work every day.

I start with the new Start menu, and for many of you, that's all you'll ever need. The Start menu coverage here is the best you'll find anywhere because I don't assume that you know Windows and I step you through everything you need to know both with a touchscreen and a mouse.

Then I dig in to the desktop and take you through all the important pieces.

I don't dwell on technical mumbo jumbo, and I keep the baffling jargon to a minimum. At the same time, though, I tackle the tough problems you're likely to encounter, show you the major road signs, and give you lots of help where you need it the most.

Whether you want to get two or more email accounts set up to work simultaneously, turn your tiles a lighter shade of pale, or share photos of your Boykin Spaniel in OneDrive, this is your book. Er, I should say ten books. I've broken out the topics into ten minibooks, so you'll find it easy to hop around to a topic — and a level of coverage — that feels comfortable.

I didn't design this book to be read from front to back. It's a reference. Each chapter and each of its sections are meant to focus on solving a particular problem or describing a specific technique.

Windows 10 All-in-One For Dummies should be your reference of first resort, even before you consult Windows Help and Support. There's a big reason why: Windows Help was written by hundreds of people over the course of many, many years. Some of the material was written ages ago, and it's confusing as all get-out, but it's still in Windows Help for folks who are tackling tough legacy problems. Some of the Help file terminology is inconsistent and downright misleading, largely because the technology has changed so much since some of the articles were written. Finding help in Help frequently boggles my mind: If I don't already know the answer to a question, it's hard to figure out how to coax Help to help. Besides, if you're looking for help on connecting your iPad to your PC or downloading pictures from your Galaxy phone, Microsoft would rather sell you something different. The proverbial bottom line: I don't duplicate the material in Windows 10 Help and Support, but I point to it if I figure it can help you.

A word about Windows 10 versions: Microsoft is trying to sell the world on the idea that Windows 10 runs on everything — desktops, laptops, tablets, phones, assisted reality headsets, huge banks of servers, giant conference room displays, refrigerators, and toasters. While that's literally true — Microsoft can call anything Windows 10 if it wants — for those of us who work on desktops and laptops,

Windows 10 is Windows 10. If you're getting Windows 10 on a tablet, you need to check to see if it's the version that runs on phones. Windows 10 Mobile has some small resemblance to what's presented here, but this book won't take you through the tough times.

Foolish Assumptions

I don't make many assumptions about you, dear reader, except to acknowledge that you're obviously intelligent, well-informed, discerning, and of impeccable taste. That's why you chose this book, eh?

Okay, okay. The least I can do is butter you up a bit. Here's the straight scoop: If you've never used Windows, bribe your neighbor (or, better, your neighbor's kids) to teach you how to do four things:

» Play a game with your fingers (if you have a touchscreen) or with a mouse (if you're finger-challenged). Any of the games that ship with Windows 10, or free games in the Windows Store, will do. If your neighbor's kids don't have a different recommendation, try the new Microsoft Solitaire Collection.

» Start File Explorer.

» Get on the web.

» Turn Windows off. (Click or tap the Start icon in the lower left of the screen, click the universal on/off button thingy, and then click Shut down.)

That covers it. If you can play a game, you know how to turn on your computer, log in if need be, touch and drag, and tap and hold down. If you run File Explorer, you know how to click a taskbar icon. After you're on the web, well, it's a great starting point for almost anything. And if you know that you need to use the Start menu, you're well on your way to achieving Windows 10 Enlightenment.

And that begins with Book 1, Chapter 1.

Icons Used in This Book

Some of the points in *Windows 10 All-in-One For Dummies* merit your special attention. I set off those points with icons.

When I'm jumping up and down on one foot with an idea so absolutely cool that I can't stand it anymore, I stick a tip icon in the margin. You can browse any chapter and hit its highest points by jumping from tip to tip.

When you see this icon, you get the real story about Windows 10 — not the stuff that the Microsoft marketing droids want you to hear — and my take on the best way to get Windows 10 to work for you. You find the same take on Microsoft, Windows, and more at my eponymous website, www.AskWoody.com.

You don't need to memorize the information marked with this icon, but you should try to remember that something special is lurking.

Achtung! Cuidado! Thar be tygers here! Anywhere that you see a warning icon, you can be sure that I've been burnt — badly. Mind your fingers. These are really, really mean suckers.

Okay, so I'm a geek. I admit it. Sure, I love to poke fun at geeks. But I'm a modern, New Age, sensitive guy, in touch with my inner geekiness. Sometimes, I just can't help but let it out, ya know? That's where the technical stuff icon comes in. If you get all tied up in knots about techie-type stuff, pass these paragraphs by. (For the record, I managed to write this entire book without telling you that an IPv4 address consists of a unique 32-bit combination of network ID and host ID, expressed as a set of four decimal numbers with each octet separated by periods. See? I can restrain myself sometimes.)

Beyond the Book

At the time I wrote this book, I covered Windows 10 Anniversary Update, version 1607. Microsoft promises to keep Windows 10 continuously updated, but it isn't clear exactly when or how much. For details about significant updates or changes that occur between editions of this book, go to www.dummies.com, search for *Windows 10 All-in-One For Dummies,* and open the Download tab on this book's dedicated page.

In addition, the cheat sheet for this book has handy Windows shortcuts and tips on other cool features worth checking out. To get to the cheat sheet, go to www.dummies.com, and then type *Windows 10 All-in-One For Dummies* Cheat Sheet in the search box.

Where to Go from Here

That's about it. It's time for you to crack this book open and have at it.

If you haven't yet told Windows 10 to show you filename extensions, flip to Book 3, Chapter 1. If you haven't yet set up the File History feature, go to Book 8, Chapter 1. If you're worried about Microsoft keeping a list of all the searches that you conduct *on your own computer,* check out Book 2, Chapter 5.

ASK
WOODY.COM

Don't forget to bookmark my website: www.AskWoody.com. It keeps you up to date on all the Windows 10 news you need to know — including notes about this book, the latest Windows bugs and gaffes, patches that are worse than the problems they're supposed to fix, and much more — and you can submit your most pressing questions for free consultation from The Woodmeister himself.

See ya! Shoot me mail at woody@AskWoody.com.

Sometimes, it's worth reading the Intro, eh?

1

Starting Windows 10

Contents at a Glance

Chapter 1

Windows 10 4 N00bs

D on't sweat it. We all started out as n00bs (newbies).

If you've never used an earlier version of Windows, you're in luck — you don't have to force your fingers to forget so much of what you've learned. Windows 10 is completely different from any Windows that has come before. It's a melding of Windows 7 and Windows 8 and 8.1, tossed into a blender, speed turned up full, poured out on your screen.

If you heard that Windows 8 was a dog, you heard only the printable part of the story. By clumsily forcing a touchscreen approach down the throats of mouse-lovers everywhere, Windows 8 alienated the touch-first people, drove the mousers nuts, and left everybody — aside from a few diehards — screaming in pain.

Windows 10 brings a kinder, gentler approach for the 1.7 billion or so people who have seen the Windows desktop and know a bit about struggling with it. Yes, Win10 will expose you to those tappy phone-style tiles, but they aren't nearly as intrusive, or as scary, as you think.

Some of you are reading this book because you specifically chose to run Windows 10. Some of you are here because Windows 10 came preinstalled on a new computer. Some of you are here because your work forced you to upgrade to Win10. Some of you are here because you fell victim to Microsoft's much-maligned "Get Windows 10" campaign or you figured you better get on Win10 while the gettin's good. Whatever the reason, you've ended up on a pretty good operating system and — as long as you understand and respect its limitations — it should serve you well.

So you're sitting in front of your computer, and this thing called Windows 10 is staring at you. Except the screen (see Figure 1-1), which Microsoft calls the lock screen, doesn't say *Windows,* much less *Windows 10.* In fact, the screen doesn't say much of anything except the current date and time, with maybe a tiny icon or two that shows you whether your Internet connection is working, how many unopened emails await, or whether you should just take the day off because your holdings in AAPL stock soared again.

You may be tempted to just sit and admire the gorgeous picture, whatever it may be, but if you use your finger or mouse to swipe up from the bottom, or press any key on an attached keyboard, you see the login screen, possibly resembling the one in Figure 1-2. If more than one person is set up to use your computer, you'll see more than one name.

That's the login screen, but it doesn't say *Login* or *Welcome to Win10 Land* or *Howdy* or even *Sit down and get to work, Bucko.* It has names and pictures for only the people who can use the computer. Why do you have to click your name? What if your name isn't there? And why in the %$#@! can't you bypass all this garbage, log in, and get your email?

FIGURE 1-2:
The Windows 10
login screen.

Good for you. That's the right attitude.

Windows 10 ranks as the most sophisticated computer program ever made. It cost more money to develop and took more people to build than any previous computer program — ever. So why is it so blasted hard to use? Why doesn't it do what you want it to do the first time? For that matter, why do you need it at all?

Someday, I swear, you'll be able to pull a PC out of the box, plug it into the wall, turn it on, and then get your email, look at the news, or connect to Facebook — bang, bang, bang, just like that, in ten seconds flat. In the meantime, those stuck in the early 21st century have to make do with PCs that grow obsolete before you can unpack them, software so ornery that you find yourself arguing with it, and Internet connections that surely involve turtles carrying bits on their backs.

If you aren't comfortable working with Windows and you still worry that you may break something if you click the wrong button, welcome to the club! In this chapter, I present a concise, school-of-hard-knocks overview of how all this hangs together and what to look for when buying a Windows computer. It may help you understand why and how Windows has limitations. It also may help you communicate with the geeky rescue team that tries to bail you out, whether you rely on the store that sold you the PC, the smelly guy in the apartment downstairs, or your 8-year-old daughter's nerdy classmate.

Hardware and Software

At the most fundamental level, all computer stuff comes in one of two flavors: hardware or software. *Hardware* is anything you can touch — a computer screen, a mouse, a hard drive, a DVD drive (remember those coasters with shiny sides?). *Software* is everything else: email messages, that letter to your Aunt Martha, digital pictures of your last vacation, programs such as Microsoft Office. If you shoot a bunch of pictures, the pictures themselves are just bits — software. But they're probably sitting on some sort of memory card inside your phone or camera. That card's hardware. Get the difference?

Windows 10 is software. You can't touch it. Your PC, on the other hand, is hardware. Kick the computer screen, and your toe hurts. Drop the big box on the floor, and it smashes into a gazillion pieces. That's hardware.

Chances are very good that one of the major PC manufacturers — Lenovo, HP, Dell, Acer, ASUS, or Toshiba, for example — or maybe even Microsoft, with its Surface line, or even Apple, made your hardware. Microsoft, and Microsoft alone, makes Windows 10.

When you bought your computer, you paid for a license to use one copy of Windows on the PC you bought. The PC manufacturer paid Microsoft a royalty so it could sell you Windows along with your PC. (That royalty may have been, in fact, zero dollars, but it's a royalty nonetheless.) You may think that you got Windows from, say, Dell — indeed, you may have to contact Dell for technical support on Windows questions — but, in fact, Windows came from Microsoft.

If you upgraded from Windows 7 or 8.1 to Windows 10, you may have received a free upgrade license — but it's still a license, whether you paid for it or not. You can't give it away to someone else.

REMEMBER

These days, most software, including Windows 10, asks you to agree to an End User License Agreement (EULA). When you first set up your PC, Windows asked you to click the Accept button to accept a licensing agreement that's long enough to reach the top of the Empire State Building. If you're curious about what agreement you accepted, take a look at the official EULA repository, www.microsoft.com/en-us/Useterms/Retail/Windows/10/UseTerms_Retail_Windows_10_English.htm.

Why Do PCs Have to Run Windows?

Here's the short answer: You don't have to run Windows on your PC.

The PC you have is a dumb box. (You needed me to tell you that, eh?) To get the dumb box to do anything worthwhile, you need a computer program that takes control of the PC and makes it do things, such as show web pages on the screen, respond to mouse clicks or taps, or print résumés. An *operating system* controls the dumb box and makes it do worthwhile things, in ways that mere humans can understand.

Without an operating system, the computer can sit in a corner and count to itself or put profound messages on the screen, such as *Non-system disk or disk error* or maybe *Insert system disk and press any key when ready.* If you want your computer to do more than that, though, you need an operating system.

Windows is not the only operating system in town. The other big contenders in the PC and PC-like operating system game are Chrome OS, Mac OS, and Linux:

>> **Chrome OS:** Cheap Chromebooks have long dominated the best-seller lists at many computer retailers, and for good reason. If you want to surf the web, work on email, compose simple documents, or do anything in a browser — which covers a whole lot of ground these days — Chrome OS is all you need. Chromebooks, which by definition run Google's Chrome OS, can't run Windows programs such as Office or Photoshop (although they *can* run web-based versions of those programs, such as Office Online or the Photoshop Express Editor). In spite of the limitations, they don't get infected and have very few maintenance problems. You can't say the same about Windows: That's why you need a thousand-page book to keep Windows going. Yes, you do need a reliable Internet connection to get the most out of Chrome OS. But some parts of Chrome OS and Google's apps, including Gmail, can work even if you don't have an active Internet connection.

Chrome OS, built on Linux, looks and feels much like the Google Chrome web browser. There are a few minor differences, but in general you feel like you're working in the Chrome browser.

For friends and family who don't have big-time computer needs, I find myself recommending a Chromebook more often than not. It's easier for them, and it's easier for me to support.

>> **Mac OS:** Apple has made great strides running on Intel hardware, and if you don't already know how to use Windows or own a Windows computer, it makes a great deal of sense to consider buying an Apple computer and/or running Mac OS on it: Check out www.hackintosh.com. But, no, it isn't legal — the Mac OS End User License Agreement specifically forbids installation on a non-Apple-branded computer — and it's certainly not for the faint of heart.

That said, if you buy a Mac — say, a MacBook Air or Pro — it's very easy to run Windows 10 on it. Some people feel that the highest quality Windows environment today comes from running Windows on a MacBook, and for years I've run Windows on my MacBook Pro and Air. All you need is a program called BootCamp, and that's already installed, free, on the MacBook.

>> **Linux:** The big up-and-coming operating system, which has been up and coming for a couple of decades now, is Linux, which is pronounced "LIN-uchs." It's a viable contender for netbooks (covered in more depth at the end of this chapter). If you expect to use your PC only to get on the Internet — to surf the web and send email from the likes of your Gmail or Hotmail account — Linux can handle all that, with few of the headaches that remain as the hallmark of Windows. By using free programs such as LibreOffice (www.libreoffice.org) and online programs such as Google Apps and Google Drive (www.drive.google.com), you can even cover the basics in word processing, spreadsheets, presentations, contact managers, calendars, and more. Linux may not support the huge array of hardware that Windows offers — but more than a few wags will tell you, with a wink, that Windows doesn't support that huge of an array, either.

WINDOWS RT, RIP

Back in the early days of Windows 8, Microsoft developed a different branch of Windows that was christened *Windows RT*. New Windows RT computers at the time were generally small, light, and inexpensive, and had a long battery life and touch-sensitive displays.

Several manufacturers made Windows RT machines, but in the end the only company that sold more than a dumpster full of them was Microsoft. Microsoft's original Surface (later renamed Surface RT) and Surface 2 ran Windows RT — and even they didn't sell worth beans.

The fundamental flaw with Windows RT? It wasn't Windows. You couldn't (and can't) run Windows programs on it. You can't upgrade the machine to real Windows. But try explaining that to a garden-variety customer. Microsoft really blew it when they gave the new, odd operating system the name *Windows RT*.

Microsoft has essentially orphaned Windows RT. If you own a Windows RT device (most likely a Microsoft Surface or Surface 2), the folks in Redmond provided one last update, called Windows RT 8.1 Update 3, which plugs what little they could muster. See www.microsoft.com/surface/en-us/support/install-update-activate/ windows-8-1-rt-update-3.

In the tablet sphere, iOS and Android rule, with iOS for iPhones and iPads — all from Apple — and Android for phones and tablets from a bewildering number of manufacturers. Windows 10 doesn't exactly compete with any of them, although Microsoft tried to take on iPad with the now-defunct Windows RT (see the sidebar "Windows RT, RIP").

There's yet another branch of Windows, which is geared toward phones and tablets, especially 8-inch and smaller tablets. Windows 10 Mobile (see the sidebar) owes its pedigree to Windows Phone 8 and Windows RT. At least conceptually (and, in fact, under the hood in no small part), Microsoft has grown Windows Phone up and Windows RT down to meet somewhere in the middle.

**ASK
WOODY.COM**

While some of the nostrums in this tome apply to Windows 10 Mobile, most do not. The mobile layout's different, the approach is different, the way you interact with things is different, and most of the details are different. There is, however, some overlap in the Universal apps that can run on both Windows 10 and Windows 10 Mobile, and the tiles in many cases look the same.

What do other people choose? It's hard to measure the percentage of PCs running Windows versus Mac versus Linux. One company, Net Applications, specializes in inspecting the online records of big-name websites and tallying how many Windows computers hit those sites, compared to Apple and Linux.

WINDOWS 10 MOBILE

Generally, devices with screens smaller than 9 inches run the other kind of Windows, known (at least unofficially) as Windows 10 Mobile. Yes, there are devices larger than 9 inches that run Windows 10 Mobile and devices 8 inches and smaller with the "real" Windows 10. The general argument goes like this: If you don't need to use the traditional Windows 7-style desktop, why pay for it? Windows 10 centers on the mouse-friendly desktop. Windows 10 Mobile sticks to the tiled world, and it's much more finger-friendly.

Believe me, running the Windows desktop on a 7-inch tablet takes a tiny stylus, or a pencil sharpener for your fingertips.

This book talks about Windows 10. Although some of the topics also apply to Windows 10 Mobile, there's quite a bit of difference. Since Microsoft gave up and sold its Nokia business in May 2016, the few Windows 10 phone fans have largely given up hope.

I hesitate to mention Net Applications (www.netapplications.com), because there's a great deal of controversy surrounding its sampling and error correction methods, but it's still (arguably) the best source of information on operating system penetration.

If you look at only desktop operating systems — Windows (on desktops, laptops, 2-in-1s) and Mac OS X and Linux — the numbers in mid 2016 broke as shown in Figure 1-3.

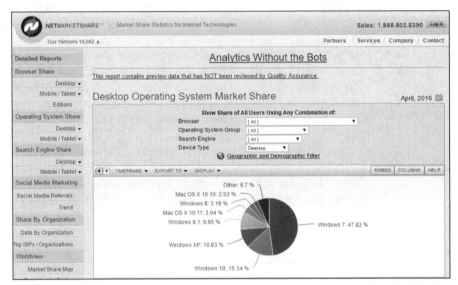

FIGURE 1-3:
Web access by desktop operating system, May 2016, worldwide.

Yes, you read the graph correctly: As of mid 2016, when Windows 10 had been out for almost a year, Win10 ran only a 15 percent market share (that is, 15 percent of the browser hits recorded by Net Applications came from Win10). Windows 8 and 8.1 together got almost as much, at 13 percent, and even old WinXP hit nearly 11 percent. Win7 was the reigning champ, with a 48 percent market share. That share is declining rapidly, though, as Microsoft pushes and shoves more Win7 customers onto Windows 10.

ASK
WOODY.COM

If you look at the bigger picture, including tablets and phones, the numbers change completely. As of May 2016, Google says that more than half of the searches it handles in the US, Japan, and ten other countries come from tablets and phones, as opposed to desktops or laptops. Back in July 2015, Andreesen Horowitz reported that the number of iOS devices (iPhones, iPads) sold per month zoomed ahead of the number of Windows PCs. Traditionally, Android phones and tablets show twice the usage rate of iOS devices. Mobile operating systems are swallowing the world — and the trend's been in mobile's favor, not Windows.

Windows was once king of the computing hill. Not so any more. Which is good news for you, the Windows customer. Microsoft's branching out to make software for phones and tablets of all stripes, and Windows itself works better with whatever phones and tablets you may like.

It's a brave new Windows world.

A Terminology Survival Kit

Some terms pop up so frequently that you'll find it worthwhile to memorize them, or at least understand where they come from. That way, you won't be caught flat-footed when your first-grader comes home and asks whether he can install a Universal app on your computer.

TIP

If you want to drive your techie friends nuts the next time you have a problem with your computer, tell them that the hassles occur when you're "running Microsoft." They won't have any idea whether you mean Windows, Word, Outlook, Hotmail, Messenger, Search, Defender, or any of a gazillion other programs — and they won't know if you're talking about a Microsoft program on Windows, the Mac, iPad, iPhone, or Android.

Windows, the *operating system* (see the preceding section), is a program. So are computer games, Microsoft Office, Microsoft Word (the word processor part of Office), Google Chrome (the web browser made by Google), Xbox Video, those nasty viruses you've heard about, that screen saver with the oh-too-perfect fish bubbling and bumbling about, and others.

An *app* or a *program* is *software* (see the earlier "Hardware and Software" section in this chapter) that works on a computer. *App* is modern and cool; *program* is old and boring, *application* manages to hit both gongs, but they all mean the same thing.

A *Universal Windows* app is a program that, at least in theory, runs on any version of Windows 10. By design, Universal apps (also called Universal Windows Platform, or UWP, apps) should run on Windows 10 on a desktop, a laptop, a tablet, a phone — and even on an Xbox game console, a giant wall-mounted Surface Hub, a HoloLens augmented reality headset, and possibly Internet of Things tiny computers.

WARNING

For most people, "Universal" does not mean what they might think it means. Universal Windows apps *don't* work on Windows 8.1 or Windows 7. They don't even run on Windows RT tablets (see the "Windows RT, RIP" sidebar). They're universal only in the sense that they'll run on Windows 10. In theory.

REMEMBER

A special kind of program called a *driver* makes specific pieces of hardware work with the operating system. For example, your computer's printer has a driver, your monitor has a driver, your mouse has a driver, and Tiger Woods has a driver (several, actually, and he makes a living with them). Wish that everyone were so talented.

Many drivers ship with Windows, even though Microsoft doesn't make them. The hardware manufacturer's responsible for making its hardware work with your Windows PC, and that includes building and fixing the drivers. (Yes, if Microsoft makes your computer, Microsoft's responsible for the drivers, too.) Sometimes you can get a driver from the manufacturer that works better than the one that ships with Windows.

When you stick an app or program on your computer — and set it up so it works — you *install* the app or program (or driver).

When you crank up a program — that is, get it going on your computer — you can say you *started* it, *launched* it, *ran* it, or *executed* it. They all mean the same thing.

If the program quits the way it's supposed to, you can say it *stopped, finished, ended, exited,* or *terminated.* Again, all these terms mean the same thing. If the program stops with some sort of weird error message, you can say it *crashed, died, cratered, croaked, went belly up, jumped in the bit bucket,* or *GPFed* (techspeak for "generated a General Protection Fault" — don't ask), or employ any of a dozen colorful but unprintable epithets. If the program just sits there and you can't get it to do anything, no matter how you click your mouse or poke the screen, you can say the program *froze, hung, stopped responding,* or *went into a loop.*

A *bug* is something that doesn't work right. (A bug is not a virus! Viruses work as intended far too often.) US Navy Rear Admiral Grace Hopper — the intellectual guiding force behind the COBOL programming language and one of the pioneers in the history of computing — often repeated the story of a moth being found in a relay of an ancient Mark II computer. The moth was taped into the technician's logbook on September 9, 1947. (See Figure 1-4.)

The people who invented all this terminology think of the Internet as being some great blob in the sky — it's *up,* as in "up in the sky." So if you send something from your computer to the Internet, you're *uploading.* If you take something off the Internet and put it on your computer, you're *downloading.*

The *cloud* is just a marketing term for the Internet. Saying that you put your data "in the cloud" sounds so much cooler than saying you copied it to storage on the Internet. Programs can run in the cloud — which is to say, they run on the Internet. Just about everything that has anything to do with computers can now be done in the cloud. Just watch your pocketbook.

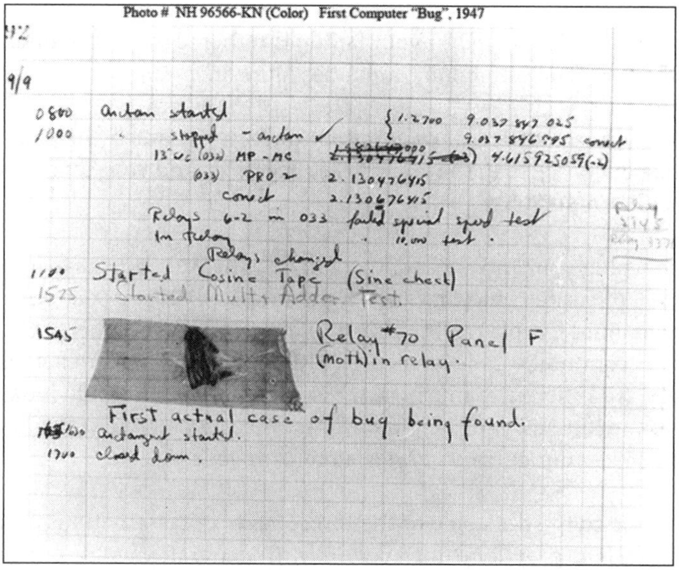

Photo # NH 96566-KN (Color) First Computer "Bug", 1947

FIGURE 1-4:
Admiral Grace
Hopper's log of
the first actual
case of a bug
being found.

Source: US Navy

REMEMBER

If you use *cloud storage*, you're just sticking your data on some company's computer. Put a file in Microsoft OneDrive, and it actually goes onto one of Microsoft's computers. Put it in Google Drive, and it goes to Google's storage in the sky. Move it to Dropbox, and it's sitting on a Dropbox computer.

When you put computers together, you *network* them, and if your network doesn't use wires, it's commonly called a *Wi-Fi network*. At the heart of a network sits a box, commonly called a *hub*, or a *router,* that computers can plug in to. If the hub has rabbit ears on top for wireless connections, it's usually called a *Wi-Fi router.* (Some Wi-Fi routers may not have antennae outside.) Yes, there are fine lines of distinction among all these terms. No, you don't need to worry about them.

There are two basic ways to hook up to the Internet: *wired* and *wireless.* Wired is easy: You plug it into a router or some other box that connects to the Internet. Wireless falls into two categories: Wi-Fi connections, as you'll find in many homes, coffee shops, airports, and some exceptionally enlightened cities' common areas; and cellular (mobile phone–style) wireless connections.

Cellular Wireless Internet connections are usually identified with one of the G levels: 2G, 3G, 4G, or maybe even 5G. Each G level should be faster than its predecessor.

This part gets a little tricky. If your phone can connect to a 3G or 4G network, it may be possible to set your phone up to behave like a Wi-Fi router: Your computer talks to the phone, the phone talks to the Internet over its 3G or 4G connection.

That's called *tethering* — your laptop is tethered to your phone. Not all phones can tether, and not all phone companies allow it.

Special boxes called *Mobile Hotspot* units work much the same way: The Mobile Hotspot connects to the 3G or 4G connection, and your laptop gets tethered to the Mobile Hotspot box.

If you plug your Internet connection into the wall, you have *broadband,* which may run via *fiber* (a cable that uses light waves), *DSL* or *ADSL* (which uses regular old phone lines), *cable* (as in cable TV), or *satellite.* The fiber, DSL, cable, or satellite box is commonly called a *modem,* although it's really a *router.* Although fiber optic lines are inherently much faster than DSL or cable, individual results can be all over the lot. Ask your neighbors what they're using and then pick the best. If you don't like your current service, vote with your wallet.

Turning to the dark side of the force, Luke, the distinctions among *viruses, worms,* and *Trojans* grow blurrier every day. In general, they're programs that replicate and can be harmful, and the worst ones blend different approaches. *Spyware* gathers information about you and then phones home with all the juicy details. *Adware* gets in your face, all too frequently installing itself on your computer without your knowledge or consent. *Ransomware* scrambles (or threatens to scramble) your data and demands a payment to keep the data intact. I tend to lump the three together and call them *scumware* or *crapware* or something a bit more descriptive and less printable.

If a bad guy (and they're almost always guys) manages to take over your computer without your knowledge, turning it into a zombie that spews spam by remote control, you're in a *botnet.* (And yes, the term *spam* comes from the immortal *Monty Python* routine that's set in a cafe serving Hormel's SPAM luncheon meat, the chorus bellowing "lovely Spam, wonderful Spam.") Check out Book 9 for details about preventing scumware and the like from messing with you.

The most successful botnets employ *rootkits* — programs that run underneath Windows, evading detection because normal programs can't see them. The number of Windows 10 computers running rootkits is probably two or three or four orders of magnitudes less than the number of zombified XP computers. But as long as Windows XP computers are out there, botnets will continue to be a major threat to everyone.

This section covers about 90 percent of the buzzwords you hear in common parlance. If you get stuck at a party where the bafflegab is flowing freely, don't hesitate to invent your own words. Nobody will ever know the difference.

What, Exactly, Is the Web?

Five years from now (although it may take ten), the operating system you use will be largely irrelevant, as will be the speed of your computer, the amount of memory you have, and the number of terabytes of storage that hum in the background. Microsoft will keep milking its cash cow, but the industry will move on. Individuals and businesses will stop shelling out big bucks for Windows and the iron to run it. Instead, the major push will be online. Rather than spend money on PCs that become obsolete the week after you purchase them, folks will spend money on big data pipes: It'll be less about me and more about us. Why? Because so much more is "out there" than "in here." Count on it.

But what is the Internet? This section answers this burning question (if you've asked it). If you don't necessarily wonder about the Internet's place in space and time just yet, you will . . . you will.

REMEMBER

You know those stories about computer jocks who come up with great ideas, develop the ideas in their basements (or garages or dorm rooms), release their products to the public, change the world, and make a gazillion bucks?

This isn't one of them.

The Internet started in the mid-1960s as an academic exercise — primarily with the RAND Corporation, the Massachusetts Institute of Technology (MIT), and the National Physical Laboratory in England — and rapidly evolved into a military project, under the US Department of Defense Advanced Research Project Agency (ARPA), designed to connect research groups working on ARPA projects.

By the end of the 1960s, ARPA had four computers hooked together — at UCLA, SRI (Stanford), UC Santa Barbara, and the University of Utah — using systems developed by BBN Technologies (then named Bolt Beranek and Newman, Inc.). By 1971, it had 18. I started using ARPANET in 1975. According to the website www.internetworldstats.com, by the end of June 2014, the Internet had more than 3 billion users worldwide.

Today, so many computers are connected directly to the Internet that the Internet's addressing system is running out of numbers, just as your local phone company is running out of telephone numbers. The current numbering system — named *IPv4* — can handle about 4 billion addresses. The next version, named *IPv6*, can handle this number of addresses:

340,000,000,000,000,000,000,000,000,000,000,000,000

That should last for a while, don'tcha think?

Ever wonder why you rarely see hard statistics about the Internet? I've found two big reasons:

» Defining terms related to the Internet is devilishly difficult these days. (What do you mean when you say "*X* number of computers are connected to the Internet"? Is that the number of computers up and running at any given moment? The number of different addresses that are active? The number that could be connected if everybody dialed up at the same time? The number of different computers that are connected in a typical day, or week, or month?)

» The other reason is that the Internet is growing so fast that any number you publish today will be meaningless tomorrow.

Getting inside the Internet

Some observers claim that the Internet works so well because it was designed to survive a nuclear attack. Not so. The people who built the Internet insist that they weren't nearly as concerned about nukes as they were about making communication among researchers reliable, even when a backhoe severed an underground phone line or one of the key computers ground to a halt.

As far as I'm concerned, the Internet works so well because the engineers who laid the groundwork were utter geniuses. Their original ideas from 50 years ago have been through the wringer a few times, but they're still pretty much intact. Here's what the engineers decided:

» **No single computer should be in charge.** All the big computers connected directly to the Internet are equal (although, admittedly, some are more equal than others). By and large, computers on the Internet move data around like kids playing hot potato — catch it, figure out where you're going to throw it, and let it fly quickly. They don't need to check with some übercomputer before doing their work; they just catch, look, and throw.

» **Break the data into fixed-size packets.** No matter how much data you're moving — an email message that just says "Hi" or a full-color, life-size photograph of the Andromeda galaxy — the data is broken into packets. Each packet is routed to the appropriate computer. The receiving computer assembles all the packets and notifies the sending computer that everything came through okay.

» **Deliver each packet quickly.** If you want to send data from Computer A to Computer B, break the data into packets and route each packet to Computer B by using the fastest connection possible — even if that means some packets go through Bangor and others go through Bangkok.

Taken together, those three rules ensure that the Internet can take a lickin' and keep on tickin'. If a chipmunk eats through a telephone line, any big computer that's using the gnawed line can start rerouting packets over a different telephone line. If the Cumbersome Computer Company in Cupertino, California, loses power, computers that were sending packets through Cumbersome can switch to other connected computers. It usually works quickly and reliably, although the techniques used internally by the Internet computers get a bit hairy at times.

Big computers are hooked together by high-speed communication lines: the *Internet backbone.* If you want to use the Internet from your business or your house, you have to connect to one of the big computers first. Companies that own the big computers — Internet service providers (ISPs) — get to charge you for the privilege of getting on the Internet through their big computers. The ISPs, in turn, pay the companies that own the cables (and satellites) that comprise the Internet backbone for a slice of the backbone.

ASK WOODY.COM

If all this sounds like a big-fish-eats-smaller-fish-eats-smaller-fish arrangement, that's quite a good analogy.

It's backbone-breaking work, but somebody's gotta do it.

What is the World Wide Web?

People tend to confuse the World Wide Web with the Internet, which is much like confusing the dessert table with the buffet line. I'd be the first to admit that desserts are mighty darn important — life-critical, in fact, if the truth be told. But they aren't the same as the buffet line.

To get to the dessert table, you have to stand in the buffet line. To get to the web, you have to be running on the Internet. Make sense?

The World Wide Web owes its existence to Tim Berners-Lee and a few co-conspirators at a research institute named CERN in Geneva, Switzerland. In 1990, Berners-Lee demonstrated a way to store and link information on the Internet so that all you had to do was click to jump from one place — one web page — to another. Nowadays, nobody in his right mind can give a definitive count of the number of pages available, but Google has indexed more than 50 billion of them. By some estimates, there are trillions of individual web pages.

Like the Internet itself, the World Wide Web owes much of its success to the brilliance of the people who brought it to life. The following list describes the ground rules:

>> Web pages, stored on the Internet, are identified by an address, such as www.dummies.com. The main part of the web page address — dummies.com,

for example — is a *domain name.* With rare exceptions, you can open a web page by simply typing its domain name and pressing Enter. Spelling counts, and underscores (_) are treated differently from hyphens (-). Being close isn't good enough — there are just too many websites. As of this writing, DomainTools (www.domaintools.com) reports that about 300 million domain names end in .com, .net, .org, .info, .biz, or .us. That's just for the United States. Other countries have different naming conventions: .co.uk, for example, is the UK equivalent of .com.

>> Web pages are written in the funny language HyperText Markup Language (HTML). HTML is sort of a programming language, sort of a formatting language, and sort of a floor wax, all rolled into one. Many products claim to make it easy for novices to create powerful, efficient HTML. Some of those products are getting close.

>> To read a web page, you have to use a web browser. A *web browser* is a program that runs on your computer and is responsible for converting HTML into text that you can read and use. The majority of people who view web pages use Google's Chrome web browser, although Firefox, Microsoft's Internet Explorer, and the new Edge browser in Win10 are all contenders. IE is still inside Windows 10, but you have to dig deep to find it. (Hint: Click the Start icon, All Apps, Windows Accessories.) For almost all people, almost all the time, Chrome works better than Internet Explorer: It's much more secure, faster, and not as dependent on things that can go bump in the night.

>> More and more people (including me!) prefer Firefox (see www.mozilla.org) or Chrome, from Google (www.chrome.google.com). You may not know that Firefox and Chrome can run right alongside Internet Explorer and Edge, with absolutely no confusion between the two. Er, four. In fact, they don't even interact — Edge, Firefox, and Chrome were designed to operate completely independently, and they do very well playing all by themselves.

One unwritten rule for the World Wide Web: All web acronyms must be completely, utterly inscrutable. For example, a web address is a *Uniform Resource Locator,* or *URL.* (The techies I know pronounce URL "earl." Those who don't wear white lab coats tend to say "you are ell.") I describe the HTML acronym in the preceding list. On the web, a gorgeous, sunny, palm-lined beach with the scent of frangipani wafting through the air would no doubt be called SHS — Smelly Hot Sand. Sheeesh.

The best part of the web is how easily you can jump from one place to another — and how easily you can create web pages with *hot links* (also called *hyperlinks* or just *links*) that transport the viewer wherever the author intends. That's the *H* in HTML and the original reason for creating the web so many years ago.

Who pays for all this stuff?

That's the 64-billion-dollar question, isn't it? The Internet is one of the true bargains of the 21st century. When you're online — for which you probably have to pay EarthLink, Comcast, Verizon, NetZero, Juno, Netscape, Qwest, some other cable company, or another ISP a monthly fee — the Internet itself is free.

REMEMBER

Edge and Internet Explorer are free, sorta, because they come with Windows 10, no matter which version you buy. Firefox is free as a breeze — in fact, it's the poster child for open-source programs: Everything about the program, even the program code itself, is free. Google Chrome is free, too. Both Microsoft, with IE and Edge, and Google, with Chrome, keep tabs on where you go and what you do online — all the better to convince you to click an ad. Firefox collects some data, but its uses are limited.

Others involved in your security may be selling your personal information. AVG, of antivirus fame, announced in September 2015 that it would start selling browsing history data to advertisers. Your ISP may be selling your data, too.

Most websites don't charge a cent. They pay for themselves in any of these ways:

>> **Reduce a company's operating costs:** Banks and brokerage firms, for example, have websites that routinely handle customer inquiries at a fraction of the cost of H2H (er, human-to-human) interactions.

>> **Increase a company's visibility:** The website gives you a good excuse to buy more of the company's products. That's why architectural firms show you pictures of their buildings and food companies post recipes.

>> **Draw in new business:** Ask any real estate agent.

>> **Contract advertising:** Google has made a fortune. A thousand thousand fortunes.

>> **Use bounty advertising:** Smaller sites run ads, most commonly from Google, but in some cases, selected from a pool of advertisers. The advertiser pays a bounty for each person who clicks the ad and views its website — a *click-through*.

>> **Use affiliate programs:** Smaller sites may also participate in a retailer's affiliate program. If a customer clicks through and orders something, the website that originated the transaction receives a percentage of the amount ordered. Amazon is well known for its affiliate program, but many others exist.

Some websites have an entrance fee. For example, if you want to read more than a few articles on *The New York Times* website, you have to part with some substantial coin — about $15 per month for the most basic option, the last time I looked. Guess that beats schlepping around a whole lotta paper.

Buying a Windows 10 Computer

Here's how it usually goes: You figure that you need to buy a new PC, so you spend a couple weeks brushing up on the details — bits and bytes and kilobytes and megabytes and gigabytes — and comparison shopping. You end up at your local Computers Are Us shop, and the guy behind the counter convinces you that the absolutely best bargain you'll ever see is sitting right here, right now, and you'd better take it quick before somebody else nabs it.

YOU MAY NOT NEED TO PAY MORE TO GET A CLEAN PC

I hate it when the computer I want comes loaded with all that nice, "free" crapware. I'd seriously consider paying more to get a clean computer.

You don't need an antivirus and Internet security program preinstalled on your new PC. It'll just open and beg for money next month. Windows 10 comes with Windows Defender, and it works great — for free.

Browser toolbars? Puh-lease.

You can choose your own Internet service provider. AOL? EarthLink? Who needs ya?

And trialware? Whether it's Quicken or any of a zillion other programs, if you have to pay for a preinstalled program in three months or six months, you don't want it.

If you're looking for a new computer but can't find an option to buy a PC without all the "extras," look elsewhere. The big PC companies are slowly getting a clue, but until they clean up their act, you may be better served buying from a smaller retailer, who hasn't yet presold every bit that isn't nailed down. Or you can buy direct from Microsoft: Its Surface tablets are as clean as the driven snow. Pricey, perhaps. But blissfully clean.

Microsoft Stores, both online and the physical kind, sell new, clean computers from major manufacturers as part of Microsoft's Signature PC program. Before you spend money on a computer, check to see whether it's available dreck-free (usually at the same price) from the Microsoft Store. Go to www.microsoftstore.com and choose any PC. The ones on offer ship without any of the junk.

Your eyes glaze over as you look at yet another spec sheet and try to figure out one last time whether a RAM is a ROM, whether a hybrid drive is worth the effort, and whether you need a SATA 3 Gbps, SATA 6 Gbps, or eSATA, or USB 2 or 3 or C. In the end, you figure that the guy behind the counter must know what he's doing, so you plunk down your plastic and pray you got a good deal.

The next Sunday morning, you look at the ads on Newegg (www.Newegg.com) or Best Buy (www.BestBuy.com) or Amazon (www.Amazon.com) or Tiger Direct (www.TigerDirect.com) and discover you could've bought twice as much machine for half as much money. The only thing you know for sure is that your PC is hopelessly out of date, and the next time you'll be smarter about the whole process.

If that describes your experiences, relax. It happens to everybody. Take solace in the fact that you bought twice as much machine for the same amount of money as the poor schmuck who went through the same process last month.

ASK
WOODY.COM

Here's everything you need to know about buying a Windows 10 PC:

>> **Decide if you're going to use a touchscreen.** If you know that you won't be using the tiled part of Windows very much, a touchscreen won't hurt, but it probably isn't worth the additional expense. Experienced, mouse-savvy Windows users often find that using a mouse and a touchscreen at the same time is an ergonomic pain in the a . . . rm.

Unless you have fingertips the size of pinheads — or you always use a stylus — using some programs on a touchscreen is an excruciating experience. Best to leave the touching to programs that are demonstrably touch-friendly.

>> **If you're going to use the old-fashioned, Windows 7–style desktop, get a high-quality monitor, a solid keyboard, and a mouse that feels comfortable.** Corollary: Don't buy a computer online unless you know for a fact that your fingers will like the keyboard, your wrist will tolerate the mouse, and your eyes will fall in love with the monitor.

>> **Get a screen that's at least 1920 x 1080 pixels — the minimum size to play back high-definition (1080p) movies.** Although a touch-sensitive screen isn't a prerequisite for using tiled Universal apps on Windows 10, you'll probably find it easier to use tiled apps with your fingers than with your mouse. Swiping with a finger is easy; swiping with a trackpad works reasonably well, depending on the trackpad; swiping with a mouse is a disaster.

There's no substitute for physically trying the hardware on a touch-sensitive Windows 10 computer. Hands come in all shapes and sizes, and fingers, too. What works for size XXL hands with ten thumbs (present company included) may not cut the mustard for svelte hands and fingers experienced at taking cotton balls out of medicine bottles.

See the section "Inside a touch-sensitive tablet" later in this chapter.

>> **Go overboard with hard drives.** In the best of all possible worlds, get a computer with a solid-state drive (SSD) for the system drive (the C: drive) plus a large hard drive for storage, perhaps attached via a USB cable. For the low-down on SSDs, hard drives, backups, and putting them all together, see the upcoming section "Managing disks and drives."

How much hard drive space do you need? How long is a string? Unless you have an enormous collection of videos, movies, or songs, 1TB (=1,024GB = 1,048,576MB = 1,073,741,824KB = 1,099,511,627,776 bytes, or characters of storage) should suffice. That's big enough to handle about 1,000 broadcast-quality movies. Consider that the printed collection of the US Library of Congress runs about 10TB.

If you're getting a laptop or Ultrabook with an SSD, consider buying an external 1TB or larger drive at the same time. You'll use it. External hard drives are cheap and plug-in easy to use.

Or you can just stick all that extra data in the cloud, with OneDrive, Dropbox, Google Drive, or some competitor. See Book 6, Chapter 1 to get started. For what it's worth, I used Dropbox in every phase of writing this book.

>> **Everything else they try to sell ya pales in comparison.**

If you want to spend more money, go for a faster Internet connection and a better chair. You need both items much more than you need a marginally faster, or bigger, computer.

Inside the big box

In this section, I give you just enough information about the inner workings of a desktop or laptop PC that you can figure out what you have to do with Windows. In the next section, I talk about touch-enabled tablets, the PCs that respond to touch. Details can change from week to week, but these are the basics.

The big box that your desktop computer lives in is sometimes called a *CPU*, or *central processing unit* (see Figure 1-5). Right off the bat, you're bound to get confused, unless somebody clues you in on one important detail: The main computer chip inside that big box is also called a CPU. I prefer to call the big box "the PC" because of the naming ambiguity, but you've probably thought of a few better names.

FIGURE 1-5:
The enduring, traditional big box.

Courtesy of Dell Inc.

The big box contains many parts and pieces (and no small amount of dust and dirt), but the crucial, central element inside every PC is the motherboard. (You can see a picture of a motherboard here: www.asus.com/Motherboards/M5A99X_EVO/).

You find the following items attached to the motherboard:

>> **The processor, or CPU:** This gizmo does the main computing. It's probably from Intel or AMD. Different manufacturers rate their CPUs in different ways, and it's impossible to compare performance by just looking at the part number. Yes, i7 CPUs usually run faster than i5s, and i3s are the slowest of the three, but there are many nuances. Unless you tackle very intensive video games, build your own audio or video files, or recalculate spreadsheets with the national debt, the CPU doesn't really count for much. In particular, if you're streaming audio and video (say, with YouTube or Netflix) you don't need a fancy processor. If in doubt, check out the reviews at www.tomshardware.com and www.anandtech.com.

>> **Memory chips and places to put them:** Memory is measured in megabytes (1MB = 1,024KB = 1,048,576 characters), gigabytes (1GB = 1,024MB), and terabytes (1TB = 1,024GB). Microsoft recommends a minimum of 2GB main memory. Unless you have an exciting cornfield to watch grow while Windows 10 saunters along, aim for 4GB or more. Most computers allow you to add more memory to them, and boosting your computer's memory to 4GB from 2GB makes the machine much snappier, especially if you run memory hogs such as Office, InDesign, or Photoshop. If you leave Outlook open and work with it all day and run almost any other major program at the same time, 8GB isn't overkill. If you're going to make your own videos, you probably need more. But for most people, 4GB is plenty and 8GB will run everything well.

>> **Video chipset:** Most motherboards include remarkably good built-in video. If you want more video oomph, you have to buy a video card and put it in a card slot. Advanced motherboards have multiple PCI card slots, to allow you to strap together two video cards and speed up video even more. If you want to run a VR or AR headset, such as an Oculus Rift, you're going to need a much more capable video setup. For more information, see the "Screening" section in this chapter.

>> **Card slots (also known as expansion slots):** Laptops have very limited (if any) expansion slots on the motherboard. Desktops generally contain several expansion slots. Modern slots come in two flavors: PCI and PCI-Express (also known as PCIe or PCI-E). Most expansion cards use PCI, but very fast cards — including, notably, video cards — require PCIe. Of course, PCI cards don't fit in PCIe slots, and vice versa. To make things more confusing, PCIe comes in four sizes — literally, the size of the bracket and the number of bumps on the bottoms of the cards is different. The PCIe 1x is smallest, the relatively uncommon PCIe 4x is considerably larger, and PCIe 8x is a bit bigger still. PCIe 16x is just a little bit bigger than an old-fashioned PCI slot. Most video cards these days require a PCIe 16x slot. Or two.

If you're buying a monitor separately from the rest of the system, make sure the monitor takes video input in a form that your PC can produce. See the upcoming section "Screening" for details.

>> **USB (Universal Serial Bus) connections:** The USB cable has a flat connector that plugs in to your slots. USB 3 is considerably faster than USB 2, and any kind of USB device can plug in to a USB 3 slot, whether or not the device itself supports USB 3 level speeds.

USB Type-C (often called USB C) is a completely different kind of cable that takes its own kind of slot. It has two big advantages. The plug is reversible, so it's impossible to plug it in upside-down. And you can run a considerable amount of power through a USB-C, making it a good choice for power supplies.

Make sure you get plenty of USB slots — at least two, preferably four, or more. Pay extra for a USB C slot or two. More details are in the section "Managing disks and drives," later in this chapter.

>> **Lots of other stuff:** You never have to play with this other stuff, unless you're very unlucky.

Here are a few upgrade dos and don'ts:

>> **Don't** let a salesperson talk you into eviscerating your PC and upgrading the CPU: i7 isn't that much faster than i5; a 3.0-GHz PC doesn't run a whole lot faster than a 2.4-GHz PC, and a dual-quad-core ChipDuoTrioQuattroQuinto stuck in an old motherboard doesn't run much faster than your original slowpoke.

>> When you hit 4GB in main memory, **don't** expect big performance improvements by adding more memory, unless you're running Chrome all day with 25 open tabs, or putting together videos.

>> On the other hand, if you have an older video card, **do** consider upgrading it to a faster card, or to one with 1GB or more of on-board memory. They're cheap. Windows 10 takes good advantage of it.

>> Rather than nickel-and-dime yourself to death on little upgrades, **do** wait until you can afford a new PC, and give away your old one.

TIP

If you decide to add memory, have the company that sells you the memory install it. The process is simple, quick, and easy — if you know what you're doing. Having the dealer install the memory also puts the monkey on his back if a memory chip doesn't work or a bracket snaps.

Inside a touch-sensitive tablet

Although touch-sensitive tablets have been on the market for more than a decade, they didn't really take off until Apple introduced the iPad in 2010. Since the iPad went ballistic, every Windows hardware manufacturer has been clamoring to join the game. Even Microsoft has entered the computer-manufacturing fray with its line of innovative tablets known as Surface.

The old Windows 7–era tablets generally required a *stylus* (a special kind of pen), and they had very little software that took advantage of touch input. The iPad changed all that.

**ASK
WOODY.COM**

The result is a real hodge-podge of Windows tablets, many kinds of 2-in-1s (which have a removable keyboard, as shown in Figure 1-6, and thus transform to a genuine tablet), and notebooks with all sorts of weird hinges, including some that flip around like an orangutan on a swing.

As sales of Windows machines plummets, the choice has never been broader. All major PC manufacturers now offer traditional clamshell notebooks, as well as some variant on the 2-in-1, many still have desktops, and more than a few even make Chromebooks!

I did most of the touch-sensitive work in this book on a Dell XPS-15 with a gorgeous 4K touchscreen (see Figure 1-7). The Infinity Edge screen makes the entire machine only slightly larger than most 13-inch laptops.

FIGURE 1-6:
Microsoft Surface Pro tablets typify the 2-in-1 combination of removable slates with tear-away keyboards.

Courtesy of Microsoft

FIGURE 1-7:
The Dell XPS-15 that I used to write this book.

Courtesy of Dell Inc.

With a 6th generation (Skylake class) i7-6700 chip, 16GB main memory and a 512GB solid-state drive, it's the fastest, most capable PC I've ever owned — much more powerful than my production desktop machines. The 4K screen simply blew me away. One USB-2 and two USB-3 ports, an HDMI output for high-definition monitors (or TVs!), and a separate SD card reader, which can hold up to 512GB, add up to an incomparable Win10 touch experience. It's 4.5 pounds, with all-day battery life, a rock solid keyboard, a responsive trackpad, and a separate GeForce video card with its own 2GB of storage. Those are all attributes you should seek when buying a Windows 10 tablet.

ASK
WOODY.COM

Of course, that kind of oomph comes at a price. That's the other part — quite possibly the constraining part — of the equation. A couple thousand bucks for a desktop replacement is great, but if you just want a Windows 10 laptop, you can find respectable, traditional Windows 10 laptops (netbooks, whatever you want to call them), with or without touchscreens, for a few hundred.

Microsoft's Surface Pro 4 (Figure 1-6) lists for $1,000 or so, including the keyboard. The Surface Book, which doesn't suffer from the bouncy keyboard on the Pro, goes for $1,500 up, and it includes the keyboard. Microsoft's SB and SP4 went through a long shakeout period — it took more than six months to get the bugs ironed out of the hardware drivers — but they now work quite respectably.

That said, if a Chromebook or an iPad or an Android tablet will do everything you need to do, there's no reason to plunk down lots of money for a Windows 10 tablet. None at all.

If you're thinking about buying a Windows 10 tablet, keep these points in mind:

REMEMBER

>> **Focus on weight, heat, and battery life.** Touch-sensitive tablets are meant to be carried, not lugged around like a suitcase, and the last thing you need is a box so hot it burns a hole in your pants, or a fan so noisy you can't carry on a conversation.

>> **Make sure you get multi-touch.** Some manufacturers like to skimp and make tablets that respond only to one or two touch points. You need at least four, just to run Windows 10, and ten wouldn't hurt. Throw in some toes and ask for 20, if you want to be ornery about it.

>> **The screen should run at 1366x768 pixels or better.** Anything smaller will have you squinting to look at the desktop.

>> **Get a solid-state drive.** In addition to making the machine much, much faster, a solid-state drive (SSD) also saves on weight, heat, and battery life. Don't be overly concerned about the amount of storage on a tablet. Many people with Win10 tablets end up putting all their data in the cloud with, for example, OneDrive, Google Drive, Dropbox, or Box. See Book 6, Chapter 1.

>> **Try before you buy.** The screen has to be sensitive to your big fingers, and look good, too. Not an easy combination. I also have a problem with bouncy keyboards. Better to know about the limitations before you fork over the cash.

>> **Make sure you can return it.** If you have experience with a "real" keyboard and a mouse, you may find that you hate using a tablet to replicate the kinds of things you used to do with a laptop or desktop PC.

OLED VERSUS LED

OLED (organic light-emitting diode) screens are coming. You'll see them on TVs, computer monitors, laptop screens, tablets, and even phones, and the prices are headed down fast. Can or should they supplant LED screens, which have led the computer charge since the turn of the century? That's' a tough question with no easy answer.

First, understand that an LED screen is actually an LCD screen — an older technology — augmented by backlighting or edge lighting, typically from LEDs or fluorescent lamps. A huge variety of LED screens are available, but most of the screens you see nowadays incorporate IPS (in-plane switching) technology, which boosts color fidelity and viewing angles.

OLED is a horse of a different color. IPS LED pixels (considered far superior to the older TN LED pixels) turn different colors, but they rely on the backlight or sidelight to push the color to your eyes. OLED (pronounced "oh-led") pixels make their own light. If you take an LED screen into a dark room and bring up a black screen, you can see variations in the screen brightness because the backlight intensity changes, if only a little bit. OLED blacks, by (er) contrast, are uniform and thus deeper.

All sorts of new techniques are being thrown at LED, and LED screens are getting better and better. HDR (high dynamic range) improvements, for example, make LED pictures stand out in ways they never could before. Quantum dots improve lighting and color. Many people feel that, at this point, OLEDs have blacker blacks, but the best LEDs produce better brights.

The huge difference is in price: OLED screens are still two to eight or more times more expensive than LED. The price of OLED is dropping rapidly, though. In addition, OLEDs don't last as long as LEDs — say, a decade with normal use. There's also some concern that OLEDs draw more power — and will burn through a laptop battery — faster than LCDs, but some contest that statement. Much depends on the particular LED and OLED you compare.

As the hardware market matures, you can expect to see many variations on the tablet theme. It ain't all cut and dried.

Screening

The computer monitor or screen — and LED, LCD, OLED, and plasma TVs — use technology that's quite different from old–fashioned television circuitry from your childhood. A traditional TV scans lines across the screen from left to right, with hundreds of them stacked on top of each other. Colors on each individual line vary all over the place. The almost infinitely variable color on an old-fashioned TV combined with a comparatively small number of lines makes for pleasant, but fuzzy, pictures.

By contrast (pun absolutely intended, of course), computer monitors, touch-sensitive tablet screens, and plasma, LED, OLED, and LCD TVs work with dots of light called *pixels*. Each pixel can have a different color, created by tiny, col-ored gizmos sitting next to each other. As a result, the picture displayed on com-puter monitors (and plasma and LCD TVs) is much sharper than on conventional TV tubes.

REMEMBER

The more pixels you can cram on a screen — that is, the higher the screen resolution — the more information you can pack on the screen. That's impor-tant if you commonly have more than one word-processing document open at a time, for example. At a resolution of 800x600, two open Word documents placed side by side look big but fuzzy, like caterpillars viewed through a dirty magnify-ing glass. At 1280x1024, those same two documents look sharp, but the text may be so small that you have to squint to read it. If you move up to wide-screen territory — 1920x1080 (full HD), or even 2560x1440 — with a good monitor, two documents side-by-side look stunning. Run up to 4K technology, at 3840x2160 or better — the resolution on the XPS-15 — and you'll need a magnifying glass to see the pixels.

A special-purpose computer called a *graphics processing unit (GPU)*, stuck on your video card or possibly integrated into the CPU, creates everything that's shown on your computer's screen. The GPU has to juggle all the pixels and all the colors, so if you're a gaming fan, the speed of the GPU's chip (and, to a lesser extent, the speed of the monitor) can make the difference between a zapped alien and a lost energy shield. If you want to experience Windows 10 in all its glory, you need a fast GPU with at least 1GB (and preferably 2GB or more) of its own memory.

Computer monitors and tablets are sold by size, measured diagonally (glass only, not the bezel or frame), like TV sets. Just like with TV sets, the only way to pick a good computer screen over a run-of-the-mill one is to compare them side by side or to follow the recommendation of someone who has.

Managing disks and drives

Your PC's memory chips hold information only temporarily: Turn off the electric-ity, and the contents of main memory go bye-bye. If you want to reuse your work, keeping it around after the plug has been pulled, you have to save it, typically on a disk, or possibly in the *cloud* (which means you copy it to a location on the Internet).

The following list describes the most common types of disks and drives:

>> **SD/xD/CF card memory:** Many smaller computers, and some tablets, have built-in SD card readers. (Apple and some Google tablets don't have SD — the companies would rather sell you more on-board memory, at inflated prices!) You probably know Secure Digital (SD) cards best as the kind of memory used in digital cameras, or possibly phones (see Figure 1-8). A microSD cards may slip into a hollowed-out card that is shaped like, and functions as, an SD card.

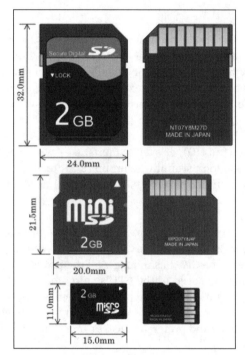

FIGURE 1-8:
Comparative sizes of an SD, a miniSD, and a microSD card.

Source: Skcard.svg, Wikimedia

TIP

Even now, long after the demise of floppy disks, many desktop computer cases have drive bays built for them. Why not use the open spot for a multifunction card reader? That way, you can slip a memory card out of your digital camera (or your Dick Tracy wristwatch, for that matter) and transfer files at will. SD card, miniSD, microSD card, xD card, CompactFlash, memory stick — whatever you have — the multifunction readers cost a pittance and read almost everything, including minds.

» **Hard drive:** The technology's changing rapidly, with traditional hard disk drives (HDDs) now being rapidly replaced by *solid-state drives* (SSDs) with no moving parts, and to a lesser extent *hybrid drives* that bolt together a rotating drive with an SSD. Each technology has benefits and drawbacks. Yes, you can run a regular HDD drive as your C: drive, and it'll work fine. But SSD-goosed systems, on tablets, laptops, or desktops, run like greased lightning.

The SSD wins as speed king. After you use an SSD as your main system (C:) drive, you'll never go back to a spinning platter, I guarantee. SSDs are great for the main drive, but they're still expensive for storing pictures, movies, and photos. They may someday supplant the old whirling dervish drive, but price and technical considerations (see the sidebar "Solid-state drives have problems, too") assure that hard drives will be around for a long time. SSDs feature low power consumption and give off less heat. They have no moving parts, so they don't wear out like hard drives. And, if you drop a hard drive and a solid- state drive off the Leaning Tower of Pisa, one of them may survive. Or maybe not.

Hybrid drives combine the benefits and problems of both HDDs and SSDs. Although HDDs have long had *caches* — chunks of memory that hold data before being written to the drive, and after it's read from the drive — hybrid drives have a full SSD to act as a buffer.

If you can stretch the budget, start with an SSD for the system drive, a big hard drive (one that attaches with a USB cable) for storing photos, movies, and music, and get *another* drive (which can be inside your PC, outside attached with a USB cable, or even on a different PC on your network) to run File History (see Book 8, Chapter 1).

TECHNICAL STUFF

If you want full on-the-fly protection against dying hard drives, you can get three hard drives — one SSD, and two hard drives, either inside the box or outside attached with USB or eSATA cables — and run Storage Spaces (see Book 7, Chapter 4).

Ultimately, though, most people opt for a fast SSD for files needed immediately, coupled with cloud storage for the big stuff. Now that Google offers free unlimited photo storage — and with the rise of data streaming instead of purchased CDs — the need for giant hard drives has definitely hit the skids.

For the enthusiast, a three-tier system, with SSDs storing data you need all the time, intermediate backup in the cloud, and multi-terabyte data repositories hanging off your PC, seems to be the way to go. Privacy concerns (and the, uh, intervention of various governments) have people worried about cloud storage. Rightfully so.

» **CD, DVD, or Blu-ray drive:** Of course, these types of drives work with CDs, DVDs, and the Sony Blu-ray discs, which can be filled with data or contain music or movies. CDs hold about 700MB of data; DVDs hold 4GB, or six times as much as a CD. Dual-layer DVDs (which use two separate layers on top of the disc) hold about 8GB, and Blu-ray discs hold 50GB, or six times as much as a dual-layer DVD.

Fewer and fewer machines these days come with built-in DVD drives: If you want to schlep data from one place to another, a USB drive works fine — and going through the cloud is even easier. For most storage requirements, though, big, cheap USB drives are hard to beat.

TIP

Unless you want to stick a high-definition movie on a single disc or play Blu-ray discs that you buy or rent in your local video store, 50GB of data on a single disc is overkill. Most Windows 10 users who still want a DVD will do quite well with a dual-layer DVD-RW drive, for the princely sum of $30 or so. You can always use a dual-layer drive to record regular (single-layer) DVDs or CDs.

>> **USB drive or key drive:** Treat it like it's a lollipop. Half the size of a pack of gum and able to hold an entire PowerPoint presentation or two or six, plus a half dozen full-length movies, flash memory (also known as a jump drive, thumb drive, or memory stick) should be your first choice for external storage space or for copying files between computers. (See Figure 1-9.) You can even use USB drives on many DVD players and TV set-top boxes.

Pop one of these guys in a USB slot, and suddenly Windows 10 knows it has another drive — except that this one's fast, portable, and incredibly easy to use. Go for the cheapest flash drives you can find: Most of the "features" on fancy key drives are just, uh, Windows dressing.

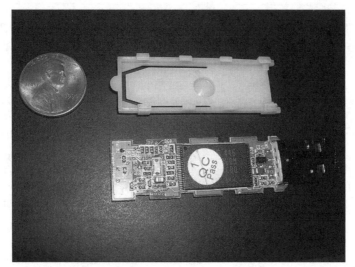

FIGURE 1-9:
The inside of a USB drive.

Source: Nrbelex, Wikimedia

SOLID-STATE DRIVES HAVE PROBLEMS, TOO

Although I love my SSD system drives and would never go back to rotating hard disk drives (HDDs), SSDs aren't perfect.

SSDs don't have any moving parts, and it looks like they're more reliable than HDDs. But when an HDD starts to go belly up, you can usually tell: whirring and gnashing, whining and groaning. Expiring SSDs don't give off any advanced warning signals. Or at least sounds.

When an HDD dies, you can frequently get the data back, although it can be expensive and time-consuming. When an SSD goes, you rarely get a second chance.

SSDs have to take care of lots of internal bookkeeping, both for trimming unused space and for load balancing to guarantee uniform wear patterns. SSDs actually slow down after you've used them for a few weeks, months, or years. The speed decrease is usually associated with the bookkeeping programs kicking in over time.

Finally, the SSD's own software has to be ultra-reliable. SSDs don't lay down tracks sequentially like HDDs. They hopscotch all over the place, and the firmware inside the SSD needs to keep up.

TIP

What about USB 3? If you have a hard drive that sits outside of your computer — an *external drive* — or a USB drive, it'll run faster if it's designed for USB 3 and attached to a USB 3 connector. Expect performance with USB 3 that's three to five times as fast as USB 2. For most other outside devices, USB 3 is overkill, and USB 2 works just as well.

This list is by no means definitive: New storage options come out every day.

Making PC connections

Your PC connects to the outside world by using a bewildering variety of cables and connectors. I describe the most common in this list:

>> **USB (Universal Serial Bus) cable:** This cable has a flat connector that plugs in to your PC, known as *USB A* (see Figure 1-10). The other end is sometimes shaped like a D (called *USB B*), but smaller devices have tiny terminators (usually called *USB mini* and *USB micro,* each of which can have two different shapes).

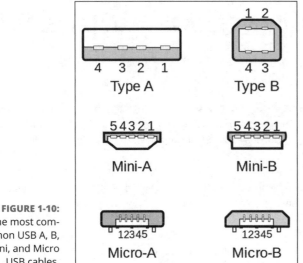

FIGURE 1-10:
The most com-
mon USB A, B,
Mini, and Micro
USB cables.

Source: Jdthood, Wikimedia

TECHNICAL
STUFF

ASK
WOODY.COM

USB 2 connectors will work with any device, but hardware — such as a hard drive — that uses USB 3 will run much faster if you use a USB 3 cable and plug it into the back of your computer in a USB 3 port. USB 2 works with USB 3 devices, but you won't get the speed. Note that not all PCs have USB 3 ports!

USB is the connector of choice for just about any kind of hardware — printer, scanner, phone, camera, portable hard drive, and even the mouse. Apple iPhones and iPads use a USB connector on one side — to plug in to your computers — but the other side is Thunderbolt (common on Apple devices, not so common on Windows PCs), and doesn't look or act like any other connector.

If you run out of USB connections on the back of your PC, get a USB hub with a separate power supply and plug away.

USB-C is a special kind of USB connection that supports very fast data trans-mission, and high levels of power. You know when you have USB-C because it's impossible to insert the plug upside-down — both sides work equally well. It's becoming the go-to choice for connecting peripherals and, in some cases, power supplies.

>> **LAN cable:** Also known as a CAT-5, CAT-6, or RJ-45 cable, it's the most common kind of network connector. It looks like an overweight telephone plug (see Figure 1-11). One end plugs in to your PC, typically into a network interface *card* (or *NIC,* pronounced "nick"), a network connector on the motherboard. The other end plugs in to your network's hub (see Figure 1-12) or switch or into a cable modem, DSL box, router, or other Internet connection-sharing device.

FIGURE 1-11:
RJ-45 Ethernet
LAN connector.

Source: David Monniaux, Wikimedia

FIGURE 1-12:
The back of a
home router.

Source: Raysonho, Wikimedia

>> **Keyboard and mouse cable:** Most mice and keyboards (even cordless mice and keyboards) come with USB connectors.

>> **DVI-D and HDMI connectors:** Although older monitors still use legacy, 15-pin, HD15 VGA connectors, most monitors and video cards now use the small HDMI connector (see Figure 1-13), which transmits both audio and video over one cable. Some older monitors don't support HDMI, but do take a DVI-D digital cable (see Figure 1-14).

TIP

If you hope to hook up your new TV to your PC, make sure your PC can connect to the TV with the right kind of cable. Or use Chromecast from your Chrome browser and a Chromecast dongle stuck in your TV — see Book 10, Chapter 2.

FIGURE 1-13:
HDMI has largely
supplanted the
old VGA and
DVI-D video
adapters.

Source: D-Kuru, Wikimedia

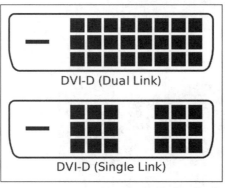

DVI-D (Dual Link)

DVI-D (Single Link)

FIGURE 1-14:
Two different
kinds of DVI-D
cables — they
work well, but
don't carry audio.

Source: Hungry Charlie, Wikimedia

TECHNICAL
STUFF

Some really old monitors still use the ancient 15-pin VGA connector, the one shaped like a *D*. Avoid VGA if you can. Old-fashioned serial (9-pin) and parallel (25-pin) cables and Centronics printer cables are growing as scarce as hen's teeth. Hey, the hen doesn't need them, either.

>> **Bluetooth** is a short-distance wireless connection. Once upon a time, Bluetooth was very finicky and hard to set up. Since the recent adoption of solid standards, Bluetooth's become quite useful.

Futzing with video, sound, and multitudinous media

Unless you're using a tablet, chances are pretty good that you're running Windows 10 on a PC with at least a little oomph in the audio department. In the simplest case, you have to be concerned about four specific sound jacks (or groups of sound jacks) because each one does something different. Your machine may not have all four (are you feeling inadequate yet?), or it may look like a patch board at a Slayer concert, but the basics are still the same.

Here's how the four key jacks are usually marked, although sometimes you have to root around in the documentation to find the details:

>> **Line In:** This stereo input jack is usually blue. It feeds a stereo audio signal — generally from an amplified source — into the PC. Use this jack to receive audio output into your computer from an iPad, cable box, TV set, radio, CD player, electric guitar, or other audio-generating box.

>> **Mic In:** This jack is usually pink. It's for unamplified sources, like most microphones or some electric guitars. If you use a cheap microphone for Skype or another VoIP service that lets you talk long distance for free, and the mic doesn't have a USB connector, plug in the microphone here. In a pinch, you can plug any of the Line In devices into the Mic In jack — but you may hear only mono sound, not stereo, and you may have to turn the volume way down to avoid some ugly distortion when the amplifier inside your PC increases the strength of an already-amplified signal.

>> **Line Out:** A stereo output jack, usually lime green, which in many cases can be used for headphones or patched into powered speakers. If you don't have fancy output jacks (such as the Sony-Philips SPDIF), this is the source for the highest-quality sound your computer can produce. If you go for a multi-speaker setup, this is for the front speaker.

>> **Rear Surround Out:** Usually black, this jack isn't used often. It's intended to be used if you have independent, powered rear speakers. Most people with rear speakers use the Line Out connector and plug it into their home theater systems, which then drives the rear speakers; or they use the HDMI cable (see the preceding section) to hook up to their TVs. If your computer can produce full surround sound output, and you have the amplifier to handle it, you'll get much better results using the black jack.

ASK
WOODY.COM

Many desktop computers have two more jacks: Orange is a direct feed for your subwoofer, and the gray (or brown) one is for your side speakers. Again, you have to put an amplifier between the jacks and your speakers.

Fortunately, PC-savvy 4-channel amplifiers can handle the lime (front speaker) and black (rear speaker) lines, 6-channel amps may be able to handle all but the gray, and 8-channel amps will take all four: lime (front speaker), orange (subwoofer, or center back), black (rear), and gray (side).

With a sufficiently bottomless budget, you can make your living room sound precisely like the 08R runway at Honolulu International.

Laptops typically have just two jacks, pink for Mic In and lime for Line Out. If you have a headphone with a mic, that's the right combination. It's also common to plug powered external speakers into the lime jack.

Tablets and phones usually have an earphone jack, which works just like a lime green Line Out jack.

High-end audio systems may support optical connections. Check both the computer end of the connection and the speaker/receiver end to make sure they'll line up.

TIP

PC manufacturers love to extol the virtues of their advanced sound systems, but the simple fact is that you can hook up a rather plain-vanilla PC to a home stereo and get good-enough sound. Just connect the Line Out jack on the back of your PC to the Aux In jack on your home stereo or entertainment center. *Voilà!*

Netbooks and Ultrabooks

I really fell in love with an ASUS netbook while working with Windows 7. But then along came the iPad, and at least 80 percent of the reason for using a netbook disappeared. Sales of *netbooks* — small, light, inexpensive laptops — have not fared well, and I don't see a comeback any time soon. Tablets just blow the doors off netbooks, and 2-in-1s just mopped up the remains.

Ultrabooks are a slightly different story. Intel coined (and trademarked) the term *Ultrabook* and set the specs. For a manufacturer to call its piece of iron an Ultrabook, it has to be less than 21mm thick, run for five hours on a battery charge, and resume from hibernation in seven seconds or less. In other words, it must work a lot like an iPad.

Intel threw a $300 million marketing budget at Ultrabooks, but they fizzled. Now the specs seem positively ancient, and the term *Ultrabook* doesn't have the wow factor it once enjoyed.

Right now, I'm having a great time with all the new form factors: I mention the XPS-15, Surface Book, and Surface Pro 4 earlier in this chapter. I worked with a trapezelike machine for a bit, but always worried about snapping the carrier off. There's no one-size-fits-all solution. Now, depending on the situation, I'm just as likely to grab my iPad Pro as I head out the door, or curl back with a Chromebook to watch Netflix. I use Android phones and iPhones, too, all the time.

If you're in the market for a new machine, drop by your favorite hardware store and just take a look around. You might find something different that strikes your fancy. Or you may decide that you just want to stick with a boring desktop machine with a mechanical keyboard and three monitors the size of football fields.

Guess what I work on.

What's Wrong with Windows 10?

Microsoft made a lot of mistakes in Windows 10's first year of existence. Chief among them was the widely despised "Get Windows 10" campaign. Combining the worst of intrusive malware, forced updates, bad interface design, presumptive implementation, and a simple lack of respect for Windows 7 and 8.1 customers, Get Windows 10 (GWX), to me, represents the lowest point in the history of Windows. Microsoft just didn't give a hairy rat's patoutie who they stomped on, as they pushed and pushed and pushed to get everybody on Windows 10.

Which is a shame, really, because Windows 10 is a great operating system.

**ASK
WOODY.COM**

Many people who used to trust Microsoft, more or less, lost all trust in the wake of GWX, and it's hard to blame them. I've been writing books about Windows and Office for 25 years, and I think GWX is the most customer-antagonistic effort Microsoft has ever undertaken.

Trust in Microsoft is at the core of what you need to understand about Windows 10.

Here's what I feel every Windows 10 customer should know:

>> **Forced updates:** Most Windows 10 customers don't have any choice about updates; when Microsoft releases a patch, it gets applied, unless you go to near-Herculean lengths to block them (see http://www.infoworld.com/article/3053701/microsoft-windows/block-windows-10-forced-updates-without-breaking-your-machine-part-2.html). I've railed against automatic updating for more than a decade V — bad patches have driven many machines and their owners to the brink. The GWX debacle has shown that Microsoft has little respect for what you want to do with your computer. With Win10, you don't have much choice.

>> **Privacy concerns:** Microsoft's following the same path blazed by Google and Facebook and, to a lesser extent, Apple and many other tech companies. They're all scraping information about you, snooping on what you're doing, in an attempt to sell you things. I don't think Microsoft is any worse than the others, but I don't think it's any better either. I talk about reducing the amount of data that Microsoft collects about you in Book 2, Chapter 6, but the simple fact is that nobody knows exactly what data is being collected, or how it's being used.

I think that data snooping will be the focus of extensive legislation over the next decade and one of the major battles of our time. The problem, of course, is that the people who control the laws also control the organizations that circumvent the laws.

>> **Massive dearth of apps:** Five years ago, apps were a nice part of using an iPhone or iPad. Now, many people rely on them to get their work done and to keep their lives sunny side up. Microsoft missed the ball with UWP apps — they never caught on, and with the demise of a viable Microsoft phone ecosystem, developers have little incentive to make UWP apps. That means we're all going to be using Win32 apps — the kind that were revolutionary 20 years ago — on our Windows machines for the foreseeable future.

ASK
WOODY.COM

I've learned how to block Microsoft's forced updating — details are in my Info-World Woody on Windows blog, http://www.infoworld.com/article/3053701/ microsoft-windows/block-windows-10-forced-updates-without-breaking- your-machine-part-2.html. I've come to peace with the fact that Microsoft's snooping on me. (Hey, I've used Google's Chrome browser for years, and it's been harvesting data the entire time.) And when I want the convenience of a specific app, I'll pick up my phone, tablet, or Chromebook.

But that's just me. You may have good reason to want to switch to another computing platform. Certainly, Windows will give you more headaches and heartaches than the alternatives. But it gives you more opportunities, too.

Welcome to my world.

Chapter 2

Windows 10 for the Experienced

f you're among the 1.7 billion or so souls on the planet who have been around the block with Windows 8/8.1, Windows 7, Windows Vista, or Windows XP, you're in for a shock.

Although Windows 10 will look vaguely familiar to long-time desktop users, the details are very different. And if you've conquered the Metro side of Windows 8.1 (which is the only side of Windows 8), you're going to be in for a pleasant surprise.

If You Just Upgraded from Win7 or 8.1 to Win10

Before we dig into an examination of the new nooks and crannies in Windows 10, I'd like to pause for a second and let you know about an option you may or may not have.

If you upgraded from Windows 7 or 8.1 to Windows 10 in the past 30 days, and you don't like Windows 10, you can roll back to your old version. This works for only 30 days because a scheduled program comes in and wipes out the backup after 30 days. But if you're in under the wire and want to roll back, here's how. Note that this technique is only for upgraders; it doesn't apply to new Windows 10 systems or computers in which you installed Windows 10 by wiping out the hard drive. If you love Win10 or don't qualify for the rollback, jump down to the next section.

The method for moving back is easy:

1. **Make sure you have your old password.**

   If your original Windows 7 or Windows 8.1 system had login IDs with passwords, you'll need those passwords to log in to the original accounts. If you changed the password while in Windows 10 (local account), you need your old password, not your new one. If you created a new account while in Windows 10, you have to delete it before reverting to the earlier version of Windows.

2. **Make a backup.**

   Before you change any operating system, it's a good idea to make a full system backup. Many people recommend Acronis for the job, but Windows 10 has a good system image program as well that is identical to the Windows 7 version. However, the program is hard to find. To get to the system image program, in the Win10 Cortana search box, type **Windows Backup**, press Enter, click Create a System Image (on the left), and follow the directions.

3. **Run the reset.**

   Choose the Start icon, the Settings icon, Update & Security, and then Recovery. You see an entry to Go Back to Windows 7 or Go Back to Windows 8.1, depending on the version of Windows from whence you came.

   If you don't see the Go Back option and are using an administrator account, you've likely fallen victim to one of the many gotchas that surround the upgrade. See the next part of this section, but don't get your hopes up.

4. **Choose to keep files or wipe them out.**

   If you chose Go Back to a Previous Windows, you're given a choice analogous to the choice you made when you upgraded to Windows 10, to either Keep My Files or Remove Everything. See Figure 2-1. The former keeps your files (as long as they're located in the usual places), so changes you made to them in Windows 10 will appear back in Windows 7 (or 8.1). The latter wipes out all your files, apps, and settings, as you would expect.

5. **Tell Microsoft why you don't like Win10.**

   The Windows rollback software wants to know why you're rolling back, offers to check for updates in a last-ditch attempt to keep you in the Windows 10 fold, warns you that you'll have to reinstall some programs after going back (a problem I didn't encounter with my rather pedestrian test programs), thanks you for trying Windows 10, and then lets you go back.

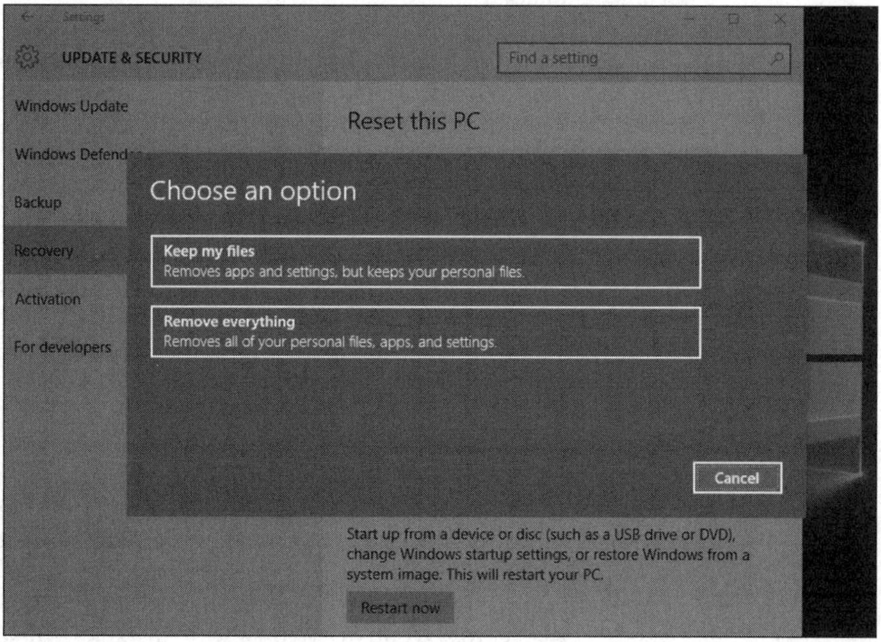

FIGURE 2-1:
When you roll back to Windows 7 or 8.1, you can choose to save your files or not.

Windows 10 for the Experienced

6. **Click Next.**

After a while (many minutes, sometimes hours), you arrive back at the Windows 7 (or 8.1) login screen.

7. **Click a login ID and provide a password.**

You're ready to go with your old version.

ASK WOODY.COM

I found, in extensive testing, that the Keep My Files option does, in spite of the warning, restore apps (programs) and settings to the original apps and settings (the ones that existed when you upgraded from Win7 to Win10). Any modifications made to those programs (for example, applying security updates to Office programs) while using Windows 10 will not be applied when you return to Win7; you have to apply them again.

On the other hand, changes made to your regular files while working in Windows 10 — edits made to Office documents, for example, or to new files created while working with Windows 10 — may or may not make it back to Windows 7. I had no problems with files stored in My Documents; edits made to those documents persisted when Windows 10 rolled back to Windows 7. But files stored in other locations (specifically, in the \Public\Documents folder or on the desktop) didn't make it back: Word docs created in Win10 simply disappeared when rolling back to Win7, even though they were on the desktop or in the Public Documents folder.

TIP

One oddity may prove useful: If you upgrade to Windows 10, create or edit documents in a strange location, and then roll back to Windows 7 (or 8.1), those documents may not make the transition. Amazingly, if you then upgrade again to Windows 10, the documents may reappear. You can retrieve the "lost" documents, stick them in a convenient place (such as on a USB drive or in the cloud), roll back to Windows 7, and pull the files back again.

Important lesson: Back up your data files before you revert to an earlier version of Windows. If you lose a file while going from Windows 7 to Windows 10, you can usually find it from inside Win10 in the hidden Windows.old folder. But when you go back from Win10 to Win7, there is no Windows.old folder.

If you can't get Windows to roll back and absolutely detest Windows 10, you're up against a tough choice. The only option I've found that works reliably is to reinstall the original version of Windows from scratch. On some machines, the old recovery partition still exists and you can bring back your old version of Windows by going through the standard recovery partition technique (which varies from manufacturer to manufacturer), commonly called a factory restore. More frequently, you get to start all over with a fresh install of Windows 7 or 8.1.

A Brief History of Windows 10

So you've decided to stick with Win10? Good.

Pardon me while I rant for a bit.

Microsoft darn near killed Windows — and most of the PC industry — with the abomination that was Windows 8. Granted, there were other forces at work — the ascendancy of mobile computing, touchscreens, faster cheaper and smaller hardware, better Apples, and other competition — but to my mind the number one factor in the demise of Windows was Windows 8.

ASK
WOODY.COM

We saw PC sales drop. After Windows XP owners replaced their machines in a big wave in late 2014 and early 2015, responding to the end of support for XP, we saw PC sales drop even more. Precipitously. Steve Ballmer confidently predicted that Microsoft would ship 400 million machines with Windows 8 preinstalled in the year that followed Windows 8's release. The actual number was closer to a quarter of that. Normal people like you and me went to great lengths to avoid Windows 8, settling on Windows 7.

Windows 8.1, which arrived a nail-biting year after Windows 8, improved the situation a little bit, primarily by not forcing people to boot to the tiled Metro Start screen.

The team inside Microsoft that brought us the wonderful forced Windows 8 Metro experience were also responsible, earlier, for the Office ribbon. Many of us old-timers grumbled about the ribbon, saying Microsoft should at least present an alternative for using the older menu interface. It never happened. Office 2007 shipped with an early ribbon, and subsequent versions have been even more ribbon-ified since. Here's the key point: Office 2007 sold like hotcakes, in spite of the ribbon, and it's been selling in the multi-billion-dollar range ever since.

As a result, the Office interface team figured they knew what consumers wanted, and old-timers were just pounding their canes and waggling toothless gums.

The entire Office 2007 management team was transplanted, almost intact, to the Windows 8 effort. They saw an opportunity to transform the Windows interface, and they took it, over the strenuous objections of many of us in the peanut gallery. I'm convinced they figured it would play out like the Office ribbon. It didn't. Windows 8 is, arguably, the largest software disaster in Microsoft's history.

Essentially all the Windows 8 management team — including some very talented and experienced people — left Microsoft shortly after Win8 shipped. With a thud. Their boss, Steve Ballmer, left Microsoft too. Ballmer's still the largest individual shareholder in Microsoft, with 333,000,000 shares at last count, worth $17 billion and change.

In their place, we're seeing an entirely new generation of Windows managers, raised in the cloud, but more than willing to listen to reason. The current head of the Windows effort, Terry Myerson, was in charge of Windows Phone — and before that, Windows Exchange Server. Head honcho Satya Nadella not only knows cloud computing, he invented lots of the Microsoft pieces.

That said, Microsoft's traditional PC market has sunk into a funk, and it appears to be on a slow ride into the sunset. Or it may just turn belly up and sink, anchored with mounds of iPhones, iPads, MacBooks, Galaxy Tabs, and Chromebooks. Or maybe, just maybe, Windows 10 will breathe some life back into the 30-year-old veteran. Yes, Windows 1.0 shipped in November 1985.

However things play out, at least we have an (admittedly highly modified) Start menu to work with, as you can see in Figure 2-2.

The first release of Windows 10, dubbed build 10240 (or just RTM by us old guys), came out on July 29, 2015. The second release, called version 1511 or the November update, arrived in November 2015. (1511 = November 2015, get it?) It had only a few improvements.

THE "GET WINDOWS 10" DEBACLE

No description of the recent history of Windows, however brief, can gloss over the fear and loathing that Microsoft induced with its Get Windows 10, or GWX, campaign.

The campaign started shortly after the RTM release in July 2015, with a little-noticed program known as KB 3035583. In October 2015, Microsoft started force-updating Windows 7 and 8.1 computers to Windows 10, without the owners' knowledge or consent. A loud scream arose and, a week after the forced upgrades started, they suddenly stopped. But the GWX campaign continued, showing increasingly persistent ads for Windows 10, all the symptoms of nagware and even malware. Microsoft proved that it could reach into your Windows 7 machine and start the upgrade to Windows 10, whether you wanted it or not.

The resultant clamor — from an unexpected appearance of a Win10 upgrade notification on a weather forecaster's live news show, to Windows experts fretting over their relatives and friends, to more than 1 million posts on a Chinese blog — should have convinced Microsoft to back off. It didn't. If you bump into people who don't trust Windows, or Microsoft, they have good reason.

The third release, known variously as the anniversary update and version 1607, came out in August 2016 (they missed the numbering system by a bit). I call it Win 10.2, but I'm old-fashioned that way. You can call it anything you like. Win 10.2 includes all sorts of improvements, such as the new Start menu layout, an improved Action/Notification Center, Hand-Off/Continuum features that almost nobody uses, Ink Workspace, which is great for Surface Books and Pros but not much else, along with big changes to Cortana and enough improvements to the Microsoft Edge browser that it's actually usable.

REMEMBER

The Different Kinds of Windows Programs, Er, Apps

Windows 10 runs two very different kinds of programs. Permit me to go back to basics.

Computer programs (call them applications or apps if you want) that you and I know work by interacting with an operating system. Since the dawn of Windows time, give or take a bit, Windows apps have communicated with Windows through a specific set of routines (application program interfaces or APIs) known colloquially and collectively as Win32. With rare exceptions, Windows desktop apps — the kind you use every day — take advantage of Win32 APIs to work with Windows.

In early June 2011, at the All Things D D9 conference in California, Steve Sinofsky and Julie Larson-Green gave their first demo of Windows 8. As part of the demo, they showed off new immersive or Metro apps, which interact with Windows in a very different way. They use the newly minted (and still evolving) API set known as Windows Runtime or, more commonly, the WinRT API.

TECHNICAL
STUFF

Microsoft started calling the WinRT based apps "immersive" and "full screen." Most of the world settled on Microsoft's internal code name, Metro. Microsoft, however, has since changed the name to Modern UI, then Windows 8, Windows Store App, New User Interface, Microsoft Design Language, Microsoft style design, and more recently Modern and Universal. The preferred terminology at the moment is *Universal Windows Platform (UWP) app,* although the tech support folks revert to *Universal app* all the time. I continue to use the term *Metro* in normal conversation, but in this book, to minimize confusion, I use the term Universal Windows app.

Don't be confused. (Ha!) They all mean the same thing: Those are the names for Universal Windows applications that run with the WinRT API.

TECHNICAL
STUFF

Universal Windows (Modern, Metro) apps have many other characteristics: They're sandboxed — stuck inside a software cocoon that isolates the programs so that it's hard to spread infections through them. They can be easily interrupted, so their power consumption can be minimized; if a Universal Windows app hangs, it's almost impossible for the app to freeze the machine. But at their heart, Universal Windows apps are written to use the WinRT API.

Windows 8 and 8.1 (and Server 2012) support the WinRT API — Universal apps run on the Metro side of Windows 8, not on the desktop. ARM-based processors also run the WinRT API. You can find ARM architecture processors in many phones and tablets. In theory, Universal apps should run on any Windows 10 computer — a desktop, a laptop, a tablet, a phone, a wall-mounted Surface Hub, an Xbox, and even a HoloLens headset. In practice, however, it ain't quite so simple. For example, only the simplest Universal app that works in Windows 10 will run in Windows 8. So "Universal" is something of an aspiration, not a definition.

REMEMBER

In Windows 10, Universal Windows (Modern/Metro/Tiled) apps run in their own boxes, right there on the desktop. Look at the Weather app — a Universal Windows app — shown in Figure 2-3.

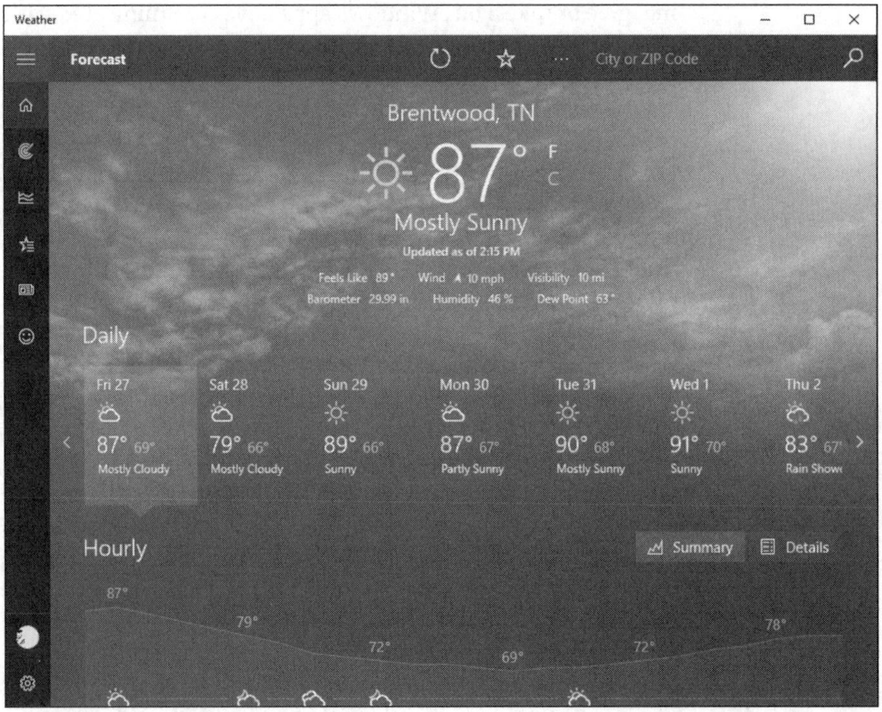

FIGURE 2-3:
The Windows 10 Weather app is a Universal Windows app because it's based on the WinRT API. See the distinctive design?

All the other Windows programs — the ones you've known since you were still wet behind the WinEars — are now called Windows Desktop apps. Three years ago, you would've just called them programs, but now they have a new name. After all, if Apple can call its programs *apps*, Microsoft can, too. Technically, old-fashioned Windows programs (Windows Desktop apps) are built to use the Win32 API.

HOW DID WE GET INTO THIS NICE MESS

Microsoft's been making tablet software for more than 10 years, and it never put a dent in the market. Never did get it. Apple started selling tablet software in 2010, and selling tons of it. Boy howdy. Now Microsoft's diving in to get a piece of the touch-enabled action.

There's a big difference in approaches. Apple started with a telephone operating system, iOS, and grew it to become the world's best-selling tablet operating system. There's very little difference between iOS 9 on an iPhone and iOS 9 on an iPad: Applications written for one device usually work on the other, with a few obvious changes, such as screen size. On the other hand, Apple's computer operating system, OS X (say "oh ess ten"), is completely different. It's built and optimized for use with a Mac computer. Apple is slowly changing the programs, er, apps on both iOS and OS X so they resemble each other and work together. But the operating systems are fundamentally quite different (even though, yes, iOS did originally start with the Mac OS Darwin foundation).

When Windows 7 was finished, Steve Sinofsky and crew decided to take a fundamentally different tack. Instead of the good people at Microsoft growing their phone software up, they decided to grow their computer operating system down. (The fact that the phone software at that point drew nearly universal scorn could've been part of the reason.) Windows 8 grew out of that decision: There's a touch-friendly part and a mouse- and keyboard-friendly part. The two aren't mutually exclusive: You can use your mouse on the Metro Start screen and in the tiled full-screen apps; you can use your greasy thumb on an old-fashioned Windows desktop app. But the approach is different, the design is different, and the intent is different.

Windows 10 goes back to Windows Start menu roots and tries to grow the same concept down even further, to Windows Phone. Microsoft will be able to say that Windows covers all the bases, from lowly smartphones to gigantic workstations (and server farms, for that matter). The fact that the "Windows" running in each of the device classes is quite different kinda gets swept under the rug.

ASK
WOODY.COM

Unfortunately, there's a huge difference between Universal Windows apps and Windows Desktop apps. For starters:

>> **Windows Desktop apps are on the way out.** Microsoft won't abandon them or the Win32 API anytime soon, but with the exception of a few big money-milking programs and utilities and niche programs from small developers, Windows Desktop apps are starting to be viewed as legacy apps, ones ultimately headed to the bone farm.

>> **Universal Windows apps — the ones that run on the WinRT API — are the future.** Microsoft rebuilt the aging Windows Desktop app Internet Explorer and turned it into the Universal Windows app called Microsoft Edge. Microsoft is trying hard to replace Windows Desktop app versions of Office with snappier, analogous (and finger-friendly) Universal Windows apps. Of course, the Universal version of Office doesn't have anywhere near as many features as the Desktop version.

>> **Windows Desktop apps and Universal Windows apps are starting to look the same.** Developers want you to look at their programs and think, "Oh, hey, this is a snappy new version."

>> **Universal Windows apps really are better.** Don't shoot me. I'm just the messenger. Now that we can run those newfangled tiled Universal Metro whoozamajiggers in their own resizable windows on the Windows desktop, the underlying new WinRT plumbing beats the pants off Win32. WinRT apps don't bump into each other as much, they (generally) play nice in their own sandboxes, they won't take Windows down with them, and they don't have all the overhead of those buggy Win32 calls.

If you're going to stay with Windows, it's time to get with the system and learn about this new tiled stuff.

Here's a quick guide to what's new — and what's still the same — with some down-and-dirty help for deciding whether you truly need Windows 10.

What's New for the XP Crowd

Time to fess up. You can tell me. I won't rat you out.

If you're an experienced Windows XP user and you're looking at Windows 10, one of two things happened: Either your trusty old XP machine died and you *had* to get Win10 with a new PC, or a friend or family member conned you into looking into Win10 to provide tech support.

Am I right, or am I right? Hey, as of this writing, something like 10 percent of all Windows online use comes from Windows XP. Yeah, you read that number right. Win7 may dominate, but XP is still alive and well even though Microsoft doesn't support it.

If you're thinking of making the jump from XP to Win10, and you're going to stick with a keyboard (as opposed to going touch-only, or touch-mostly, heaven help ya), you have two big hurdles:

>> Learning the ways of tiled Universal Windows apps (which I outline in the next section, "What's New for Windows 7 and Vista Victims")

>> Making the transition from XP to Windows 7 because the Win10 desktop works much like Windows 7

Are you sure you want to tackle the learning curve? Er, curves? See the nearby sidebar about switching to a Mac.

That said, if you didn't plunge into the Windows 7 or Vista madness, or the Windows 8/8.1 diversion, and instead sat back and waited for something better to come along, many improvements indeed await in Windows 10.

WOULDN'T IT BE SMARTER TO GET A MAC?

Knowledgeable Windows XP users may find it easier — or at least more rewarding — to jump to a Mac, rather than upgrading to Windows 10. I know that's heretical. Microsoft will never speak to me again. But there's much to be said for making the switch.

Why? XP cognoscenti face a double whammy: learning Windows 7 (for the Win10 desktop) and learning how to deal with Metro/Modern Universal Windows apps. If you don't mind paying the higher price — and, yes, Macs are marginally more expensive than PCs, feature-for-feature — Macs have a distinct advantage in being able to work easily in the Apple ecosystem: iPads, iPhones, the App Store, iTunes, iCloud, and Apple TV all work together remarkably well. That's a big advantage held by Apple, where the software, hardware, cloud support, and content all come from the same company. "It just works" may be overblown, but there's more than a nugget of truth in it. Give or take a buggy iOS update.

Yes, Macs have a variant of the Blue Screen of Death. Yes, Macs do get viruses. Yes, Macs have all sorts of problems. Yes, you may have to stand in line at an Apple Store to get help — I guess there's a reason why Microsoft Stores seem so empty.

If you're thinking about switching sides, I bet you'll be surprised at the similarities between Mac OS X and Windows XP.

Improved performance

Windows 10 (and Windows 8 and 7 before it) actually places fewer demands on your PC's hardware. I know that's hard to believe, but as long as you have a fairly powerful video card, and 2GB or more of main memory, moving from XP to Win10 will make your PC run faster.

ASK
WOODY.COM

If you don't have a powerful video card, and you're running a desktop system, you can get one for less than $100, and extra memory costs a pittance. I've upgraded dozens of PCs from XP to Win10, and the performance improvement is quite noticeable. You laptop users aren't so lucky because laptop video is usually soldered in.

Better video

Windows 10 doesn't sport the Aero interface made popular in Vista and Win7, but some of the Aero improvements persist.

TIP

The *Snap Assist* feature in Windows 10 lets you drag a window to an edge of the screen and have it automatically resize to half-screen size — a boon to anyone with a wide screen. Sounds like a parlor trick, but it's a capability I use many times every day. You can even snap to the four corners of the screen, and the desktop shows you which open programs can be clicked to fill in the open spot (see Figure 2-4).

Windows 10's desktop shows you thumbnails of running programs when you hover your mouse cursor over a program on the taskbar (see Figure 2-4).

Video efficiency is also substantially improved: If you have a video that drips and drops in XP, the same video running on the same hardware may go straight through in Windows 10.

A genuinely better browser is emerging

Internet Explorer lives in Windows 10, but it's buried deep. If you're lucky, you'll never see it when you use Win10. IE is an old, buggy, bloated slug with incredibly stupid and infection-prone "features": ActiveX, COM extensions, custom crap-filled toolbars, and don't get me started on Silverlight. IE deserves to die, if only in retaliation for all the infections it's brought to millions of machines.

In its place, the new, light, standards-happy, fast Microsoft Edge is everything IE should be, without the legacy garbage. Microsoft built Edge from the ground up as a Universal Windows app — a new WinRT API-based tiled app that runs on the desktop in its own resizable window.

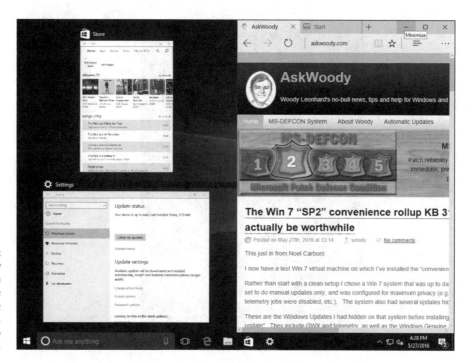

FIGURE 2-4:
Drag a window
to the edge or a
corner, and the
other available
windows appear,
ready for you to
click into place.

It's a poster boy for the new apps that are coming down the pike. It took Microsoft forever to build, but the final result is well worth the effort.

Unfortunately, Edge is still an unfinished work. Few people use it because it lacks many important browser features. The situation's slowly improving, though, and Edge may well be ready for prime time at some point.

If you live in fear of IE getting you infected and/or hate the massive IE patches now appearing every month, Microsoft Edge will be a refreshing change.

Cortana

Apple has Siri. Google has Google Now. Amazon has Alexa. Microsoft has Cortana, the Redmond version of an AI-based personal assistant, shown in Figure 2-5. Unlike Siri and Now, though, Cortana has taken over the Windows search function, so it has a larger potential footprint than its AI cousins, which comes with a double edge. At the same time, Cortana really, really wants to scan everything on your computer, coming and going — all the better to help you with, my dear.

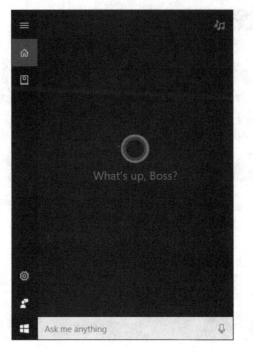

What's up, Boss?

Ask me anything

I tell you much more about Cortana in this book — she has a chapter all to herself, Book 3, Chapter 6 — but I'll drop a little tidbit here, tailored for those Windows XP fans among you who may just be a bit intimidated by a talking helper-droid.

You see, Cortana has a history.

Back in 2001, Microsoft released a game called Halo: Combat Evolved. In Halo: CE, you, the player, take the role of the Master Chief, a kinda-human kinda-cyber soldier known as Master Chief Petty Officer John-117. Cortana is part of you, an artificial intelligence that's built into a neural implant in your body armor. After saving Captain Keyes, Cortana and the Master Chief go into a map room called the Silent Cartographer, and . . . well, you get the idea. Cortana is smooth and creepy and omniscient, just like the Windows 10 character.

ASK
WOODY.COM

Right now, depending on how you measure, Cortana is likely the least intelligent of the assistants, with Google on top, and Siri and Alexa vying for second place. That may change over time. In fact, some day Cortana may scan this paragraph and call me to task for my impertinence — bad blot on my record, served up to our robotic overlords.

Other improvements

Many other features — not as sexy as Cortana but every bit as useful — put Windows 10 head and shoulders above XP. The standout features include:

REMEMBER

» **The taskbar:** I know many XP users swear by the old Quick Launch toolbar, but the taskbar, after you get to know it, runs rings around its predecessor. Just one example is shown in Figure 2-3 earlier in this chapter.

» **A backup worthy of the name:** Backup was a cruel joke in Windows XP. Windows 7 did it better, but Windows 10 makes backup truly easy, particularly with File History (see Book 8, Chapter 1).

» **A less-infested notification area:** XP let any program and its brother put an icon in the notification area, near the system clock. Windows 10 severely limits the number of icons that appear and gives you a spot to click if you really want to see them all. Besides, notifications are supposed to go in the Action pane, on the right. See Book 2, Chapter 3.

» **Second monitor support:** Although some video card manufacturers managed to jury-rig multiple monitor support into the Windows XP drivers, Windows 10 makes using multiple monitors one-click easy.

» **Homegroups:** Windows 10, like Windows 7, lets you put together all the PCs in a trusted environment and share among them quite easily.

» **Easy wireless networking:** All sorts of traps and gotchas live in the Windows XP wireless programs. Windows 10 does it much, much better.

» **Search:** In Windows XP, searching for anything other than a filename involved an enormous kludge of an add-on that sucked up computer cycles and overwhelmed your machine. In Windows 10, search is part of Windows itself, and it works quickly.

On the security front, Windows 10 is light years ahead of XP. From protection against rootkits to browser hardening, and a million points in between, XP is a security disaster — Microsoft no longer supports it — while Windows 10 is relatively (not completely) impenetrable.

Although Windows 10 isn't the XP of your dreams, it's remarkably easy to use and has all sorts of compelling new features.

What's New for Windows 7 and Vista Victims

Anything that works with Windows 7, 8, or 8.1 — and almost everything from Vista — will work in Windows 10. Programs, hardware, drivers, utilities — just about anything.

That's a remarkable achievement, particularly because your Windows Desktop apps/Legacy programs (there's that *L* word again) have to peacefully coexist with the WinRT API–based Windows/Universal/Modern/Metro apps.

Windows 10 does have lots going for it. Let me skip lightly through the major changes between Windows 7 and Windows 10.

Getting the hang of the new Start menu

By now, you've no doubt seen the tiles on the right of the Start menu (refer to Figure 2-6).

FIGURE 2-6:
The Windows 10 desktop.

If you're coming to Windows 10 from Windows 7 — without taking a detour through Windows 8 — those tiles are likely to represent your greatest conceptual hurdle. They're different, but in many ways they're familiar.

Do you remember gadgets in Win7? See Figure 2-7. They actually started in Vista. Many people (who finally found them) put tiles for clocks on their desktops. I also used to use the CPU gadget and on some machines the Weather gadget.

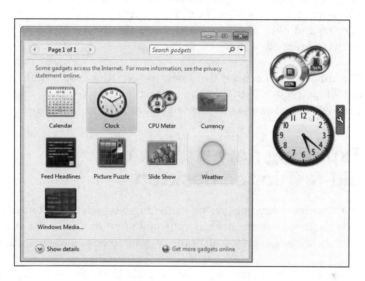

FIGURE 2-7:
Windows 7
gadgets — at
least from the
interface point
of view — work
much like the
new Universal
Windows
app tiles.

In Windows 10, you have a layout that's more or less similar to Windows 7, but it has fantastically good gadgets. Microsoft rebuilt all the plumbing in Windows to support these really good gadgets. Those updated, enormously powerful gadgets are now called Universal Windows apps.

The new gadgets/Universal Windows apps run in resizable windows on the desktop. They can do phenomenal things. In fact, Microsoft Edge is quite superior to Internet Explorer, even if it doesn't yet have all the bells and whistles. Internet Explorer gets the heave-ho. Edge, which runs as a gadget/Universal Windows app, becomes the new default browser.

Tiles for these gadgets/Universal Windows apps appear to the right of the list of programs in the Win10 Start menu.

REMEMBER

Here's the big picture, from the Win7 perspective: Windows 10 has a desktop, and it's more or less analogous to the desktop in Windows 7. It doesn't have a Windows 8/8.1–style Metro view. Doesn't need a Metro view: The gadgets (or Metro apps or Universal Windows apps) now behave themselves and run in resizable windows on the desktop.

In Windows 10, you can switch from a finger-friendly view of the desktop to a mouse-friendly view and back. The finger-friendly view — called tablet mode — has larger gadget tiles, opens the gadgets at full-screen, and hides most of the text. It takes three clicks to change modes. Or you can plug or unplug your keyboard, and Windows will ask if you want to switch modes.

Here's the ace in the hole: Programmers who write programs for these new gadgets can have their gadgets run, with a varying amount of modification, on Windows 10 for PCs, Windows 10 for tablets without a keyboard, Windows 10 phones, and even Xbox. At least, that's the theory. Remains to be seen how it works in practice.

The only way you can get these new gadgets/Universal Windows apps is through the Windows Store, so — again, at least in theory — they should be well vetted, checked for malware, and generally in good shape, before you can install them.

Exploring new stuff in the old-fashioned desktop

You'll notice many improvements to long-neglected portions of the Windows 7–style desktop. For example, if you copy more than one file at a time, Windows actually keeps you on top of all the copying in one window. Imagine that.

A new and much better *Task Manager* rolls in all the usage reporting that's been scattered in different corners of Windows (see Figure 2-8). The new Task Manager even gives you hooks to look at programs that start automatically, and to stop them if you like. Some serious chops. See Book 8, Chapter 4.

File Explorer (formerly known as Windows Explorer) takes on a new face and loses some of its annoying bad habits. You may or may not like the new Explorer, but at least Windows 10 brings back the up arrow to move up one folder — a feature that last appeared in Windows XP. That one feature, all by itself, makes me feel good about the new File Explorer. Explorer also now offers native support for ISO files. About time.

Taking a cue from iPad . . . er, other tablets, Windows 10 also offers a one-stop system restore capability. Actually, it offers three capabilities: *PC Reset* wipes everything off the machine and then reinstalls Windows 10. *PC Refresh* goes through the same motions but retains your data, apps from the Windows Store, and settings. And Start Fresh pulls in a brand-spanking-new version of Windows 10. Note that PC Refresh zaps out your legacy Windows Desktop apps and doesn't put them back. See Book 8, Chapter 2.

Task Manager

File Options View

Processes	Performance	App history	Startup	Users	Details	Services			
Name					34% CPU	68% Memory	29% Disk	0% Network	
Apps (3)									
Microsoft Edge					0%	11.5 MB	0 MB/s	0 Mbps	
Task Manager					1.6%	8.3 MB	0.1 MB/s	0 Mbps	
Windows Explorer					0%	19.8 MB	0.1 MB/s	0 Mbps	
Background processes (22)									
Application Frame Host					0%	7.0 MB	0 MB/s	0 Mbps	
Browser_Broker					0%	1.4 MB	0 MB/s	0 Mbps	
Casting protocol connection lis...					0%	0.7 MB	0 MB/s	0 Mbps	
COM Surrogate					0%	0.5 MB	0 MB/s	0 Mbps	
COM Surrogate					0%	0.9 MB	0 MB/s	0 Mbps	
Cortana					0%	0.1 MB	0 MB/s	0 Mbps	
Cortana Background Task Host					0%	3.0 MB	0 MB/s	0 Mbps	
Host Process for Windows Tasks					0%	3.2 MB	0.1 MB/s	0 Mbps	
InstallAgent					0%	1.1 MB	0 MB/s	0 Mbps	

Fewer details   End task

FIGURE 2-8:
The new and greatly improved Task Manager.

TIP

Storage Spaces requires at least two available hard drives — not including the one you use to boot the PC. If you can afford the disk space, Windows 10 can give you a fully redundant, hot backup of everything, all the time. If a hard drive dies, you disconnect the dead one, slip in a new one, grab a cup of coffee, and you're up and running as if nothing happened. If you run out of disk space, stick another drive in the PC or attach it with a USB cable, and Windows figures it all out. It's a magical capability that debuted in Windows Home Server, now made more robust. See Book 7, Chapter 4 for more on Storage Spaces.

Backup gets a major boost with an Apple Time Machine work-alike called *File History.* You may not realize it, but Windows 7 had the capability to restore previous versions of your data files. Windows 10 offers the same functionality, but in a much nicer package — so you're more likely to discover that it's there. See Book 8, Chapter 1. Unfortunately, Windows 10 drops the capability to create whole-disk ghost backups — you need to buy a third-party program such as Acronis if a full backup is in your future.

Power options have changed significantly. Again. The new options allow Windows to restart itself much faster than ever before. See Book 7, Chapter 1.

TECHNICAL STUFF

If you ever wanted to run a Virtual Machine inside Windows, Microsoft has made *Hyper-V* available, free. It's a rather esoteric capability that can come in very handy if you need to run two different copies of an operating system on one machine. You must be running a 64-bit version of Windows 10 Pro (or Enterprise), with at least 4GB of RAM. See Book 8, Chapter 4.

What's New for Windows 8 and 8.1 Users

You're joking, right?

Windows 10 is a no-brainer if you already have Windows 8 or 8.1. If you're still running Windows 8, drop everything right now, and follow the instructions in Book 1, Chapter 4 to install Windows 10.

Okay, I'll backtrack a bit. If you're a big fan of the tiled Metro side of Windows 8 or 8.1, you probably won't be happy with Windows 10, at least at first. There's no Charms bar, the taskbar always takes up part of the screen, Metro apps aren't completely immersive because they have title bars, and the full-screen tablet mode in Windows 10 isn't exactly comparable to the Metro side of Windows 8.

But if you use a mouse, even a little bit, or the desktop side of Windows 8/8.1, there's absolutely no question in my mind that you'll be happier with Windows 10.

Here's what you'll find when shifting from Win8 to Win10:

>> The Start menu — need I say more?

>> Big new features (detailed in the next section), along with a bunch of small tweaks really make life easier. Even in tablet mode, you'll find all sorts of things to love about Windows 10.

>> Universal Windows apps are updated and greatly improved.

>> OneDrive is built-in. You don't need to install a separate app.

WARNING

On the downside, OneDrive in Windows 10 works differently from how it does in Windows 8.1. The placeholders that many Windows 8.1 customers have come to know and love disappear in Windows 10. In Windows 8.1, files in OneDrive, in the cloud, aren't automatically synced and stuck on the Win 8.1 machine. Instead, small file previews called placeholders live on the Win 8.1 machine and act much like the whole file. When you bring up Explorer, for example, you riffle through placeholders. If you click a file that's only a placeholder, OneDrive runs out and quickly downloads the file, feeding it to you or your program.

A problem arises if you're disconnected from the cloud when you want to open a file. By all appearances, the file's on your computer — but it isn't.

There are other problems. If you have a gazillion photos in OneDrive, and you crank up OneDrive on a Windows 8.1 machine with a tiny hard drive, just the placeholders can take up all the space on the hard drive.

Windows 10 changes all that, making the sync process much more convoluted, eliminating the old placeholders. Many people — rightfully — don't like that change. But, in my experience, it's the only significant feature that's getting the axe in moving from Windows 8.1 to Windows 10.

Windows 10 is, in many ways, what Windows 8 should've been. If Microsoft had been listening to its experienced Windows customers, Win8 never would've seen light of day.

What's New for All of Windows

Permit me to take you on a whirlwind tour of the most important new features in Windows 10 — of which there are many.

The Start menu

Unless you've been living on an alternate Windows desktop, you know that Win10 sports a new Start menu, with shortcuts on the left, a list of all your programs in the middle, and Windows 8–style tiles on the right.

Figures 2-2 and 2-6 earlier in this chapter show the Start menu. In Figure 2-9, I show you the Start menu with the phone-dialer style index; you get to it by clicking the Start icon and then clicking one of the headings for the app groups (A, B, and so on).

You have very few customizing options for the Start menu — for example, you can't drag entries onto the Most Used list in the top left, or drag items from the list on the left and turn them into tiles on the right. Tiles on the right can be resized to small (one-quarter the size of a medium tile), medium, wide (two single-size slots, as with the Store and Mail tiles in the screen shot), and large (twice the size of wide). You can click and drag, group and ungroup tiles on the right, and give groups custom names.

You can resize the Start menu, within certain rigid limits. You can adjust it vertically in small increments, but trying to drag things the other way is limited to big swaths of tiles: Groups of tiles remain three wide, and you can add or remove only entire columns. You can drag tiles from the right side of the Start screen onto the desktop for easy access.

Although it's possible to manually remove all the tiles on the right (right-click each, Unpin from Start), the big area for tiles doesn't shrink beyond one column.

FIGURE 2-9:
The Start menu,
with the index
that lets you jump
to apps quickly.

In tablet mode, Start looks quite different, although many of the options are the same. See Figure 2-10.

I talk about personalizing the Start menu in Book 3, Chapter 2, and working with tablet mode in Book 3, Chapter 3.

Microsoft Edge

Long overdue — and for many of us, a real surprise — Microsoft Edge (Figure 2-11) finally sheds the albatross that is Internet Explorer. Edge is a stripped-down, consciously standards-compliant, screamingly fast shell of a browser, ready to take on just about any website anywhere. Microsoft Edge may see Microsoft taking back the mindshare it's been steadily losing on the browser front for the past decade or so. As of this writing, though, Google's Chrome rules the roost.

ASK
WOODY.COM

Edge doesn't replace Internet Explorer — IE still lurks, but it's buried in the Start⇨Windows Accessories list. Microsoft Edge is, however, the default web browser, with its own tile on the right side of the Start menu and its own icon on the taskbar. IE continues to use the old Trident rendering engine, while Edge has the newer Edge. That makes it faster, lighter, and much more capable of playing nicely with websites designed for Firefox and Chrome.

FIGURE 2-10:
Start in tablet
mode, which
you can see
by clicking the
Notification icon
in the lower-right
corner.

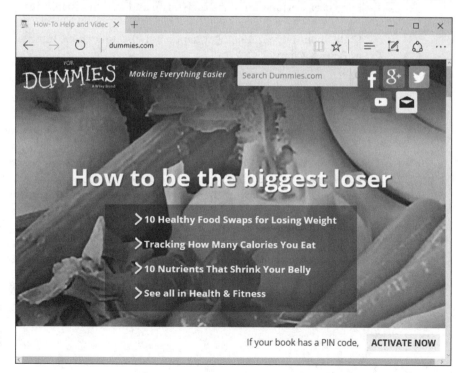

FIGURE 2-11:
Edge finally,
finally lets you cut
the IE cord . . . if
you want to.

Edge is a Universal Windows app (formerly Universal app, formerly Metro app) that runs inside its own window on the desktop, like every other WinRT API-based Universal Windows app. IE is an old-fashioned Windows Desktop app, and the difference is like a Tesla III versus a 1958 Edsel.

Adobe Flash Player can be turned on and off with a simple switch in Settings. There's a reading view as well, which helps on smaller screens. Click the OneNote icon in the upper right, and all the OneNote markup tools become available. And you can Print as PDF.

REMEMBER

Where IE was frequently infected by wayward Flash programs and bad PDF files, Edge is relatively immune. And all the flotsam that came along with IE — the ancient (and penetrable) COM extensions, wacko custom toolbars, even Silverlight — are suddenly legacy and rapidly headed to a well-deserved stint in the bit bucket.

On the other hand, Edge will eventually, we're told, support Google Chrome-like extensions, which play in their own sandboxes, staying isolated. Instead of the spaghetti mess with IE add-ons, we finally have some Microsoft-sponsored order. It's about time.

Edge uses Cortana for voice assistance and search capabilities.

I talk about Edge in Book 5, Chapter 1. I also talk about Internet Explorer, briefly, in Book 3, Chapter 5.

Cortana

Although Apple partisans will give you a zillion reasons why Siri rules, and Googlies swear the superiority of Google Now, Cortana partisans think Microsoft rules the AI roost, of course. Unlike Siri and Now, though, Cortana has taken over the Windows search function — which you can see in Figure 2-12 — so it has a larger potential footprint than its AI cousins, which comes with a double edge.

Cortana occupies the search box to the right of the Start button. She (forgive my anthropomorphism) also appears when you click or tap the Search tile, on the right side of the Start menu. Cortana works only when connected to the Internet, and it's severely limited unless you use a Windows account. You can control some aspects of Cortana's inquisitiveness by clicking the hamburger icon in the upper-left corner (and shown in the margin).

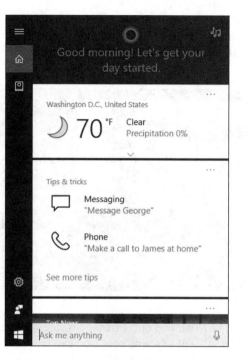

FIGURE 2-12:
Cortana knows all, sees all, and takes over your search function.

REMEMBER

Frequently overlooked in Cortana discussions: everything — absolutely everything — that you search for on your computer gets sent, through Cortana, to Microsoft's giant database in the sky. Cortana's Notebook, as your personal repository is called, can be switched off, and entries can be manually deleted, but Microsoft's banking on you leaving it on.

Cortana improves as it gathers more information about you — yes, by snooping on what you do. But it also improves as Microsoft hones its artificial intelligence moxie, on the back end.

Microsoft has ported Cortana to both iOS (Apple phones and tablets) and Android, although the extent of its integration/usefulness remains to be seen. No, you won't be able to use Google Search with Cortana.

In actual use, there's no question that Google's AI is superior to all the others, with Siri and Alexa each occupying different niches. Cortana's well adapted to Windows 10, but she isn't all that smart. I talk about Cortana in Book 3, Chapter 6.

Virtual desktops and task view

Windows has had virtual (or multiple) desktops since Windows XP, but before Windows 10 you had to install a third-party app — or something like Sysinternals desktop, from Microsoft — to get them to work. Windows 10 implements virtual desktops (Figure 2-13) so they're actually useful.

FIGURE 2-13:
Task view (shown here) displays all the multiple desktops you've set up.

ASK WOODY.COM

Don't let the terminology freak you out: Virtual desktops are just multiple desktops, and vice versa. If you want to sound cool, you can talk about optimizing your virtual desktops, but people in the know will realize you're just flipping between multiple desktops.

Multiple desktops are very handy if you tend to multitask. You can set up one desktop to handle your mail, calendar, and day-to-day stuff, and another desktop for your latest project or projects. Got a crunch project? Fire up a new desktop. It's a great way to put a meta-structure on the work you do every day.

To start a new desktop, press Win+Ctrl+D, or bring up the task view — the environment where you can work directly with multiple desktops — by clicking the Task View icon to the right of the Cortana Search bar (and shown in the margin) and then clicking or tapping the + sign in the lower-right corner. Windows can be moved between desktops by right-clicking and choosing Move To. Alt+Tab still rotates among all running windows. Clicking an icon in the taskbar brings up the associated program, regardless of which desktop it's on.

I talk about multiple desktops in Book 3, Chapter 4.

Security improvements

I'm told that Pliny the Elder once described the alarm system of ancient Rome by saying, "Even when the dogs sleep, the goose watches."

By that standard, Windows 10 has been goosed.

With Windows 8, Microsoft somehow found a new backbone — or decided that it can fend off antitrust actions — and baked full antivirus, antispyware, antiscumstuff protection into Windows itself. Windows 10 continues to use exactly the same protection as Windows 8/8.1.

Although the 'Softies resurrected an old name for the service — *Windows Defender* — the antivirus protection inside Windows 10 is second to none. And it's free.

Microsoft is also encouraging hardware manufacturers to use a boot-up process called *UEFI*, as a replacement to the decades-old BIOS. UEFI isn't exactly a Windows 10 feature, but it's a requirement for all PCs that carry the Windows 10 (or Windows 8) logo. UEFI can help protect you from rootkits by requiring digital signatures on any operating system that gets loaded. See Book 9, Chapter 3.

Other Universal Windows apps

Microsoft has given most of its built-in apps a much-needed makeover.

Mail and **Calendar,** unlike their Windows 8.1 analogs, actually work. You don't need to feel like the 90-pound weakling on the beach if you crank them up. I use Gmail and Google Calendar, but the new Windows Mail app is definitely a contendah. I talk about Mail and Calendar (which are really one app with two different viewpoints) in Book 4, Chapter 1.

People is a derivative of the Windows Phone People Sense app. It doesn't do much. I talk about it in Book 4, Chapter 2.

Groove Music and **Movies & TV** have replaced the useless Windows 8.1 Xbox Music and Xbox Video apps. They're surprisingly capable and tie into Microsoft's streaming service. (It took Microsoft only half a decade to put together a decent streaming service.) Look at Book 4, Chapter 5 for more.

The new **Photos** app is a dud. If you do anything at all with photos, other than file them and maybe remove some red-eye from time to time, you're far better off with a free online alternative — or do yourself a favor and try Google Photos, www.photos.google.com, which I talk about in Book 4, Chapter 3.

The **Weather** app shows more weather and less sappy background than its Windows 8.1 counterpart. I cover it along with the other Bing apps — News, Money, Sports, Extortion — in Book 5, Chapter 3.

Even the **Windows Store** is better than it used to be — damning with faint praise, for sure. Look for some actual improvements in Book 5, Chapter 4.

What you lose

OneDrive in Windows 10 doesn't work anything like it did in Windows 8 and 8.1, primarily because Microsoft is doing away with placeholder or smart file behavior — where thumbnails of files are stored on your machine and pulled down from OneDrive only as needed. I talk about that in the "What's New for Windows 8 and 8.1 Users" section, earlier in this chapter. If you're coming to Windows 10 from Windows 7, don't worry about it. You never knew what you're missing.

WARNING

Although Microsoft hasn't talked much about it, the fact is that all the old Windows Live programs are disappearing. Windows Live is, in fact, dead. Windows 8 killed it, and Windows 10 drove a stake through its heart. If you use any of the Windows Live apps in Windows 7 (or Vista or XP, for that matter), your old Live apps are still available, but it doesn't look like Microsoft is going to do much with them. They certainly aren't getting any support.

Why? The Windows 10 Windows/Universal/Metro tiled apps cover many of the Live bases. Consider these:

>> **Windows Live ID** (formerly known as Microsoft Wallet, Microsoft Passport, .NET Passport, and Microsoft Passport Network), which now operates from the Windows Live Account site (confused yet?), is rebranded Microsoft Your Account and referred to informally as your *Microsoft Account.*

>> **Windows Live OneDrive** has already turned into just plain *OneDrive.* Parts of Ray Ozzie's Windows Live Mesh — formerly Live Mesh, Windows Live Sync, and Windows Live FolderShare — have folded into OneDrive, although Microsoft has squashed PC-to-PC sync; the only way to synchronize files is through the OneDrive cloud. It appears as if Mesh has met its match.

>> **Windows Live Mail** has officially fallen out of favor, with Microsoft announcing that it won't support WLM with any Microsoft accounts. Expect Microsoft to push the new *Universal Windows Mail* as a core Windows communications app. Ditto for Windows Live Calendar.

>> **Windows Live Contacts** is now the *Universal Windows People app.*

>> **Windows Live Photo Gallery** morphed into the *Universal Windows Photos* app.

>> **Windows Live Messenger** is dead. It's been replaced by Skype — or Facebook, or any of a zillion competitors. I use Line, but that's a story for Book 5, Chapter 2.

It's not just the Live apps that are dying. Some of the old Windows programs — **Media Center** being a good example — are just dead.

Some people feel that losing **Adobe Reader** (and other browser add-ins) in Edge is a bad thing. I disagree strongly. Reader (and Flash, which is insulated in Edge) have brought on more pain and misery — and hijacked systems — than they're worth. Microsoft's own ActiveX technology, which won't run on Edge, is another malware magnet that deserves to die, as do browser helper objects, home page hijackers, custom toolbars, and much more. You can run all those add-ins in the Legacy desktop version of Internet Explorer, if you absolutely must.

Some other odd missing pieces include the following:

WARNING

>> **ClearType** doesn't run on the Universal Windows apps' interface, at all. It's still on the old-fashioned desktop, but your Windows/Universal/Metro tiles apps can't use it.

Note that this is different from Microsoft's ClearType HD technology, a marketing term for the monitors on Microsoft Surface tablets. I have no idea why Microsoft used the same term for both.

>> **Flip 3D** is gone. Little more than a parlor trick, and rarely used, the Windows Key+Tab used to show a 3D rendering of all running programs and flip among them. Stick a fork in it. Now it cycles among desktops.

Do You Need Windows 10?

ASK
WOODY.COM

With the drubbing I gave Windows 8 and Windows 8.1 in the press — and in my *For Dummies* books — you might think that I'd come down hard on Windows 10.

Nope.

I've been using Windows 10 in various stages for almost a year now, and I still love it. This is from a guy who works in front of a monitor about 16 hours a day, 7 days a week (at least during book-writing season). I use a mouse or trackpad, and I'm proud of it. Windows 10, to my mind, is a great operating system, and it's a big improvement over Windows 8. I know, damning with faint praise again.

If you use a keyboard and a mouse with Windows 8 or 8.1, you need Windows 10. It's that simple.

Switching over to touch computing isn't quite so clear-cut. I have a couple of touch tablets, and I review dozens more, and for simple demands — mail, web, media playing, TV casting — I still prefer Chrome OS. It's simpler, less prone to infuriating screw-ups, less prone to infection, and less demanding for patches.

On the other hand, if you need one of the (many!) Universal Windows apps or Windows Desktop apps that don't run on Chrome OS, and you have a touch-first environment, Windows 10 ain't a bad choice.

One thing's for sure. This isn't recycled old Windows 8 garbage. With Windows 10, Microsoft has taken a bold step in the right direction — one that accommodates both old desktop fogies like me and the more mobile newcomers (like me, too, I guess).

I haven't felt this good about a Microsoft product since the original release of Windows 7. I just wish Microsoft hadn't pushed so hard with the Get Windows 10 campaign. It still leaves a bad taste in my mouth.

Chapter 3

Which Version?

P ermit me to dispel two rumors, right off the bat. Windows 10 isn't exactly free. And it isn't the last version of Windows.

You probably heard either or both of those rumors from well-regarded mainstream publications, and what you heard was wrong.

ASK WOODY.COM

Here are the facts:

>> From July 29, 2015 (when Win10 RTM was released) to July 29, 2016, you could upgrade from a genuine copy of Win7 or Win8.1 to Win10 for free. At the time this book went to press, you can't, although hope springs eternal. For the latest info on free or reduced-price upgrades, drop by www.AskWoody.com.

If you're building a new PC, you have to buy Windows 10. And if you buy a new PC with Windows 10 preinstalled, the PC manufacturer (probably) paid for Windows 10.

>> Microsoft may drop the numbering system — so Windows 10 in the future will become, simply, Windows — but there will always be version numbers. I tell you how to find yours in this chapter. The number 10 is, was, and always will be a marketing fantasy.

If you haven't yet bought a copy of Windows, you can save yourself some headaches and more than a few bucks by buying the right version the first time. And if you're struggling with the 32-bit versus 64-bit debate, illumination — and possibly some help — is at hand.

Counting the Editions

Windows 10 appears in six different major editions, uncounted numbers of minor editions, and three of the major editions are available in 32-bit and 64-bit incarnations. That makes nine different editions of Windows to choose from.

Fortunately, most people need to concern themselves with only two editions, and you can probably quickly winnow the list to one. Contemplating the 32-bit conundrum may exercise a few extra gray cells, but with a little help, you can probably figure it out easily.

In a nutshell, the four desktop/laptop Windows versions (and targeted customer bases) look like this:

REMEMBER

>> **Windows 10 (also known as Windows 10 Home)** — the version you probably want — works great unless you specifically need one of the features in Windows 10 Pro. A big bonus for many of you: This version makes all the myriad Windows languages — 96 of them, from Afrikaans to Yoruba — available to anyone with a normal, everyday copy of Windows, at no extra cost.

>> **Windows 10 Pro** includes everything in Windows 10 Home plus the capability to attach the computer to a corporate domain network; the Encrypting File System and BitLocker (see the "Encrypting File System and BitLocker" sidebar later in this chapter) for scrambling your hard drive's data; Hyper-V for running virtual machines; and the software necessary for your computer to act as a Remote Desktop host — the "puppet" in an RD session.

>> **Windows 10 Enterprise** is available only to companies that buy into Microsoft's Volume License program — the (expensive) volume licensing plan that buys licenses to every modern Windows version. Enterprise offers a handful of additional features, but they don't matter unless you're going to buy a handful of licenses or more.

>> **Windows 10 Education** looks just like Windows 10 Enterprise, but it's available only to schools, through a program called Academic Volume Licensing.

Those four editions run only on Intel (and AMD) processors. They're traditional Windows.

Windows Vista and Windows 7 both had Ultimate editions, which included absolutely everything. Win10 doesn't work that way. If you want the whole enchilada, you have to pay for volume licensing.

Windows Media Center — the Windows XP–era way to turn a PC into a set-top box — is no longer available in any version of Windows 10. Do yourself a favor and buy a Chromecast, or use your cable company's DVR if you really have to record TV.

Two more editions of Windows 10 run only Universal Windows apps. That bears repeating: **These versions of Windows don't run old-fashioned Windows programs.** They're designed for Windows Phone and small (roughly 8-inch or smaller) tablets. Here are the options:

» **Windows 10 Mobile** is what you probably think of when you think Windows Phone. It's all grown up now, and it'll run on small tablets, but it's still a phone at heart. By not including the Windows desktop, or running old-fashioned Windows programs, Windows 10 Mobile can run on less powerful computers, including both Intel and ARM processors. (ARM processors, traditionally, have powered phones. That's changing, though.)

» **Windows 10 Mobile Enterprise** adds a few features to Windows 10 Mobile, which is of interest only if you need to connect your phone to a corporate network.

This book covers Windows 10 (Home) and Windows 10 Pro. Most of the content is applicable also to Windows 10 Enterprise and Windows 10 Education. Only a little bit of the content applies to Windows 10 Mobile and Windows 10 Mobile Enterprise.

Before you tear your hair out trying to determine whether you bought the right version or which edition you should buy your great-aunt Ethel, rest assured that choosing the right version is much simpler than it first appears. Flip to "Narrowing the choices," later in this chapter. If you're considering buying a cheap version now and maybe upgrading later, I suggest that you first read the next section, "Buying the right version the first time," before you make up your mind.

Buying the right version the first time

What if you aim too low? What if you buy Windows 10 and decide later that you really want Windows 10 Pro? Be of good cheer. Switching versions ain't as tough as you think.

WHAT HAPPENED TO WINDOWS PHONE?

Windows Phone turned into a multibillion-dollar tragedy that sent tens of thousands of people to the unemployment line and put a major drain on Finland's economy.

Finnish company Nokia pioneered the Windows phone and sold millions of them. Nokia sales started drifting off, and Microsoft was faced with a big choice: Either prop up Nokia or lose its only major outlet for the Windows Phone software. Long story short, Microsoft sent one of its execs to lead Nokia, ultimately buying Nokia in April 2014 for $7.2 billion. Three months later, Microsoft announced it was laying off 18,000 Nokia employees.

Fifteen months later, the Nokia phone business had crashed and Microsoft wrote off $7.6 billion in acquisition costs. In May 2016, after several more rounds of layoffs and write-offs, Microsoft announced it was selling the Nokia brand and its smartphones to Foxconn, the company best known for manufacturing computers throughout Asia.

Microsoft sold the remnants of the Nokia brand for $350 million, and Foxconn immediately announced plans to sell Android phones. Windows Phone — now Windows 10 Mobile — self-immolated in a multibillion pile of dollar dust.

ASK
WOODY.COM

Microsoft chose the feature sets assigned to each Windows version with one specific goal in mind: Maximize Microsoft profits. If you want to move from Windows 10 (Home) to Windows 10 Pro (the only upgrade available to individuals), you need to buy the Windows 10 Pro Pack. To buy an upgrade, choose the Start icon, the Settings icon, Update & Security, Activation, and then choose Go to Store.

Upgrading is easy and cheap, but not as cheap as buying the version you want the first time. That's also why it's important for your financial health to get the right version from the get-go.

Narrowing the choices

You can dismiss two regular Windows editions and both Windows Mobile editions out of hand:

>> **Windows 10 Enterprise** is an option only if you want to pay through the nose for five or more Windows licenses, through the Volume Licensing program. Microsoft may change its mind — either lower the price for small bunches of

licenses and/or make the Enterprise version available to individuals — but as of this writing, Enterprise is out of the picture for most of you. There are some tricks, but in general they aren't worth the hassle.

>> **Windows 10 Education,** similarly, can be purchased only in large quantities. If you're a student, faculty member, or staff member at a licensed school, you must contact the IT department to get set up.

>> **Windows 10 Mobile** comes on a dwindling number of new machines and is available as an upgrade to old Windows phones. You can't buy a copy and slap it on that cheap tablet you have sitting in the basement.

>> **Windows 10 Mobile Enterprise** comes only in large quantities, just like Windows 10 Enterprise.

ENCRYPTING FILE SYSTEM AND BITLOCKER

Encrypting File System (EFS) is a method for encrypting individual files or groups of files on a hard drive. EFS starts after Windows boots: It runs as a program under Windows, which means it can leave traces of itself and the data that's being encrypted in temporary Windows places that may be sniffed by exploit programs. The Windows directory isn't encrypted by EFS, so bad guys (and girls!) who can get access to the directory can hammer it with brute-force password attacks. Widely available tools can crack EFS if the cracker can reboot the, uh, crackee's computer. Thus, for example, EFS can't protect the hard drive on a stolen laptop/notebook. Windows has supported EFS since the halcyon days of Windows 2000.

BitLocker was introduced in Vista and has been improved since. BitLocker runs *underneath* Windows: It starts before Windows starts. The Windows partition on a BitLocker-protected drive is completely encrypted, so bad guys who try to get to the file system can't find it.

EFS and BitLocker are complementary technologies: BitLocker provides coarse, all-or-nothing protection for an entire drive. EFS lets you scramble specific files or groups of files. Used together, they can be mighty hard to crack.

BitLocker To Go provides BitLocker-style protection to removable drives, including USB drives.

That leaves you with plain vanilla Windows 10, unless you have a crying need to do one of the following:

>> **Connect to a corporate network.** If your company doesn't give you a copy of Windows 10 Enterprise, you need to spend the extra bucks and buy Windows 10 Pro.

>> **Play the role of the puppet — the *host* — in a Remote Desktop interaction.** If you're stuck with Remote Desktop, you must buy Windows 10 Pro.

Note that you can use Remote Assistance, any time, on any Windows PC, any version. (See Book 7, Chapter 2.) This Win10 Pro restriction is specifically for Remote Desktop, which is commonly used inside companies, but not used that frequently in the real world.

Many businesspeople find that *LogMeIn,* a free alternative to Remote Desktop, does everything they need and that Remote Desktop amounts to overkill. LogMeIn lets you access and control your home or office PC from any place that has an Internet connection. Look at its website, www.logmein.com.

>> **Provide added security to protect your data from prying eyes or to keep your notebook's data safe even if it's stolen.** Start by determining whether you need Encrypting File System (EFS), BitLocker, or both (see the "Encrypting File System and BitLocker" sidebar). Win10 Pro has EFS and BitLocker — with BitLocker To Go tossed in for a bit o' lagniappe.

>> **Run Hyper-V.** Some people can benefit from running *virtual machines* inside Windows 10. If you absolutely must get an old Windows XP program to cooperate, for example, running Hyper-V with a licensed copy of Windows XP may be the best choice. For most people, VMs are an interesting toy, but not much more.

TIP

Choosing 32-bit versus 64-bit

If you've settled on, oh, Windows 10 as your operating system of choice, you aren't off the hook yet. You need to decide whether you want the 32-bit flavor or the 64-bit flavor of Windows 10. (Similarly, Windows 10 Pro and Enterprise are available in a 32-bit model and a 64-bit model.)

Although the 32-bit and 64-bit flavors of Windows look and act the same on the surface, down in the bowels of Windows, they work quite differently. Which should you get? The question no doubt seems a bit esoteric, but just about every new PC nowadays uses the 64-bit version of Windows for good reasons:

>> **Performance:** The 32-bit flavor of Windows — the flavor that everyone was using a few years ago and many use now — has a limit on the amount of memory that Windows can use. Give or take a nip here and a tuck there, 32-bit Windows machines can see, at most, 3.4 or 3.5 gigabytes (GB) of memory. You can stick 4GB of memory into your computer, but in the 32-bit world, anything beyond 3.5GB is simply out of reach. It just sits there, unused. That's why you see 32-bit Windows these days only on tiny, cheap tablets and mobile devices.

**ASK
WOODY.COM**

The 64-bit flavor of Windows opens your computer's memory, so Windows can see and use more than 4GB — much more, in fact. Whether you need access to all that additional memory is debatable at this point. Five years from now, chances are pretty good that 3.5GB will start to feel a bit constraining.

REMEMBER

Although lots of technical mumbo jumbo is involved, the simple fact is that programs are getting too big, and Windows as we know it is running out of room. Although Windows can fake it by shuffling data on and off your hard drive, doing so slows your computer significantly.

>> **Security:** Security is one more good reason for running a 64-bit flavor of Windows. Microsoft enforced strict security constraints on drivers that support hardware in 64-bit machines — constraints that just couldn't be enforced in the older, more lax (and more compatible!) 32-bit environment.

WARNING

And that leads to the primary problem with 64-bit Windows: drivers. Many, many people have older hardware that simply doesn't work in any 64-bit flavor of Windows. Their hardware isn't supported. Hardware manufacturers sometimes decide that it isn't worth the money to build a solid 64-bit savvy driver, to make the old hardware work with the new operating system. You, as a customer, get the short end of the stick.

Application programs are a different story altogether. The 64-bit version of Office 2010 is notorious for causing all sorts of headaches: You're better off running 32-bit Office 2010, even on a 64-bit system (yes, 32-bit programs run just fine on a 64-bit system, by and large). Office 2013 and 2016 don't have the 64-bit shakes; they work fine on either 32-bit or 64-bit Windows. Some programs can't take advantage of the 64-bit breathing room. So all is not sweetness and light.

Now that you know the pros and cons, you have one more thing to take into consideration: What does your PC support? To run 64-bit Windows, your computer must support 64-bit operations. If you bought your computer any time after 2005 or so, you're fine — virtually all the PCs sold since then can handle 64-bit. But if you have an older PC, here's an easy way to see whether your current computer can handle 64 bits: Go to Steve Gibson's SecurAble site, at `www.grc.com/securable.htm`. Follow the instructions to download and run the SecurAble program. If your computer can handle 64-bit operations, SecurAble tells you.

Which Version?

If you have older hardware — printers, scanners, USB modems, and the like — that you want to use with your Windows computer, do yourself a favor and stick with 32-bit Windows. It's unlikely that you'll start feeling the constraints of 32 bits until your current PC is long past its prime. On the other hand, if you're starting with completely new hardware — or hardware that you bought in the past five or six years — and you plan to run your current PC for a long, long time, 64-bit Windows makes lots of sense. You may end up cursing me when an obscure driver goes bump in the night. But in the long run, you'll be better prepared for the future.

Which Version of Windows Are You Running?

You may be curious to know which version of Windows you're running on your current machine. Here's the easy way to tell:

>> If your Start screen resembles the one in Figure 3-1, you have some version of Windows 8, 8.1, RT, or RT 8.1. Swipe from the right or hover your mouse cursor in the lower-right corner, and then choose Change PC Settings. Click or tap PC and Devices, then PC Info. You get a report like the one in Figure 3-2.

FIGURE 3-1:
A Start screen like this is a dead giveaway for 8, 8.1, or RT.

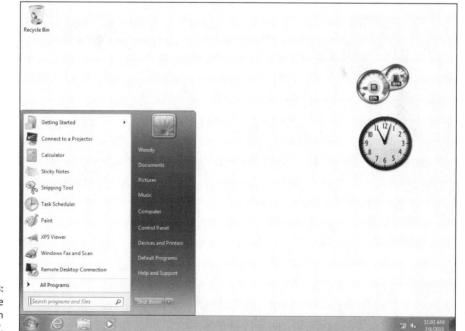

FIGURE 3-2:
This machine
runs 64-bit
Windows 8.1 Pro.

>> If you have a desktop like the one in Figure 3-3, you're running some version of Windows 7. Click the Start icon in the lower-left corner, then Control Panel ⇨ System ⇨ Security. Under System, click View Amount of RAM and Processor Speed. You see a report like the one in Figure 3-4.

FIGURE 3-3:
Here's a telltale
desktop in
Windows 7.

Which Version?

FIGURE 3-4:
This is Windows 7
Pro Service
Pack 1, 64-bit.

» If your desktop doesn't look like Figure 3-1 or Figure 3-3, you're running
Windows Vista or XP. Click the Start icon in the lower-left corner, then click
Control Panel ➪ System ➪ Security. Under System, click View Amount of RAM
and Processor Speed.

If you have a 64-bit system installed already, you should upgrade to a 64-bit version of Windows 10. If you currently have a 32-bit system, check Steve Gibson's
site, as mentioned in the preceding section.

Chapter 4

Upgrades and Clean Installs

ASK
WOODY.COM

've been upgrading Windows machines since I moved from Windows 286 (a souped-up version of Windows 2.0) to Windows 3.0 on my trusty Gateway PC in 1990. All the upgrade took was five of those newfangled high-density (1.2MB) five-and-a-quarter-inch floppies. Since then, I don't know how many systems I've upgraded over the years, how many times, but the count certainly runs more than a thousand.

During all those upgrades, I've sworn and kicked and moaned about in-place upgrades. They never worked. Sooner or later, putting a new version of Windows on top of an old one, without wiping out the old version, led to heartache, yanks of pulled hair, and screams of anguish. With Windows 8.1, for the first time ever, I changed my tune. Windows 10 in-place upgrades are even smoother. I talk about my near-religious conversion in this chapter.

Can your PC handle Windows 10? Probably. I talk about that in this chapter too, along with details about running upgrades, both online and from the DVD-based System Builder edition, creating a backup DVD, and what to do if your PC dies. I cover upgrading from Windows 7 or 8 to Windows 10.

TIP

I also sandwich in a few tips about getting the crap off new PCs — or how to avoid getting a junker altogether. It's shameful that Microsoft lets Windows PC vendors stick all that junk on their new PCs, but that's how things shake out. Imagine how the fans would wail if Apple charged extra for clean, decrapified Macs.

If you're here because Windows 10 is misbehaving and you want to tear out its beating heart and stomp on it . . . you're in the wrong place. After Windows 10 is installed on your PC, it's very rare indeed that you have to install it again. Instead, look into resetting or restoring your PC, a topic I cover in Book 8, Chapter 2.

By the way, if you're upgrading an installation for schools, Microsoft has a useful guide here: `https://blogs.msdn.microsoft.com/ukfe/2016/05/24/windows-10-upgrade-guide-for-schools/`.

Do You Qualify for an Online Upgrade?

If your current PC runs Windows 7 Service Pack 1 or Windows 8.1 with the Update 1 installed (also known as KB 2919355), you can install Windows 10 over the top of the old system by using Microsoft's online upgrade.

Aren't sure if you have Win7 Service Pack 1? On a Windows 7 system, click the Start icon, Control Panel, System and Security, then under the System heading, click the link to View amount of RAM and processor speed. If you have Service Pack 1, you see something like the notice in Figure 4-1.

Not sure about Windows 8.1 Update (also called Update 1)? Go to the Start screen (remember that abomination?) and look in the upper-right corner. If there's a power switch and a search icon in the upper-right corner, as in Figure 4-2, you have the Update installed.

If you have Windows 7 without Service Pack 1, or if you have Windows 8 without 8.1, or 8.1 without the Update, you need to bring your machine up to snuff before you can even think about upgrading to Windows 10. Windows 7 Service Pack 1 has been around for a long while, and very few people have problems installing it. The Windows 8.1 Update isn't quite so user-friendly.

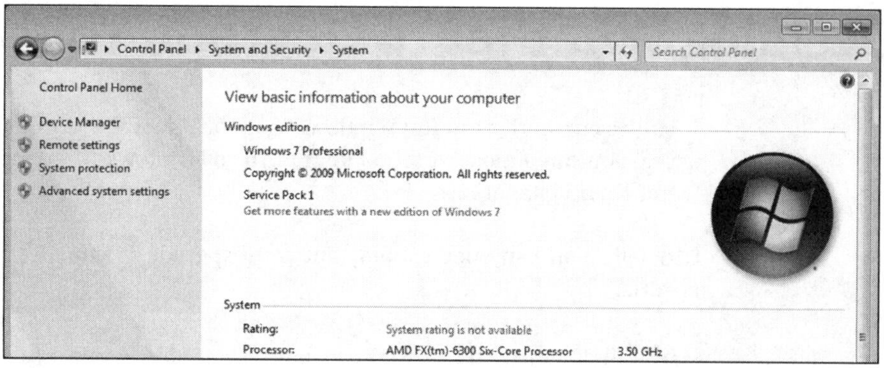

FIGURE 4-1:
Here's where you
find verification
that you have
Service Pack 1.

FIGURE 4-2:
The telltale power
and search icons
on the Start
screen for
Windows 8.1
Update 1 indicate
that you're
eligible for a
free upgrade to
Windows 10.

In any case, if you need to bring your system up to speed, turn on Automatic Update:

>> In **Windows 7,** using an administrator-level account, click the Start icon, Control Panel, and then System and Security. Under Windows Update, click the Turn Automatic Updating On or Off link. In the drop-down box, select Install Updates Automatically (recommended) and click OK.

>> In **Windows 8 or 8.1,** right-click or tap and hold down the Start icon, and choose Control Panel. Then follow the instructions in the preceding paragraph to turn on automatic updates.

Leave your computer running overnight and by the time you come back, you should be up to speed, give or take a restart or two or three.

Deciding Whether to Upgrade Your Old PC

If you're currently running Windows Vista or Windows 7 or 8 on a PC, the answer is yes, you can almost certainly upgrade it to Windows 10 — and it'll probably run faster than Vista, at least.

Officially you can (not should, but *can*) upgrade if your PC has at least these criteria:

>> **1 GHz** or faster processor — an Intel or AMD processor.

>> **2GB** of RAM memory for either the 32-bit version or the 64-bit version. (See Book 1, Chapter 3 for a discussion of bittedness.)

>> **16GB** of available hard drive space for 32-bit versions of Win10, 20GB for 64-bit. Of course, that's just for Windows. If you want to install any programs or save any data, you're going to need a leeeeeetle bit more.

>> **DirectX 9** graphics card with WDDM 1.0 or higher driver. Every video card made in the past ten years meets that requirement.

The much more difficult question of whether you *should* upgrade launches me into a metaphysical discussion. Consider how the following apply to you:

>> **If you have a touch-enabled PC, especially if you're running Windows 8 or 8.1,** there's absolutely no question you should upgrade to Windows 10. Windows 8 and 8.1 are a grotesque joke (although, admittedly, some finger-only people prefer the Win 8.1 tile layout). Get Windows 10 and you'll feel much better.

>> **If you're using a mouse and keyboard and don't plan on getting a touchscreen,** you need Windows 10 only if you really need one of the new features I mention in Book 1, Chapter 2, or if one of the Windows Store apps tickles your fancy. If the benefits there don't put a tingle down your spine, no, you don't need Windows 10. Stick with Windows 7.

ASK
WOODY.COM

I have a touch-sensitive Windows 10 notebook (Dell XPS-15), which works great. I also run a Surface Pro 4 and Surface Book from time to time, and those are Win10 born and raised. My main desktop runs Windows 10 all the time, as do several test machines. I have a couple of MacBooks that usually run Windows 10 under Boot-camp, although OS X is just a click away.

To write this book, I used several Dell products, including a lovely XPS-15, as well as the aforementioned Microsoft Surface Book and Surface Pro 4. My main machine is a cobbled-together assemblage of whatever was cheap at the time I needed it. Quite an array of equipment. My desk looks like a mess.

I love my iPad, Android Galaxy Note, and Kindle Fire. I also seriously covet my wife's iPhone. That's why I include lots of information about those dern Appley and Googlie things in this book. I find them all useful, although my life is still seriously buried in Windows.

Frankly, as things stand right now, I'm not sure I'll ever buy another desktop machine, unless the one I have turns shiny side up. I'll always need a big screen and a keyboard built like a brick house to get my work done, but even cheap laptops these days work very well, plugged into a solid keyboard, good mouse, and gorgeous monitor.

Will I ever *buy* a Windows 10 machine? Could happen.

Upgrades and
Clean Installs

Choosing Your Upgrade Path

Here are the three ways to get a Windows 10 upgrade from Windows 7 SP1 or Windows 8.1 Update:

TIP

>> **You can download the upgrade from the Internet.** This is the way I recommend to almost everybody, as long as your current computer is running a genuine copy of Windows 7 or 8.1. Your new Windows 10 installation is completely legit, 100 percent genuine, and Microsoft keeps records of the upgrade, so you can reinstall Win10 from scratch if your system ever dies.

>> **You can download a file — called an ISO file — that lets you create a bootable DVD or USB drive.** Boot from the DVD or USB, and you're off to the races. If you're using Windows 8.1, you can even run the Windows 10 installation file from inside Windows.

You can buy a Windows 10 DVD, called the System Builder Edition, in a box, through a process not unlike the one everybody used ten years ago. If you already have a copy of Windows running on your computer, this approach is not only wasteful (just try recycling the DVD jewel case!), but also a pain in the neck because you have to futz with booting from the DVD, entering a product key, deciding which partitions to nuke, and then running Windows Activation. Windows 10 may even be available, from Microsoft, on a USB drive.

REMEMBER

Whether you upgrade online or upgrade by booting from a DVD or USB drive, Windows 10 has certain restrictions:

>> **Windows Media Center won't come through.** If you paid for Windows Media Center, Microsoft says it'll give you a DVD player. Meh. But Microsoft won't let you put WMC on a Windows 10 machine or bring it across when you upgrade.

>> **If you're using OneDrive in Windows 8.1, you're going to hate what it does to your file access.** I cover the details in Book 6, Chapter 1, but the bottom line is that you're going to find it hard to use OneDrive to locate your files, unless you go through a bunch of steps to make the files visible.

>> **When upgrading from Windows 7 SP1 or 8.1 Update,** you can choose to keep your programs, some of your settings (desktop background and Internet Explorer favorites and history), and data (anything in your user folders, including Documents, Desktop, and Downloads). If you have anything stored outside of one of the user's libraries, don't count on it coming across. You may be pleasantly surprised, but it may not come through.

REMEMBER

Of course, you should always, always, always back up all your data before you perform an upgrade.

>> **When upgrading from Vista or XP,** you have to run a clean install. Nothing comes along for the ride.

>> **If you want to change from a 32-bit version of Windows to 64-bit Windows 10,** you will necessarily wipe out all your old programs and settings, as is the case with an upgrade from XP. Note, though, that not all machines are capable of moving to 64-bit Windows 10.

I take you through the upgrading details, step by step, in the next three sections.

Upgrading Windows 7 SP1 or Windows 8.1 Update to Windows 10 Online

By far, the easiest and most reliable way to upgrade from Win7 SP1 or Win 8.1 relies on Microsoft's Get Windows 10 software download page, www.microsoft.com/en-us/software-download/windows10.

Unless you have a fake copy of Windows, this is the way to go.

1. **Go to the Microsoft's Get Windows 10 software download page, at www.microsoft.com/en-us/software-download/windows10, and click the Upgrade Now box.**

    Details differ depending on which browser you use, but run the downloaded file. The upgrader responds with an End User License Agreement, as shown in Figure 4-3.

2. **Click Accept.**

    The Windows 10 compatibility checker runs. Most machines get a clean bill of health, as shown in Figure 4-4.

3. **If you receive a report about an incompatible piece of hardware or software, check into the cause of the problem.**

    In my experience, the most common stumbling blocks at this point include older, incompatible video cards, old device drivers, and odd pieces of software.

    If the compatibility checker chokes on hardware, your best bet is to buy and install replacement hardware (such as a new video card), or just dump the hardware. Trying to make older computers work with Win10 can cost as much as a new PC.

Upgrades and
Clean Installs

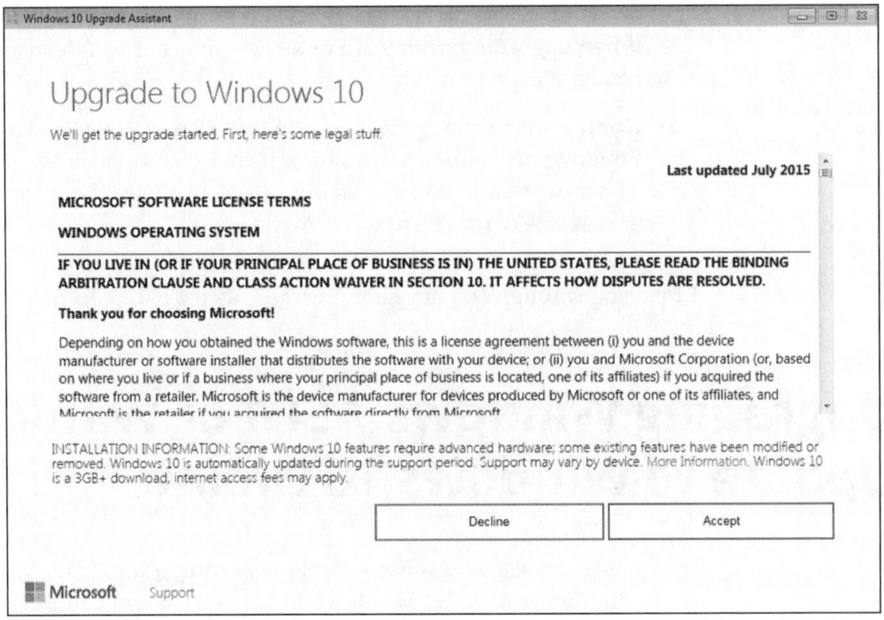

FIGURE 4-3:
The Windows 10
EULA.

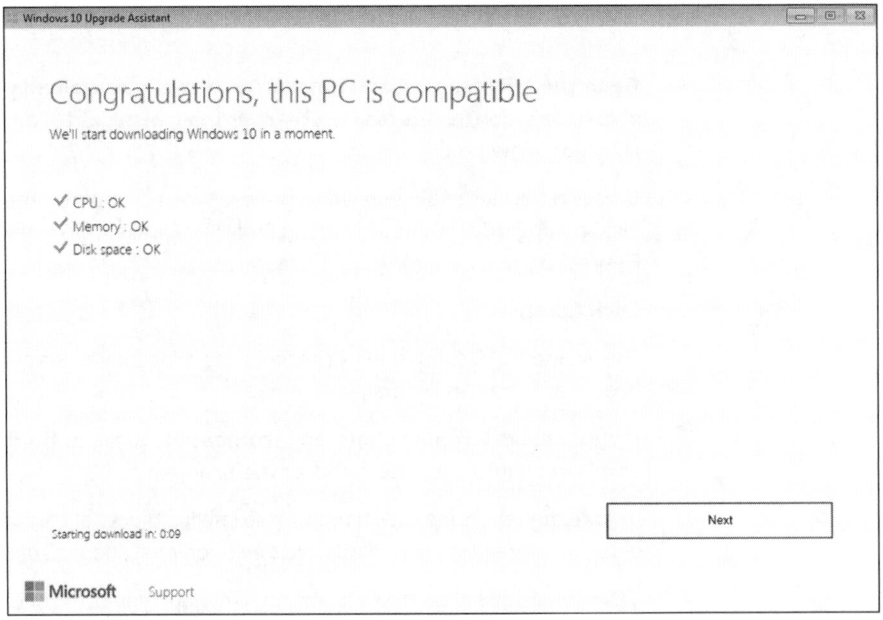

FIGURE 4-4:
If your computer
checks out, the
download starts
automatically.

Yes, Microsoft Money is an odd piece of software — and yes, it's Microsoft software. Getting Money to work on Win10 can be challenging. See `https://social.microsoft.com/Forums/en-US/home?forum=money` for some tips.

If you have Windows Media Center, it'll get a special mention — WMC doesn't come across in the upgrade and won't run on Win10. You can't do anything about it, except realize that there are much better alternatives.

If you stumble on some unusual report at this point, check out Microsoft's FAQ at `http://windows.microsoft.com/en-us/windows-10/compatibility-report-windows-10`.

4. **If you encounter a problem with a piece of software that you don't care about, relax. The installer will zap it for you. On the other hand, if you get a bad report about hardware or a driver, it would behoove you to resolve the problem before trying the upgrade again.**

   Yes, that may include buying and installing a new video card, adding more memory, or driving a stake through the cartridge of your beloved ancient printer. When everything is up to snuff, start all over at Step 1.

5. **Wait for the installer to go through the motions.**

   The installer can take a long time, particularly if you have a slow Internet connection or an overstuffed hard drive. When it's done, you see the notification in Figure 4-5.

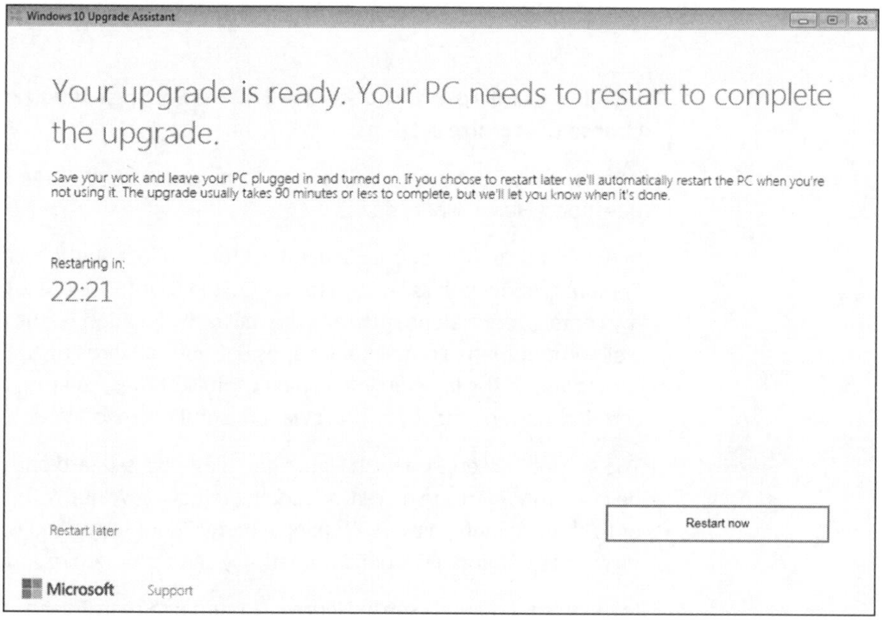

FIGURE 4-5:
When the installer is finally ready to go, here's what you see.

6. **Save any open files, close any open programs, and click Restart now. And wait. And wait.**

   When Windows comes back up for air, it'll show you a welcome screen.

CHAPTER 4 **Upgrades and Clean Installs**   95

Upgrades and
Clean Installs

7. Click Next.

You see a screen that says Get Going Fast, as shown in Figure 4-6.

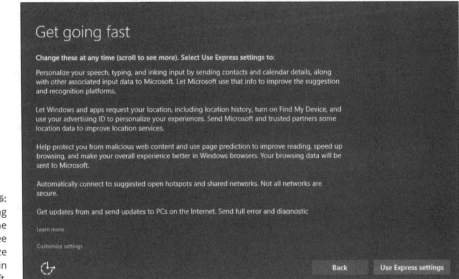

Get going fast

Change these at any time (scroll to see more). Select Use Express settings to:

Personalize your speech, typing, and inking input by sending contacts and calendar details, along with other associated input data to Microsoft. Let Microsoft use that info to improve the suggestion and recognition platforms.

Let Windows and apps request your location, including location history, turn on Find My Device, and use your advertising ID to personalize your experiences. Send Microsoft and trusted partners some location data to improve location services.

Help protect you from malicious web content and use page prediction to improve reading, speed up browsing, and make your overall experience better in Windows browsers. Your browsing data will be sent to Microsoft.

Automatically connect to suggested open hotspots and shared networks. Not all networks are secure.

Get updates from and send updates to PCs on the Internet. Send full error and diagnostic

Learn more

Customize settings

Back   Use Express settings

FIGURE 4-6:
Are you willing to take the bait? Hint: See the Customize Settings link in the lower left.

8. If you trust Microsoft, choose Use Express Settings. If you're like me, choose Customize settings.

If you choose Customize, the installer takes you through three screens of questions. Here's what I do:

In the first screen, shown in Figure 4-7, I turn off just about everything in Personalization, unless I intend to use Cortana. Unfortunately, Cortana needs my contacts and calendar details, as well as my location — she can't work very well without them. I refuse to "let apps use your advertising ID for experiences across apps." The location info can be useful at times, so I turn it on, but I'd certainly understand if you don't want to send Microsoft your location.

The second screen, shown in Figure 4-8, is an odd buzzard and is primarily devoted to Wi-Fi. I see no real advantage to having Windows hunt for hotspots or to share sign-in passes with people in my People app. And I debate on a daily basis whether I should automatically send problem reports to Microsoft.

In the third screen, shown in Figure 4-9, I turn on SmartScreen, although I'm painfully aware that this sends some of my browsing history to Microsoft. I don't use page prediction because the fraction-of-a-second improvement in speed isn't worth giving away my entire browsing history. Finally, I want to download my own updates directly from Microsoft, not share them with other PCs.

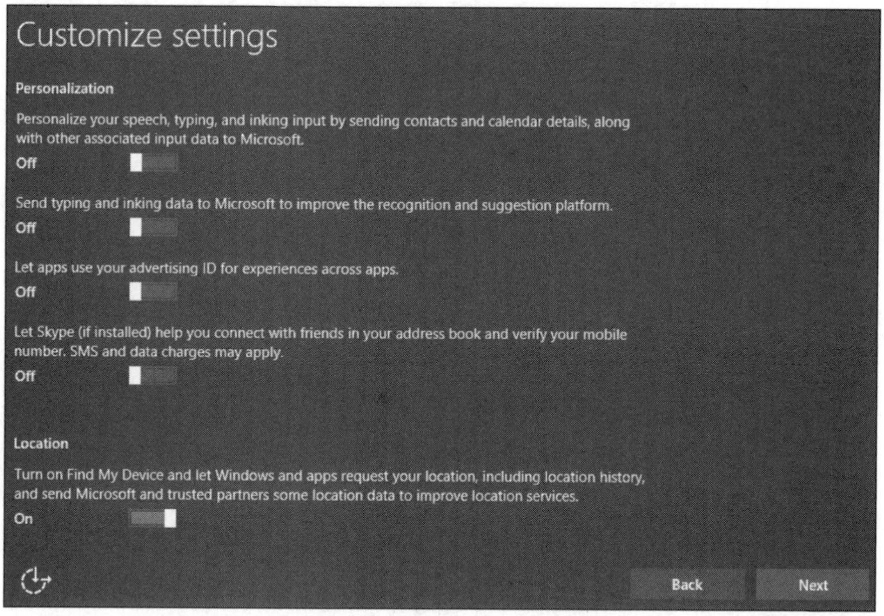

Customize settings

Personalization

Personalize your speech, typing, and inking input by sending contacts and calendar details, along with other associated input data to Microsoft.

Off

Send typing and inking data to Microsoft to improve the recognition and suggestion platform.

Off

Let apps use your advertising ID for experiences across apps.

Off

Let Skype (if installed) help you connect with friends in your address book and verify your mobile number. SMS and data charges may apply.

Off

Location

Turn on Find My Device and let Windows and apps request your location, including location history, and send Microsoft and trusted partners some location data to improve location services.

On

Back   Next

FIGURE 4-7:
Here's my
reaction to the
first screen of
privacy related
settings.

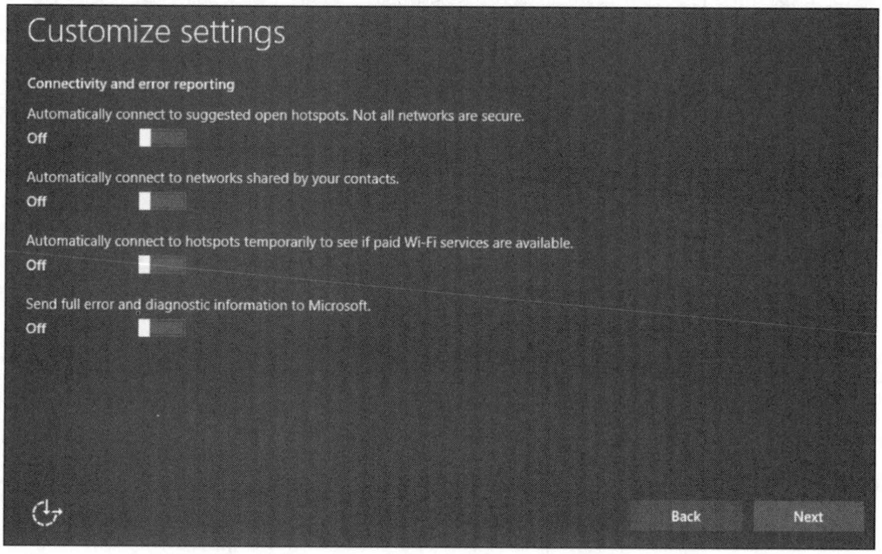

Customize settings

Connectivity and error reporting

Automatically connect to suggested open hotspots. Not all networks are secure.

Off

Automatically connect to networks shared by your contacts.

Off

Automatically connect to hotspots temporarily to see if paid Wi-Fi services are available.

Off

Send full error and diagnostic information to Microsoft.

Off

Back   Next

FIGURE 4-8:
I like to control
my own
Wi-Fi destiny,
thank you.

In the fourth screen (not shown here), Cortana raises her AI head. I confess that I like having Cortana available, even though my AI of choice is on my Google phone. (Compare Cortana and OK Google for a few minutes and you'll see why.) Still, some Cortana stuff is worthwhile when I'm working in Windows, so I click Use Cortana.

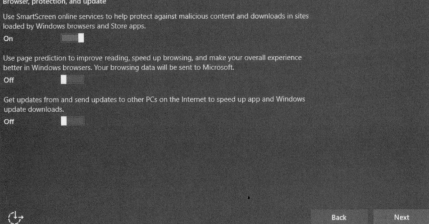

FIGURE 4-9:
Here are my choices for the third collection of privacy robbers.

In the fifth screen (also not shown here), the installer seems to be bragging about its "New apps for the new Windows" and lists the super cool features in Photos (lame, compared to Google Photos), Edge (much better than IE but still not that great), Groove Music (Spotify anybody?), and Movies & TV (where you can rent some movies from Microsoft). The point isn't to tell you about those groovy new apps. The point is to get your permission to set them all as default apps in certain situations. When you double-click a picture, for example, this screen gives Win10 permission to open the pic with the Photos app.

If you want to fight city hall, you can click the link on screen five to Let Me Choose My Default Apps. Or you can just go along for now, realizing you'll change the default file associations at some point in the future. I don't bother, and click Next.

After five privacy screens, the installer says it's "finalizing your settings" (whatever that means), goes out to lunch for a long time, shows you some swirling dots, and finally comes back with the Win10 login screen.

9. **Log in, watch the animation that says "Your files are exactly where you left them," and start using Windows 10.**

Have an upgrade problem? Microsoft has a thorough list of dozens of upgrade errors and what you can (and can't) do about them in this FAQ: `https://support.microsoft.com/en-us/kb/3107983`.

Installing Win10 from a DVD or USB Drive

If you're going to upgrade from Windows 7 SP1 or 8.1 Update to Windows 10, and you want to keep your data and programs intact, I strongly urge you to perform the online upgrade I mention in the preceding section. As long as you stick to upgrading 32-bit Win7 to 32-bit Win10 or 64-bit Win7 to 64-bit Win10, the online installer works great.

Even if you want to install a clean copy of Windows 10 — and wipe out everything — I urge you to go through the steps in the preceding section first, and then use the tools described in Book 8, Chapter 2 to run Microsoft's Start Fresh sequence.

If you really, really want to wipe your computer and install Windows 10 from scratch, do that by booting from a DVD or USB drive and running a clean install. That's the process I describe in this section.

WARNING

I can't emphasize enough that you must make full backups of all your data, write down *all* your passwords (unless they're stored online someplace such as Last-Pass), get *all* your software installation CDs and DVDs, and make yet another backup just in case, before starting this process.

If you buy a shrink-wrapped copy of Windows 10, you get a DVD (or possibly a USB drive) that's ready to boot. If you download an ISO file, follow the instructions in the sidebar "Making an ISO file usable" to turn the file into a bootable DVD or USB drive.

With a bootable USB drive or DVD in hand, you may have to adjust your computer so it boots from the USB or DVD.

MAKING AN ISO FILE USABLE

Many people get a copy of Windows 10 in the form of a single file with the filename extension .iso. Microsoft MSDN and TechNet subscribers, for example, get ISO files. An *ISO file* is just a compressed version of a DVD image. You can turn an ISO file into a bootable DVD or USB drive by using a simple tool that Microsoft provides.

To perform the magic, download Microsoft's Windows 7 USB tool, which is located at www.store.microsoft.com/Help/ISO-Tool. Run the tool. Navigate to the ISO file, and choose whether you want to burn a DVD or create a bootable USB drive. Four steps, and you're finished.

Upgrades and
Clean Installs

Here's how to go through the whole process — and survive to tell the tale:

1. **With your old version of Windows running, insert the Windows installation disk in the DVD drive, or the installation USB in a USB port.**

2. **In Win7, choose Start, Shut Down to go through a full shutdown. In Win 8.1, click the power icon next to your name on the Start screen and choose Shut Down.**

   Windows may offer to install itself while you're trying to shut down. If it does, click the Cancel button.

3. **Power off the PC, wait at least a full minute, and then turn on the power.**

   If the PC can start (or *boot*) from the DVD drive or USB drive, you see something like this on the screen: *Press any key to boot from CD* or *Press Esc to choose boot device.*

4. **Press whatever key is recommended.**

   If the PC doesn't offer to boot from the DVD drive or USB stick, you have to look in your PC's documentation for the correct setting in your PC's BIOS. If you're not familiar with your PC's BIOS, go to the website for your PC manufacturer and search for the term *change boot sequence.* The process may be complex, particularly if you have something called a UEFI secure boot enabled. Only your PC manufacturer can tell you how to deal with UEFI.

5. **When the PC boots, you may be asked if you want to go online to get the latest updates. If you do, choose Go Online to Install Updates Now and click Next.**

6. **In the Windows Setup screen, change the language if you want, click Next, and then click Install Now.**

7. **When the installer prompts for the product key, enter it. (If you have a valid key for Windows 7, 8, or 8.1 on this machine, you may use it.) When a license terms screen appears, accept it.**

   The Which Type of Installation Do You Want? dialog box, shown in Figure 4-10, appears.

8. **To wipe everything and start fresh, click Custom: Install Windows Only (Advanced).**

   The installer asks you where you want to install Windows, as shown in Figure 4-11.

9. **If the upper box has more than one entry, choose Drive Options (Advanced), click each entry in the upper box, one by one, and then click the link that says Delete. When you're finished, click Next.**

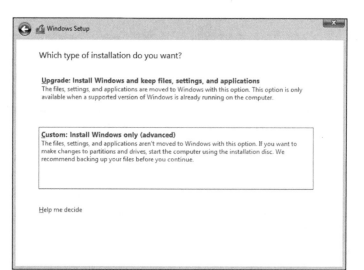

FIGURE 4-10:
Wipe everything and perform a clean install by choosing the Custom option.

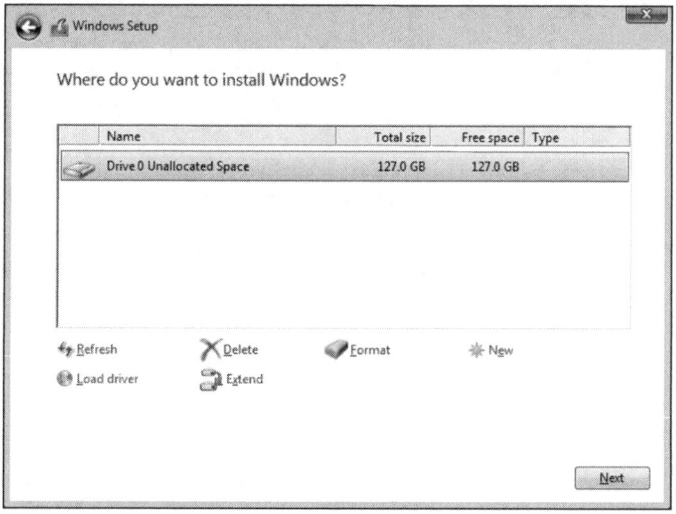

FIGURE 4-11:
Where to install Windows?

Then go have another latte . . . or two . . . or three. Your computer restarts several times.

WARNING

If you had to jimmy your BIOS in Step 4 to make your PC boot from a DVD drive or USB, you may reach an odd situation where you see the setup screen again, and your computer just sits there waiting for you to start again. If that happens, pull the DVD or USB drive out of its slot and manually restart your computer. The installer kicks back in again the second time.

Upgrades and
Clean Installs

By the time the installer comes up for air, you're ready to personalize your copy of Windows.

10. **Type a name for the PC (better if you stick to letters and numbers, no spaces or weird characters). If you're asked to set up a new account, follow the instructions in Book 2, Chapter 5 to make an intelligent choice about what kind of account to use. Click Next.**

Windows starts on the "Get Going Fast" gauntlet covered starting at Step 8 in the preceding section.

Depending on how you upgrade, there may be a step in the upgrade process where the installer asks what settings and files you want to keep. See Table 4-1 for a more detailed explanation.

TABLE 4-1   Choose What to Keep

This Choice	Means This
Keep Windows Settings	Some of your Windows settings survive the upgrade: user accounts and passwords, your desktop background, Internet Explorer favorites and history, some File Explorer settings. Other Windows settings don't survive.
Keep Personal Files	This specifically means all the files in the Users folder, including Documents, Pictures, Photos, Videos, and Desktop folders. But if you have data sitting in some other folder, stored outside Users, it may or may not make the transition, even if it's in one of your libraries.
Keep Apps	The upgrade process keeps all the application programs that are identified and understood by the upgrader. Microsoft has hundreds of thousands of programs and drivers on file — but it doesn't have every Windows program made. In addition, some programs (such as some system utilities) can't make it through the upgrade process. The problematic programs should be listed in the compatibility scan.
Nothing	This is a clean install. The upgrade routine moves several folders (Windows, Program Files, Program Files [x86], Users, and Program Data) to the windows.old folder, but all the originals are overwritten in the upgrade process. *Remember:* If you use a fingerprint reader or some other device that doesn't rely on passwords to log you in, make sure you have your password before you upgrade. The biometric data doesn't survive the upgrade.

Cleaning the Gunk Off New PCs

On your new PC, did you get a free 60-day trial for Norton Internet Security with Symantec Live Update and the trial version of WinDVD and Roxio and Quicken — and oh! — this neat discount for EarthLink?

If you bought a new computer with Windows preinstalled, the manufacturer probably sold some desktop real estate to a software company or an Internet service provider (ISP).

Oh yeah, the AOLs and Nortons of the world compensate the Sonys and Dells and HPs for services, and space, rendered.

The last thing you need is yet another come-on to sign up for AOL or an antivirus program that begs you for money every week, or a fancy manufacturer-installed driver that just sits there and sucks up space.

Some manufacturers have wised up and started offering clean PCs, for a slight premium. Microsoft stores also sell Signature editions of popular PCs — *Signature* implies that the PCs have been divested of typical manufacturer junk. Believe me, it's worth the money to get the cleanest PC you possibly can.

The easiest way to get a clean PC? Install Windows 10 from Microsoft. Use any of the methods mentioned in the preceding section and, as long as you don't bring across old programs in an upgrade, your new computer will be clean as can be. Blissfully so.

If you have a PC with all that junk, here's what you can do to remove it:

>> **Take it to a Microsoft store** (one of the bricks-and-mortar ones), where you can pay $99 for someone to take the junk off a new PC.

>> **Use a tool that removes most, if not all, the useless junk.** PC Decrapifier is a free, simple program that scans your machine and gets rid of most of the junk. Run over to www.pcdecrapifier.com.

What If the Wheels Fall Off?

So what should you do if Windows dies? Try this:

TIP

>> **If Windows came bundled with a new PC,** scream bloody murder at the vendor who sold you the %$#@! thing. Don't put up with any talk about it's a software problem; Microsoft is at fault. If you bought Windows with a new PC, the company that sold you the machine has full responsibility for making it work right. Period.

Upgrades and
Clean Installs

>> **If you upgraded from Windows 7 SP1 or Windows 8.1 Update to Windows 10 and didn't complete a custom (clean) install,** try that. You don't have much to lose, eh? Follow the instructions in the section, "Installing Win10 from a DVD or USB Drive," earlier in this chapter, and go for the Custom (Clean) Install, or run the Fresh Start routine, described in Book 8, Chapter 2.

>> **If you completed a custom (clean) install and Windows still falls over and plays dead,** man, you have my sympathies. Check with your hardware manufacturer and make sure that you have the latest BIOS version installed. (Make sure to find an instruction book; changing the BIOS is remarkably easy, if you follow the instructions.) Visit the online newsgroups, look at www. AskWoody.com, or drop by the Microsoft Answers forum, www.answers. microsoft.com, to see whether anybody there can lend a hand. If all else fails, admit defeat and reinstall your old operating system.

Life's too short.

2

Personalizing Windows

Contents at a Glance

IN THIS CHAPTER

Navigating via your fingers or via a mouse

Switching among apps

Boldly going where no mouse has gone before

Chapter 1

Getting Around in Windows

Ready to get your feet wet, but not yet up to a full plunge?

ASK WOODY.COM

Good. You're in the right place for a dip-your-toes-in kind of experience. Nothing tough in this chapter, just a bit of windows cruising. Lay of the land kind of stuff.

If you're an experienced Windows 7 or XP user, you'll find parts of Windows 10 that look a bit familiar and parts that look like they were ripped from an iPhone. If you're an experienced Windows 8.1 user, I salute you and your stamina, and I welcome you to a kinder, gentler Windows.

REMEMBER

Former Microsoft General Manager and Distinguished Engineer Hal Berenson said it best: "Consumers increasingly reject the old experiences in both their personal and work lives. For the 20-something-and-under crowd, the current Windows desktop experience is about as attractive as the thought of visiting a 19th-century dentist."

Windows 10 looks a little bit like that 19th-century dentist's office, but underneath it's gone through radical transformations.

I figure that 90 percent of the stuff that 80 percent of the people do with a computer runs just fine on a tablet or a Chromebook. So why put up with all the hassles of running Windows on a piece of iron that weighs more than your refrigerator, and breaks down twice as often? Maybe you're addicted to blue screens and frozen mice. Or maybe you're ready to leave it all behind and tap your way to something new. But if you're still solidly stuck in the Windows column, this chapter's for you.

In this chapter, I show you what's to like about both the old-fashioned side of Windows and the new Universal Windows side, how to get around if you're new to Windows, and if you're an experienced Windows hand, how to reconcile your old finger memory with the new interface. It isn't as hard as you think.

Really.

I also show you how to be input-agnostic — how to use either your fingers, or a pen, or your fork, er, mouse to get around the screen. And I give you a few not-at-all-obvious tips about how to get the most out of your consorting with the beast.

Windows' New Beginnings

The way I look at it, most people starting with Windows 10 start in one of five groups, with the largest percentage in the first group:

>> Somewhat experienced at some version of Windows and primarily comfortable with a mouse and keyboard. (More than 1.5 billion people have used Windows.)

>> Experienced at Windows but want to learn touch input.

>> Windows 8 refugee who's hoping and praying Windows 10 isn't so disorienting.

>> New to Windows, prefer to use touch.

>> New to Windows and want to visit the 19th-century dentist's office to see what all the screaming's about.

If you fall into that final group, you need to learn to use the antique interface apparatus known as a mouse and keyboard. I'm reminded of Scotty on the Enterprise picking up a mouse and saying, "Computer! Computer! Hello computer . . ." When Scotty's reminded to use the keyboard, he says, "Keyboard. How quaint." At least he didn't say, "Hey, Cortana!"

TAP OR CLICK, PAPER OR PLASTIC?

Lots of people have asked me whether I'm serious about tapping on a Windows machine. Yes, I am, and I hope you will be, too.

I tried the old stylus Windows interface, back when the luggable Windows tablets first appeared, in the Windows XP days. I hated it. I still hate it. I hated it so much that when I saw someone using an iPad, all I could think was, "Oh, that must suck." (Remember, *suck* is a technical term.)

An hour later, I tried an iPad, and suddenly using a finger was fine. More than fine, it was tremendous. When my then-18-month-old son spent a few hours playing on the iPad and started using the interface like a virtuoso, I was hooked. The tap-and-swipe interface is astonishingly easy to learn, use, and remember.

Windows 10's tap interface isn't as elegant as the iPad's. Sorry, but it's true. The main difference is that Windows has to accommodate lots of things that the iPad just doesn't do — right-click comes immediately to mind (although tablets have tap-and-hold to simulate right-click; the iPhone even has 3D touch, which goes way beyond clicking). But for many, many things that I do every day — web surfing, quickly checking email, scrolling through Twitter, catching up on Facebook, reading the news, looking at the stock market, and on and on — the touch interface is vastly superior to a mouse and keyboard. At least, it is to me.

That said, yes, you can get used to a tablet without a mouse and keyboard.

As I'm writing this book, I have three computers on my desk. One's a traditional desktop running Windows 10, and one's running the latest beta test version of Windows 10. The third is a Win10 tablet with a portable keyboard — a Surface Pro 4. When I want to look up something quickly, guess which one I use? Bzzzzzt. Wrong. I pick up my Nexus phone — or my iPad. "OK, Google, where is Timbuktu?" "Navigate to Costco." "Call the Recreation Center."

So this section offers a whirlwind tour of your new Windows 10 home that helps you start clicking and tapping your way around.

A tale of two homes

As you undoubtedly know by now, Windows 10's Start menu has two faces. They're designed to work together. You can be the judge of how well they live up to the design.

On the left side of the Start menu (see Figure 1-1), you see the Start menu that's supposed to look like the Windows 7 (and Vista and XP and 95) Start menu. On the right side of the Start menu, you see a bunch of tiles, some of which actually have useful information on them.

Although the left side of the Start menu is supposed to bring back warm, comforting memories of Windows 7 (and XP), underneath the surface, the left part of the Start menu has almost nothing in common with earlier Start menus. The old Start menu has been ripped out and replaced with this new list of links and, on the far left, a set of shortcut icons

See the funny icon in the upper-left corner (and shown in the margin)? For the mathematicians in the crowd, it looks just like an equivalence sign. In the computer world, that's known as a hamburger icon (see the nearby sidebar).

TIP

The new stab at a Start menu is both good and bad. As you'll see, the left side of the Start menu is a wimpy thing, built according to inflexible rules. If you gnawed away at the Windows 7 Start menu back in the day, you'll find that there's very little meat to the new Start menu. Conversely, the Windows 10 Start menu doesn't get screwed up as easily — or as completely — as the Windows 7 Start menu.

On the right side of the Start menu, you see a vast sea of tiles. Unlike the tiles on your iPhone or iPad or Galaxy, these tiles have some smarts: If prodded, they will tell you things that you might want to know, without opening up the associated app. In this screen shot, you can see a bit of the weather, a news story, a photo, stock market results, and a little peek at the calendar. You also see lots and lots of ads. That's the Windows tile shtick, and it's apparent here in all its glory.

THE HISTORY OF THE HAMBURGER ICON

There have been many harsh words about the lowly hamburger. On the one hand, the icon doesn't really say anything. On the other hand, so many systems and programs now use the icon that it's close to being universal. Even cross-platform.

Ends up that the hamburger icon (like so many things we take for granted today) was designed at the Xerox Palo Alto Research Center, PARC, for use on the first graphical computer, the Xerox Star. Norm Cox designed it at PARC, and you can see its first appearance at https://vimeo.com/61556918. Software designer Geoff Alday contacted Cox, and this is what he said:

"I designed that symbol many years ago as a 'container' for contextual menu choices. It would be somewhat equivalent to the context menu we use today when clicking over objects with the right mouse button. Its graphic design was meant to be very 'road sign' simple, functionally memorable, and mimic the look of the resulting displayed menu list. With so few pixels to work with, it had to be very distinct, yet simple . . . we used to tell potential users that the image was an 'air vent' to keep the window cool. It usually got a chuckle, and made the mark much more memorable."

That's why, 30 years later, Windows 10 uses the hamburger icon.

Whether you like having your news boiled down into a sentence fragment, that's for you to decide.

Unlike the left side of the Start menu, the right side with the tiles can get gloriously screwed up. You can stretch and move and group and ungroup until you're blue screened in the face.

ASK WOODY.COM

I tend to think of the tiles on the right side of the Start menu as the next generation of Windows 7 Gadgets. If you ever used Gadgets, you know that they were small programs that displayed useful information on their faces. Microsoft banned them before releasing Windows 8, primarily because they raised all sorts of security problems.

Windows 10 Start menu tiles don't have the security problems. And the infrastructure that has replaced the Gadget mentality has taken Windows to an entirely new level.

Switching to tablet mode and back

Get your computer going. Go ahead. I'll wait.

You're looking at the old-fashioned Windows desktop, right? (If you have a mouse and Windows sensed it, you're looking at the desktop. If your machine is only touch, you may be in tablet mode already.)

 Time to take a walk on the wild side. Let's flip over to tablet mode. Way down in the lower-right corner, to the right of the date and time, click the Action/ Notification Area icon. (Microsoft calls it an Action Area, but every other computer on the planet calls it a Notification area.) At the bottom, in the upper-left of the hive of shortcut icons, click Tablet Mode.

This (see Figure 1-2) is where the finger pickers live. They can tap and swipe and pinch and nudge to their heart's content.

Wait. Don't panic.

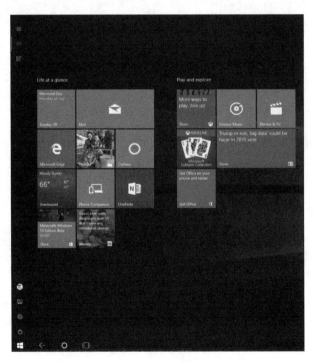

FIGURE 1-2:
Tablet mode, a good place for touch-first types.

REMEMBER

To get back to normal (I call it *desktop view* although it doesn't really seem to have a name), click or tap the Action/Notification Area icon in the lower-right corner, and click Tablet Mode once again. Like Dorothy tapping her heels together three times, you go back to where there's no place like Home.

That brings you back to Figure 1-1. Which is probably where you wanted to be.

Although tablet mode is designed for people who want to use a touchscreen, not a mouse, there's no law that says you're stuck in one persona or the other. You can flip back and forth between regular mouse-first mode and tablet mode any time.

Navigating around the Desktop

Whether you use a mouse, a trackpad, or your finger, the Windows Desktop rules as your number-one point of entry into the beast itself.

Here's a guided tour of your PC, which you can perform with either a mouse or a finger, your choice:

1. **Click or tap the Start icon.**

   You see the Start menu in Figure 1-1.

2. **Tap or click the tile on the right marked Mail.**

   You may have to Add an Email Account, but sooner or later, Microsoft's new Mail app appears, as in Figure 1-3.

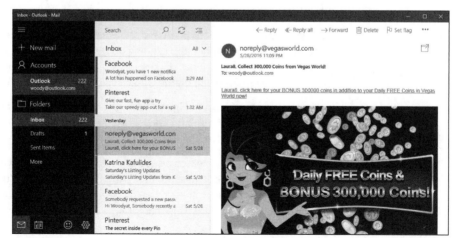

FIGURE 1-3:
The Mail app is indicative of the new Universal Windows apps.

3. Take a close look at the Mail app window.

Like other Windows windows, the Mail window can be resized by moving your mouse cursor over an edge and dragging. You can move the whole window by clicking the title bar and dragging. You can minimize the window — make it float down, to the taskbar — by clicking the horizontal line in the upper-right corner. And, finally, you can close the app by clicking the X in the upper right.

That may seem pretty trivial if you're from the Windows 7 site of the reality divide. But for Windows 8/8.1 veterans, the capability to move a Metro app window around is a Real Big Deal.

4. At the bottom in the taskbar, to the right of the Cortana "Ask me anything" puffery, click the Task View icon (shown in the margin).

The desktop turns gray, and your Mail window shrinks a bit. A New Desktop icon, shaped like a + sign, appears in the lower right.

5. Click the + (New Desktop) icon.

Windows creates a new, empty desktop, and shows it to you in task view. See Figure 1-4. Note how the Mail app shows up on Desktop 1, and Desktop 2 is blank except for your wallpaper.

FIGURE 1-4:
Windows 10 lets
you create as
many desktops as
you like.

6. Click Desktop 2, on the right. Then click or tap Start, and choose the Weather app. Finally, click the Task View icon.

Windows 10 pops back into task view, showing the Mail app running on Desktop 1 and the Weather app running on Desktop 2. In addition, the background for Desktop 2 has darkened, and you can see a slimmed-down version of the Weather app on the Desktop 2 desktop. See Figure 1-5.

7. From the screen shown in Figure 1-5, right-click (or tap and hold down on) the running Weather app and choose Move to, Desktop 1. Then click the Desktop 1 thumbnail at the bottom.

You've just successfully created a second desktop, and then moved a running application from one desktop to another. The results should look like Figure 1-6. That's a quick introduction to task view and multiple desktops, which I cover in detail in Book 3, Chapter 4.

FIGURE 1-5:
Two desktops, each with different programs running.

FIGURE 1-6:
Both of the apps are running happily on Desktop 1.

8. **X out of the Mail and Weather apps. Then click or tap the Start icon again.**

Windows brings up a more-or-less alphabetized view of all your apps, in the second column.

9. **Scroll down to Windows Accessories, click the down arrow to its right, and choose Paint.**

Windows Paint appears, just like in the good old days, as shown in Figure 1-7.

ASK
WOODY.COM

Note that the Start menu's apps list has a few collections of programs, like Windows Accessories. When you install new programs, they may build drop-down menus on the All Apps list, as you see with Windows Accessories, but far more commonly they just get dumped in the list. That gives you lots of stuff to scroll through.

Also note that the running app — Paint — has an icon down on the taskbar (in this case, on the far right) and shown in the margin. When you close Paint, the icon disappears. If you want to keep Paint on the taskbar, right-click the icon and choose Pin This Program to Taskbar. That'll save you a scroll-scroll-scroll trip through All Apps the next time you want to run Paint.

FIGURE 1-7:
The Start menu's apps list is lengthy but necessary.

10. **X out of Paint. Again, click or tap Start. This time click or tap one of the alphabetizing indexes.**

For example, click the A above Alarms & Clock. Windows shows you a telephone-like index for all your apps entries, as you can see in Figure 1-8. If you were to click, say, W, you would be immediately transported to the W part of the All Apps list.

11. **Let's take a quick look at the other notable new Universal Windows apps. At the bottom of the screen, click or tap the Edge icon (shown in the margin).**

The icon is vaguely reminiscent of the old Internet Explorer *e*. You're transported into Microsoft Edge, the new Internet browser from the folks in Redmond. See Figure 1-9.

Internet Explorer is still around if you really, really, really have to use it: Just look in Start apps under Windows Accessories, not far from where you found Paint in Step 9.

FIGURE 1-8:
The Start apps list has an index.

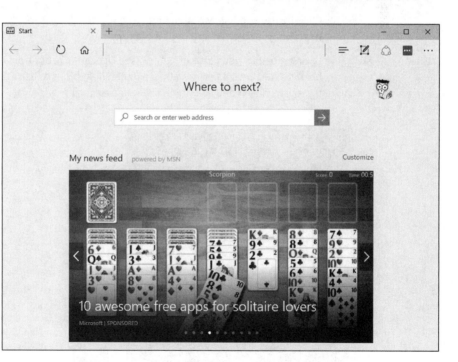

FIGURE 1-9:
Microsoft Edge takes you straight to adville; do not pass go.

REMEMBER

Microsoft is, to a first approximation anyway, abandoning Internet Explorer. That's good because IE has turned into a bloated, buggy, sinking piece of scrap. (You knew that already if you read any of my previous Windows *All-in-One For Dummies* books.) With Microsoft Edge, there's a chance that the 'Softies may actually stand a chance of one day competing against Google's Chrome browser and Firefox — both of which I still recommend.

Play with Edge for a bit — type something up in the address bar. Click or tap the + sign at the top, and add a new tab. Click some links. See how it works like a browser? Edge is actually a reasonably good browser, although it lacks some key features. See Book 5, Chapter 1 for much more info.

12. **If you haven't yet started with Cortana, give her a try. Click inside the bar that says Ask Me Anything.**

Cortana goes through some setup steps, which I describe in Book 3, Chapter 6. If you already have a Microsoft account, it's easy to get set up. (Note that you do need a Microsoft account to get personal information out of Cortana — that's how she/he/it stores your data for later retrieval.)

TECHNICAL STUFF

Cortana looks like an independent app and in some ways it is, but more than anything, Cortana is an extension of Bing, Microsoft's search engine. Anything you type in Cortana search — any sweet nothing you whisper in her ear — is destined for Bing.

13. **Click inside the Ask Me Anything box, say "Hey, Cortana," pause for a heartbeat, and then say "Tell me a joke."**

I won't attest to her sense of humor (see Figure 1-10), but Cortana has certainly been trained well. If you'd like more interesting things to ask Cortana, hop over to Google (sorry) and search for *Cortana questions.*

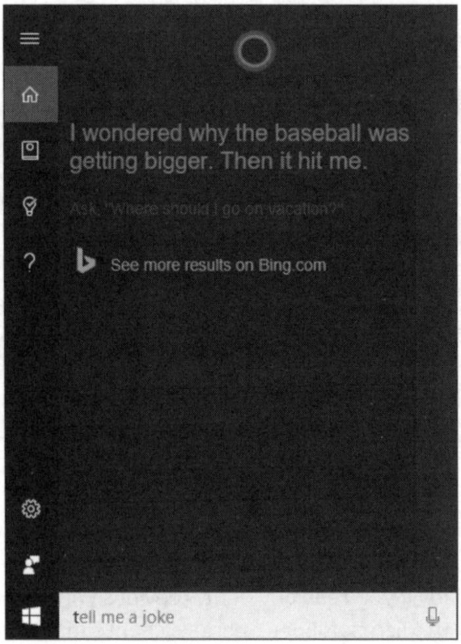

I wondered why the baseball was getting bigger. Then it hit me.

Ask "Where should I go on vacation?"

See more results on Bing.com

tell me a joke

FIGURE 1-10:
Hey, Cortana (pause, pause). Tell me a joke!

That completes the canned tour of Windows 10 highlights. There's much, much more to discover — I only scratched a thin layer of epidermis.

Take a breather.

Keying Keyboard Shortcuts

Windows 10 has about a hundred zillion — no, a googolplex — of keyboard shortcuts.

I don't use very many of them. They make my brain hurt.

REMEMBER

Here are the keyboard shortcuts that everyone should know. They've been around for a long, long time:

>> **Ctrl+C** copies whatever you've selected and puts it on the Clipboard. On a touchscreen, you can do the same thing in most applications by tapping and holding down, and then choosing Copy.

>> **Ctrl+X** does the same thing but removes the selected items — a cut. Again, you can tap and hold down, and Cut should appear in the menu.

>> **Ctrl+V** pastes whatever is in the Clipboard to the current cursor location. Tap and hold down usually works.

>> **Ctrl+A** selects everything, although sometimes it's hard to tell what "every-thing" means — different applications handle Ctrl+A differently. Tap and hold down usually works here, too.

>> **Ctrl+Z** usually undoes whatever you just did. Few touch-enabled apps have a tap-and-hold-down alternative; you usually have to find Undo on a ribbon or menu.

>> When you're typing, **Ctrl+B**, **Ctrl+I**, and **Ctrl+U** usually flip your text over to Bold, Italic, or Underline, respectively. Hit the same key combination again, and you flip back to normal.

REMEMBER

In addition to all the key combinations you may have encountered in Windows versions since the dawn of 19th-century dentistry, there's a healthy crop of new combinations. These are the important ones:

>> The **Windows key** brings up the Start menu.

>> **Alt+Tab** cycles through all running Windows programs, one by one — and each running Legacy desktop app is treated as a running program. (Windows key+Tab treats the entire desktop as one app.) See Figure 1-11.

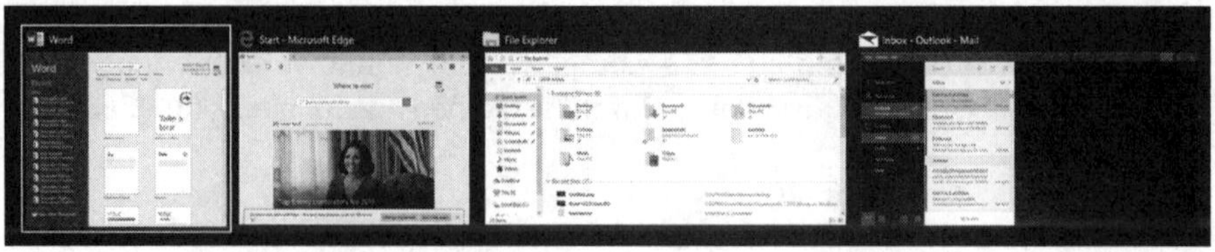
Word
Start - Microsoft Edge
File Explorer
Inbox - Outlook - Mail

FIGURE 1-11: Alt+Tab cycles through all running apps.

- **Ctrl+Alt+Del** — the old Vulcan three-finger salute — brings up a screen that lets you choose to lock your PC (flip to Book 2, Chapter 2), switch the user (see Book 2, Chapter 4), sign out, or run the new and much improved Task Manager (see Book 8, Chapter 4).

You can also right-click the Start icon or press **Windows key+X** to bring up the so-called Power User menu shown in Figure 1-12.

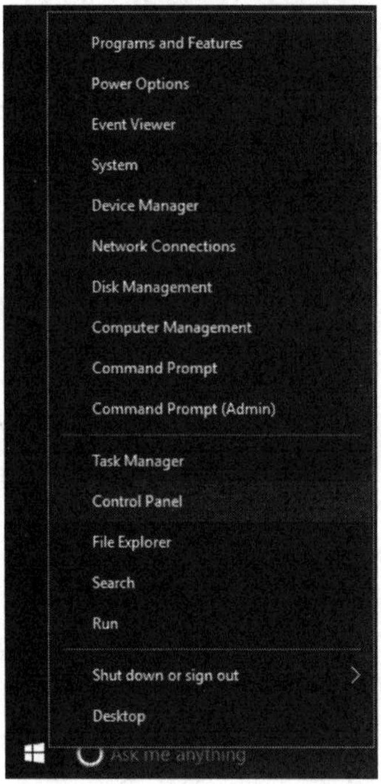
Programs and Features
Power Options
Event Viewer
System
Device Manager
Network Connections
Disk Management
Computer Management
Command Prompt
Command Prompt (Admin)
Task Manager
Control Panel
File Explorer
Search
Run
Shut down or sign out
Desktop
Ask me anything

FIGURE 1-12: The Win-X, or Power User, menu can get you into the innards of Windows.

Chapter 2

Changing the Lock and Login Screens

W indows presents three hurdles for you to clear before you can get down to work (or play, or whatever):

>> You have to get past the *lock screen.* That's a first-level hurdle so your computer doesn't accidentally get started, like the lock screen on a smartphone or an iPad.

>> If more than one person — one *account* — is set up on the computer, you have to choose which person will log in. I go into detail about setting up user accounts in Book 2, Chapter 4.

>> If a password's associated with the account, you must type it into the computer. Windows allows different kinds of passwords, which are particularly helpful if you're working on a touch-only tablet or a tiny screen like a telephone's. But the idea's the same: Unless you specifically set up an account without a password, you need to confirm your identity.

Only after clearing those three hurdles are you granted access to the Start screen and, from there, to everything Windows has to offer. In the sections that follow, you find out how you can customize the lock screen and the login methods to suit yourself.

WHAT'S NEW IN WINDOWS HELLO

Windows Hello gives an additional method for confirming your identity. Windows Hello uses biometric authentication — scanning your face or fingerprint or one day scanning your iris — as a much more secure method than passwords.

As the book went to press, Windows Hello technology (including, notably, Intel RealSense cameras) was just starting to appear on non-Microsoft hardware. Microsoft Surface Pro 4 and Surface Book both have Hello-compatible cameras, but on non-Microsoft computers the cameras aren't common. Even the Surface Pro 3's camera isn't good enough.

These are the best-known laptops that support Windows Hello: Acer Aspire V 17 Nitro, Asus N551JQ, ROG G771JM, X751LD, Dell Inspiron 15 5548, Dell Inspiron 23 7000, HP Sprout, HP Envy 15t Touch RealSense Laptop, Microsoft Surface Pro 4, Microsoft Surface Book, Lenovo B5030, ThinkPad Yoga 15, and ThinkPad E550. You can buy an add-on RealSense camera that'll support Windows Hello, but it's expensive.

Many devices support fingerprint recognition, but the specific kind of recognition demanded by Hello, once again, isn't common.

Only time will tell if Hello is reliable enough (and the hardware cheap enough!) to make a dent in the market.

If you have a pre-Windows 10 camera or fingerprint reader, chances are very good it won't work with Windows Hello. Many more details are in Microsoft's lengthy Passport guide, at https://technet.microsoft.com/en-us/itpro/windows/keep-secure/microsoft-passport-guide. (Passport is an on-again, off-again Microsoft brand that's being folded into Windows Hello.)

Working with the Lock Screen

The very first time you start Windows, and anytime you shut it down, restart, or let the machine go idle for long enough, you're greeted with the lock screen, such as the one in Figure 2-1.

You can get through the lock screen by doing any of the following:

>> Swiping up with your finger, if you have a touch-sensitive display

>> Dragging up with your mouse

>> Pressing any key on your keyboard

FIGURE 2-1:
The Windows
lock screen.

You aren't stuck with the lock screen Microsoft gives you. You can customize your picture and the little icons (or *badges*). The following sections explain how.

Using your own picture

Changing the picture for your lock screen is easy. (See the nearby sidebar "Individualized lock screens" for details about the difference between your lock screen and the system's lock screen.) Customizing the picture is a favorite trick at Windows demos, so you know it has to be easy, right? Here's how:

1. **Click or tap the Start icon, the Settings icon, and then Personalization.**

2. **On the left, choose Lock Screen.**

   The lock screen's Preview window appears.

3. **From the Background drop-down list, first try Windows Spotlight, if it's available (see Figure 2-2).**

   Windows Spotlight images come directly from Microsoft — more specifically, from Bing — and change frequently. Microsoft reserves the right to put advertising on Windows Spotlight screens, ostensibly to tell you about features in Windows that you haven't used yet. Remains to be seen whether other, uh, partners can purchase spots on the screen.

4. **From the drop-down list, choose Picture.**

   This selection (see Figure 2-3) lets you choose which picture will appear. If you like one of the pictures on offer, click it. If you'd rather find your own picture, click Browse.

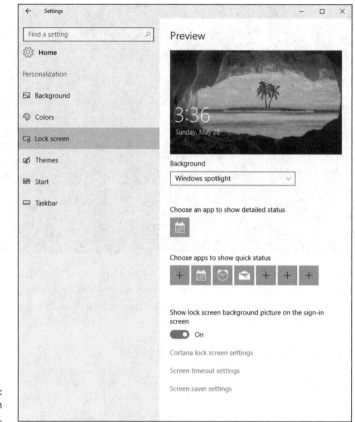

FIGURE 2-2:
Change your own
lock screen here.

You can decide whether you want your chosen picture to be overlaid with "fun facts, tips, tricks, and more on your lock screen." Oh goodie.

5. **If you find a picture you want, click it. If not, choose Slideshow in the Background drop-down box.**

   This option ties into the Albums in the Universal Windows Photos app (see Book 4, Chapter 3), or you can choose to turn a folder of pictures into a slideshow. If you decide to go with a slideshow, click the Advanced Slideshow Settings link to set whether the slideshow can be pulled from your camera roll, whether the chosen pictures have to be large enough to fit your screen, and several additional choices.

6. **After you've chosen the background itself, you can specify what apps should provide details that appear on the lock screen. See the next section for details about *Badges*.**

   You're finished. There's no Apply or OK button to tap or click.

Test to make sure that your personal lock screen has been updated. The easiest way is to go to the Start menu, click your picture in the upper-left corner, and choose Lock or Sign Out.

FIGURE 2-3:
Choose your own picture, with or without Microsoft advertising.

INDIVIDUALIZED LOCK SCREENS

If you read the Microsoft help file, you may think that Windows keeps one lock screen for all users, but it doesn't. Instead, it has a lock screen for each individual user and one more lock screen for the system as a whole.

If you're using the system and you lock it — say, tap your picture on the Metro Start screen and choose Lock — Windows shows your personal lock screen, with the badges you've chosen. If you swipe or drag to lift that lock screen, you're immediately asked to provide your password. There's no intervening step to ask which user should log in.

If, instead of locking the system when you leave it, you tap your picture and choose Sign Out, Windows behaves quite differently. It shows the system's lock screen, with the system's badges. Your lock screen and badges are nowhere to be seen. If you drag or swipe to go through the lock screen, you're asked to choose which user will log in.

Bottom line: If you change your lock screen using the techniques in this chapter, you change only *your* lock screen. Windows' idea of a lock screen stays the same.

Adding and removing apps on the lock screen

Badges are the little icons that appear at the bottom of the lock screen. They exist to tell you something about your computer at a glance, without having to log in — how many email messages are unread, whether your battery needs charging, and so on. Some badges just appear on the lock screen, no matter what you do. For example, if you have an Internet connection, a badge appears on the lock screen. If you're using a tablet or laptop, the battery status appears; there's nothing you can do about it.

Mostly, though, Windows lets you pick and choose quick status badges that are important to you. The question I most often hear about badges is, "Why not just choose them all?"

Good question. The programs that support the badges update their information periodically — every 15 minutes, in some cases. If you have a badge on your lock screen, the lock screen app that controls the badge has to wake up every so often, so it can retrieve the data and put it on the lock screen. Putting everything on the lock screen drains your computer's battery.

ASK
WOODY.COM

Corollary: If your computer has a short battery life, whittle your needs down as much as you can, and get rid of every quick status badge you don't absolutely need. But if your computer is plugged in to the wall, put all the badges you like on the lock screen.

Here's how to pick and choose your quick status badges:

1. **Click or tap the Start icon and then the Settings icon.**

2. **Choose Personalization. On the left, choose Lock Screen. On the right, scroll down.**

TIP

   At the bottom of the screen are two rows of gray icons. You can see them at the bottom of Figure 2-3.

   The first icon points to a specially anointed app that shows detailed status information on the lock screen. You get only one. In Figure 2-1, I have the date and time, which is the default choice.

   The detailed status app has to be specially designed to display the large block of information shown in Figure 2-1.

3. **Tap or click the detailed status icon, and choose which display badge you want to appear in that slot on the lock screen (see Figure 2-4).**

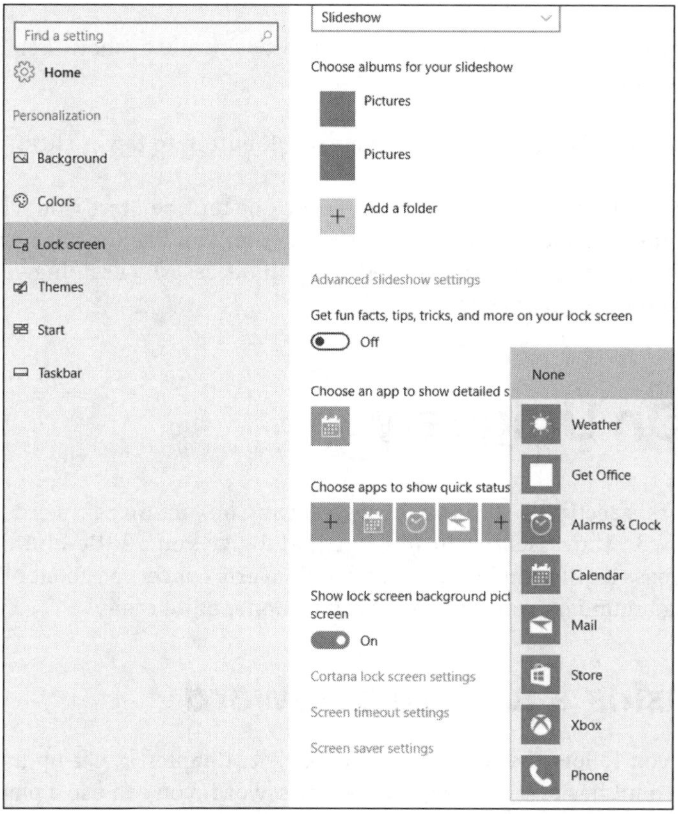

![Settings window showing Lock screen personalization options]

FIGURE 2-4:
Choose which apps' badges appear on the lock screen.

TIP

Apps must be specially designed to display the badge information on the lock screen. You're given a choice of all the apps that have registered with Windows as being capable of displaying a quick status badge on the lock screen. As you add more apps, some of them appear spontaneously on this list.

The second row, of seven icons, corresponds to seven badge locations at the bottom of the lock screen. They appear in order from left to right, starting below the time. In theory (although this doesn't always work), you can choose which badges appear, and where they appear, in order from left to right.

4. **Click each of the seven gray icons in turn, and choose an app to show its status on the lock screen.**

   If you choose Don't Show Quick Status Here, the gray icon gets a plus (+) sign, indicating that it isn't being used. No badge appears in the corresponding slot on the lock screen.

The quick status apps have to be built specifically to show their badges on the lock screen.

You're finished. There's no Apply or OK button to tap or click.

Go back out to the lock screen — click or tap the Start icon, choose your picture at the top, choose Lock — and see whether you like the changes. If you don't like what you see or you're worried about unnecessarily draining your battery with all the fluff, start over at Step 1.

Logging On Uniquely

In this section, I step you through setting up picture passwords and PINs, tell you how to show Hello your mugly ug, and give you a little hint about how you can bypass login completely, if you aren't overly concerned about other people snooping around on your PC. Yes, it can be done, quite easily.

Using a picture password

If you follow the instructions in Book 2, Chapter 4, set up an account, and the account has an everyday, ordinary password, you can use a picture password.

It's easy.

A *picture password* consists of two parts: First, you choose a picture — any picture — and then you tell Windows that you're going to draw on that picture in a particular way, such as taps, clicks, circles, and straight lines, with a finger or a mouse. The next time you want to log in to Windows, you can either type your password or you can repeat the series of clicks, taps, circles, and straight lines.

So, for example, you may have a picture of Thai dancers, as shown in the upper-right corner of Figure 2-5, and you may decide that you want your picture password to consist of tapping the forehead of the many-armed figure in the middle, then on the dancer on the left, then on the right, in that order.

That picture password is simple, fast, and not easy to guess.

Everybody I know who has a chance to switch to a picture password or PIN loves it. Whether you're working with a mouse or a stubby finger, a few taps or slides are sooo much easier than trying to remember and type a17LetterP@ssw0rd.

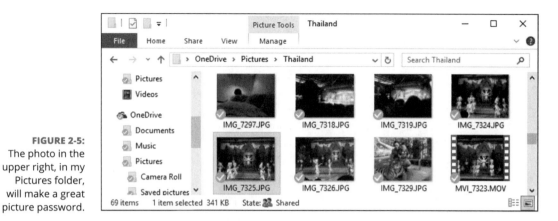

FIGURE 2-5:
The photo in the upper right, in my Pictures folder, will make a great picture password.

Microsoft has a few suggestions for making your picture password hard to crack. These include the following:

>> **Start with a picture that has lots of interesting points.** If you have just one or two interesting locations in the photo, you don't have very many points to choose from.

>> **Don't use just taps (or clicks).** Mix things up. Use a tap, a circle, and a line, for example, in any sequence you can easily remember.

>> **Don't always move from left to right.** Lines can go right to left, or top to bottom. Circles can go clockwise or counterclockwise.

REMEMBER

>> **Don't let anybody watch you sign in.** Picture passwords are worse than keyboard passwords, in some respects, because the picture password appears on the screen as you're drawing it.

ASK WOODY.COM

>> **Clean your screen.** Really devious souls may be able to figure out that trail of oil and grime is from your repeated use of the same picture password. If you can't clean your screen and you're worried about somebody following the grime trail, put a couple of gratuitous smudges on the screen. I'm sure you can find a 2-year-old who would be happy to oblige.

Here's how to change your account to use a picture password:

1. **Tap or click the Start icon, the Settings icon, and then Accounts.**

2. **On the left, choose Sign-In Options.**

   The password settings for your account appear, as shown in Figure 2-6.

3. **Under Picture Password, tap or click Add.**

   If your account doesn't yet have a password, you're prompted to provide one. If you do have a password, Windows asks you to verify your typed password.

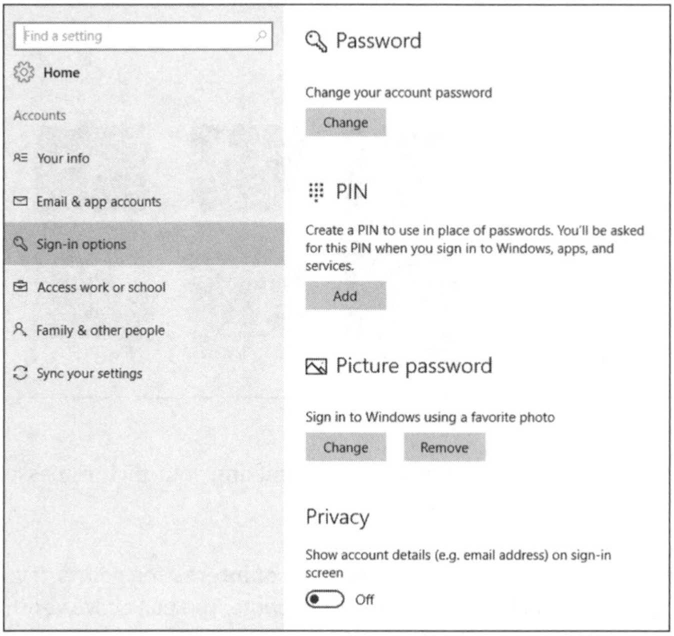

![Figure 2-6 screenshot: Windows Settings sign-in options]

Find a setting

⚙ Home

Accounts

Aⱻ Your info

✉ Email & app accounts

🔍 Sign-in options

🏢 Access work or school

👤 Family & other people

🔄 Sync your settings

🔑 **Password**

Change your account password

Change

⠿ **PIN**

Create a PIN to use in place of passwords. You'll be asked for this PIN when you sign in to Windows, apps, and services.

Add

🖼 **Picture password**

Sign in to Windows using a favorite photo

Change   Remove

Privacy

Show account details (e.g. email address) on sign-in screen

◉○ Off

FIGURE 2-6:
Your account's
password
settings.

You must have a typed password — the password can't be blank — or Windows will just log you in without any password, either typed or picture.

4. **Type your password, and then tap or click OK.**

Windows asks you to choose a picture.

5. **Tap or click Choose Picture, find a picture (remember, with ten or more interesting points), and tap or click Open.**

Your picture appears in a cropping bucket. The picture must conform to an odd shape, or it won't fit on the login screen.

6. **Slide the picture around to crop it the way you want. Then tap or click Use This Picture.**

Windows invites you to set up your gestures, as shown in Figure 2-7.

7. **Trace out the gestures exactly as you want them.**

Make sure the gestures are in the correct order and that each of the three consists of a click, a line, or a circle.

Windows then asks you to repeat your gestures. This is where you get to see how sensitive the gesture-tracking method can be.

8. **Repeat the gestures. When you get them to match (which isn't necessarily easy!), tap or click Finish.**

Your new picture password is ready.

FIGURE 2-7:
Here's where you draw your three taps/clicks, lines, and circles.

9. **Go to the Start menu, tap your picture, choose Lock, and make sure you can replicate your gestures.**

REMEMBER

If you can't get the picture password to work, you can always use your regular typed password.

Creating a PIN

Everybody has PIN codes for ATM cards, telephones, just about everything.

WARNING

Reusing PIN codes on multiple devices (and credit cards) is dangerous — somebody looks over your shoulder, watches you type your Windows PIN, and then lifts your wallet. Such nefarious folks can have a good time, unless the PINs are different. Word to the wise, eh?

PINs have lots of advantages over passwords and picture passwords. They're short and easy to remember. Fast. Technically, though, the best thing about a PIN is that it's stored on your computer — it's tied to that one computer, and you don't have to worry about it getting stored in some hacked database or stolen with your credit card numbers.

Creating a PIN is easy:

1. **Tap or click the Start icon, the Settings icon, and then Accounts.**

2. **On the left, choose Sign-In Options.**

   The password settings for your account appear (refer to Figure 2-6).

3. **Under PIN, tap or click Add.**

   Windows asks you to verify your password — it must be your typed password; a picture password won't do.

4. **Type your password, and tap or click OK.**

   Windows gives you a chance to type your PIN, as in Figure 2-8, and then retype it to confirm it. **Note:** Most ATM PINs are four digits, but you can go longer, if you want — Windows can handle just about any PIN you can throw at it.

5. **Type your PIN, confirm it, and tap or click OK.**

   You can log in with your PIN.

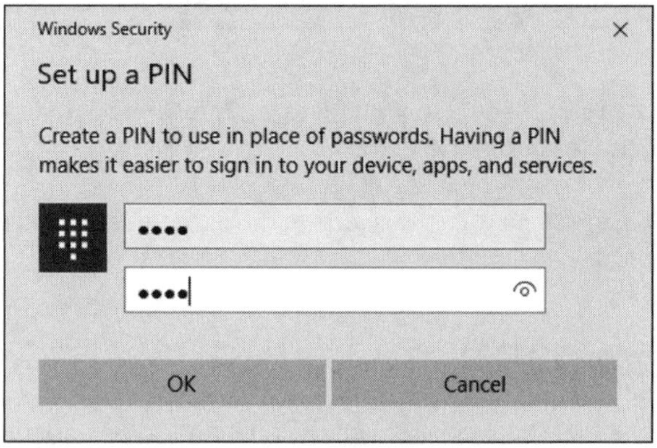

![Windows Security dialog box titled "Set up a PIN" with text "Create a PIN to use in place of passwords. Having a PIN makes it easier to sign in to your device, apps, and services." Two PIN entry fields and OK and Cancel buttons.]

FIGURE 2-8:
Creating a PIN
is easy.

Windows Hello

As we went to press, Windows Hello hardware was starting to roll out. In a nutshell, Windows Hello offers biometric authentication — way beyond a password or a PIN. The Windows Hello technology includes fingerprint, face (and, soon, iris) recognition with a specially designed camera or fingerprint reader or both.

Microsoft is gradually implementing fingerprint recognition with older finger scanners as well. But the hallmark Hello scan for your shiny face is limited to fancy cameras, included with only a limited number of computers (see the "Windows Hello" sidebar at the start of this chapter).

ASK
WOODY.COM

Frankly, I'm not a big fan of Windows Hello face recognition. I use it on the Surface Book and sometimes on the Surface Pro 4, but it isn't my cup of tea. Why? Many times, I sit in front of a PC and don't want to log in. Heresy, I know. But if I put my face anywhere near the Surface Pro when it's turned on, I'm caught like a deer in headlights — bang, there, I'm logged in and Cortana's ready to be directed.

If I want to log in to a different account, I have to manually log out and then beat Hello to the punch, which is surprisingly difficult.

If you have a computer that supports Hello face recognition, give it a try and see if you like it. If you're thinking about buying a computer specifically because it has the camera to support Hello face recognition, fuhgeddaboutit. I'll stick with a PIN or a picture, thank you very much.

How to tell if your computer supports Windows Hello? Click the Start icon, the Settings icon, Account, and then Sign-In Options. Set up a PIN using the steps in the preceding section. Then, if your machine can handle Windows Hello, there is a link in the settings page under Windows Hello.

Bypassing passwords and login

So now you have three convenient ways to tell Windows your password: You can type it, just like a normal password; you can click or tap on a picture; or you can pretend it's a phone and enter a PIN.

But what if you don't want a password? What if your computer is secure enough — it's sitting in your house, it's in your safe deposit box, it's dangling from a vine over a pot of boiling oil — and you just don't want to be bothered with typing or tapping a password?

TIP

As long as you have a Local account, it's easy. Just remove your password. Turn it into a blank. Follow the steps in Book 2, Chapter 4 to change your password but leave the New Password field blank. (Shortcut: In Figure 2-6, tap or click the Change button under Password.)

Microsoft accounts can't have blank passwords. But local accounts can.

If you have a blank password, when you click your username on the login screen, Windows ushers you to the desktop.

If only one user is on the PC and that user has a blank password, just getting past the lock screen takes you to the Start screen.

If you have a Microsoft account, you have to use your password (picture, PIN, Hello, whatever) once each time you reboot. If you don't want to be bothered after that, see the Require Sign-In drop-down choice at the top of the Sign-In options screen. Click to change the answer to "If you've been away, when should Windows require you to sign in again?" to Never.

Chapter 3

Working with the Action/Notification Center

f you've ever used a moderately sentient phone or tablet, you already know about the notification center. Different devices do it differently, but the general idea is that the phone watches and gathers notifications — little warning messages or status reports — that are sent to you. The phone or tablet gathers all the notifications and puts them in one place, where you can look at them and decide what to do from there.

In Windows 7, notifications just kind of flew by, and there weren't many of them. In Windows 8 and 8.1, you typically see many more notifications (I'm looking at you, Gmail running in Chrome), but they still fly by. There's no way in Windows 8 or 8.1 to look at old notifications. After they're off the screen — frequently for just a few seconds — that's it. And when they pile up, they can pile up and up and up and up, taking over the right edge of your screen.

Finally, with Windows 10, we have a place where Windows sticks all the notifications. Or at least some of them. Sometimes. You know, like smartphones have had for a decade or so.

What Is the Action Center?

Unfortunately, this new locus for machine notifications isn't called a notification center, as it's called in almost every operating system, in almost every language, on earth. That name's taken — Microsoft started calling the system tray, down at the lower-right corner of the screen, the notification center with Windows 8.

So we get a strange name for a common sight: It's officially called the *action center,* although everyone I know slips from time to time and calls it the notification center.

This isn't the Windows solution center (born in Windows 7, primarily for security stuff), nor is it the Windows 7 or Windows 8 action center (see Figure 3-1), which includes lots of system-related stuff, but no program notifications.

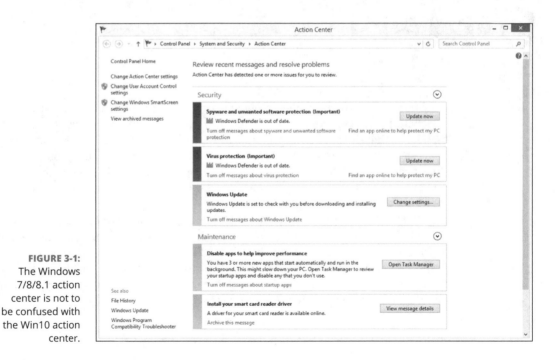

FIGURE 3-1: The Windows 7/8/8.1 action center is not to be confused with the Win10 action center.

Instead, the Windows 10 action center is, well, a real notification center. Click the icon down in the lower right of the screen (and shown in the margin) and you can see the action in Figure 3-2.

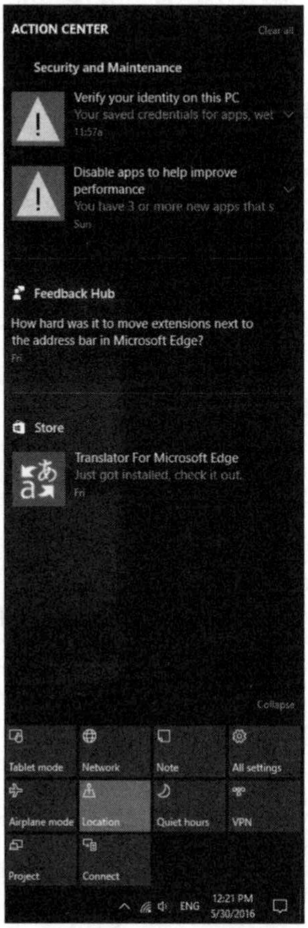

FIGURE 3-2:
The Windows
10 notific. . . er,
action center.

At the top, Windows gathers some (but by no means all) of the various programs' notifications. At the bottom, you have a bunch of quick links to various settings.

What, Exactly, Is a Notification?

ASK
WOODY.COM

Historically, Windows allowed all sorts of notifications: blinking taskbar tiles, balloon messages over the system time (in the lower-right corner), dire-looking icons in the system notification area (near the system time), or dialog boxes that appear out of nowhere, sometimes taking over your computer. Then came

Windows 8, and the powers that be started looking down on programs that jilted and cavorted, whittled and wheezed. People who write the programs have gradually become more disciplined.

Except for Scottrade, Figure 3-3, which locks out the screen, but that's another modal dialog story.

These new, politically correct notifications — the things that can happen when Windows 10 or one of its programs wants your attention — fall into three broad categories:

>> They can put rectangular notices, usually gray, in the upper-right edge of your screen, with a few lines of text. Typically, the notifications say things such as *Tap* or *Choose what happens when you insert a USB drive,* or *Turn sharing on or off.*

   These notifications are called *toaster notifications* (or sometimes just *toast*), and they're a core part of the new Universal face of Windows. It's a fabulous name because they pop up, just like toast, but on their sides, and then they disappear.

>> They can show toaster notifications on the lock screen. This is considered more dire than simply showing the notifications on tiled apps or the desktop. Why? Because the apps that create lock screen notifications may need to run, even when Windows is sleeping. And that leads to battery drainage.

>> They can play sounds. Don't get me started.

Google's never been partial to the Windows notification method, so they've built an independent notification system into the Chrome browser itself. The notifications appear in the lower-right corner of the browser. See Figure 3-4.

FIGURE 3-4:
This is Google Chrome's notification for arriving Gmail.

When you click a Chrome Gmail notification — if you're fast enough — Chrome opens the email for you, and puts it in a separate window, ready for you to reply. That's exactly the kind of response you should expect from your notifications — click them, and they do something appropriate.

These notifications are internal to Google Chrome; Windows doesn't see them and doesn't control them. As of this writing, they haven't been integrated into the Windows 10 notific. . . er, action center.

Working with Notifications

In the best of all possible worlds, Windows 10 notifications would work like Google Chrome notifications, only better: Click a Windows 10 notification, and you get transported to a description, a setting, a piece of mail, some sort of instructions, whatever.

With the Anniversary Update of Windows 10, the Windows action/notification center has become just a little more useful, primarily because you can now click a notification and expect something worthwhile to happen. In the earlier version of Windows 10, clicking a notification rarely accomplished anything useful. In the Anniversary Update, you may get a response or you may not. Don't hold your breath.

If you find that a particular program is generating notifications that you don't want to see, Windows lets you disable all notifications rather easily, or you can pick and choose which apps can send notifications and which just have to stifle their utterances.

Here's how to disable notifications:

1. **Tap or click the Start icon, the Settings icon, and then System.**

   Or you can get into Settings from the bottom of the action center (see the All Settings icon, right below Collapse, at the top right of the bottom part of Figure 3-2).

2. **On the left, choose Notifications & Actions.**

   You see the Notifications pane shown in Figure 3-5.

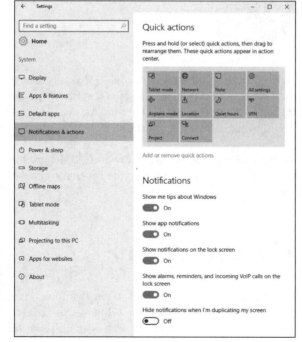

FIGURE 3-5:
Make changes to the quick action icons (more on that in the next section), or turn off notifications altogether.

3. **Turn off all notifications by finding the slider marked Get Notifications from Apps and Other Senders, and sliding it to Off.**

4. **If you would like to silence just one app, scroll down farther (see Figure 3-6), find the app, and move its slider to Off.**

   You're finished. There's no Apply or OK button to tap or click.

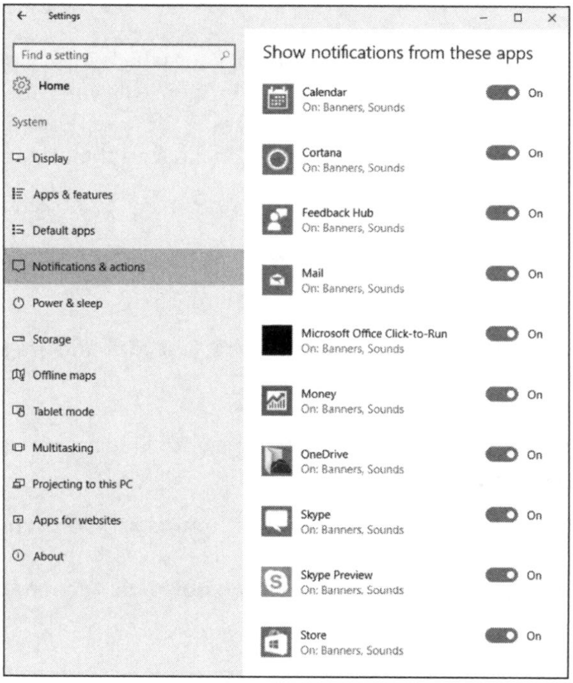

FIGURE 3-6:
You can silence notifications from individual apps.

Working with Settings Shortcuts

The action center contains a gob (that's a technical term) of shortcuts at the bottom of the Notifications pane. In Figure 3-2, I count ten of them. If the computer used a Wi-Fi connection, there would have been additional shortcuts for Wi-Fi, Bluetooth, rotation lock, battery saver, and brightness. I don't know of any definitive list of all quick action icons.

Quick actions mimic what you would find on a phone — airplane mode is an obvious analog — all readily accessible from the right side of the screen. In many cases, a quick action displays a Settings page, where you can change the individual setting, displays a pane on the right side of the screen (Connect, Project), or toggles a specific setting in, uh, Settings. The Note quick action displays the Microsoft OneNote application.

ASK
WOODY.COM

You can think of quick actions as handy shortcuts to frequently adjusted settings, or you can look at them as testimony to the diverse way Windows has settings scattered all over Hades's half acre. You decide.

You have some — but not much — control over which icons appear at the bottom of the pane. Here's how to exert as much influence as you can:

1. **Tap or click the Start icon, the Settings icon, and then System.**

   Or you can get into Settings from the bottom of the action center.

2. **On the left, choose Notifications & Actions.**

   The Notifications pane appears (refer to Figure 3-5).

3. **To move the quick actions icons around, just click and drag.**

   You can't drag a quick action off the grid.

4. **To choose additional quick action icons or to hide an icon, click the link to Add or Remove Quick Actions.**

   A list of predefined action icons appears, from which you can pick and choose.

Table 3-1 explains what each of the configurable quick action icons does.

TABLE 3-1 ## Some Quick Action Icon Results in the Action Center

Click This Icon	And This Happens
Tablet Mode	Flips the computer to tablet mode.
Brightness (100%)	Adjusts the screen brightness in 25% increments: Click once to cycle among 25%, 50%, 75%, and 100%.
Connect	Searches for wireless display and audio devices — Miracast in particular.
All Settings	Takes you to the Settings app.
Battery Saver	Cycles between two battery saver modes, dimming the display. It doesn't work if the machine is plugged in.
VPN	Displays the Settings app's Network & Internet section on VPN, where you can add a new VPN connection or connected to an existing one.
Bluetooth	Turns Bluetooth on and off.

Click This Icon	And This Happens
Rotation Lock	Prevents the screen from rotating from portrait to landscape and vice versa.
Wi-Fi	Turns Wi-Fi on and off. There's no provision to select a Wi-Fi connection.
Location	Turns the location setting on and off in the Settings app's Privacy, Location pane.
Airplane	Turns all wireless communication on and off. See the Settings app's Network & Internet, Airplane Mode setting.

Too bad you can't add your own quick actions. The action center be a convenient place to stick your own favorite programs, replicating the Win7/8.1 Start menu capability, on the right side of the screen.

Working with the Action Center

Chapter 4

Controlling Users

Microsoft reports that 70 percent of all Windows PCs have just one user account. That's a startling figure. It means that 70 percent of all Windows PCs run at the most permissive security level, all the time. It means that, on 70 percent of all Windows PCs, little Billy can install Internet Antivirus 2011 — a notorious piece of scumware — and have it bring down the whole family with a couple of simple clicks. "Sorry, Dad, but it's an antivirus program, and it said that we really need to install it, and it's just $49.95 for a three-month subscription. I thought you said that antivirus was good. They wouldn't lie about stuff like that, would they?"

ASK WOODY.COM

Although it's undoubtedly true that many PCs are each used by just one person, I think it's highly likely that people don't set up multiple user accounts on their PCs because they're intimidated. Not to worry. I take you through the ins and outs.

Even if you're the only person who ever uses your PC, you may want to create a second account — another user, as it were — even if the second user is just you. (As Pogo said, "We have met the enemy, and he is us.") Then again, you may not. And therein lies this chapter's story.

REMEMBER

If you're running Windows 10 Enterprise or Win10 Pro and your PC is connected to a big corporate network (in the parlance, a *domain*), you have little or no control over who can log in to your computer and what a logged-in user can do after she's on the machine. That's a Good Thing, at least in theory: Your company's network administrator gets to worry about all the security issues, relieving you of the hassles of figuring out whether the guy down the hall should be able to look at payroll records or the company Christmas card list. But it can also be a pain in the neck, especially if you have to install a program, like, right now, and you don't have a user account with sufficient capabilities. If your computer is attached to a domain, your only choice is to convince (or bribe) the network admin to let you in.

The nostrums in this chapter apply only to PCs connected to small networks or to stand-alone PCs. If you're on a big network, you must pay homage to the network gods. Pizza, beer, and a smile can help.

ASK WOODY.COM

Windows 10 has two separate locations that control user accounts. If you want to do only some simple stuff — create a new account, change the password, or switch to a picture password, say — you can do it all on the touch-friendly Metro tiled side of Windows 10. On the other hand, if you want to do something more challenging — set the User Account Control trigger levels, for example — you must work with the old-fashioned Windows 7–style desktop's Control Panel. I show you how to use both in this chapter.

User Account Control is a security topic, only tangentially related to user accounts. I talk about it in Book 9, Chapter 3.

Why You Need Separate User Accounts

Windows assumes that, sooner or later, more than one person will want to work on your PC. All sorts of problems crop up when several people share a PC. I set up my screen just right, with all my icons right where I can find them, and then my son comes along and plasters the desktop with a shot of Alpha Centauri. He puts together a killer Taylor Swift playlist and "accidentally" deletes my Grateful Dead playlist in the process.

It's worse than sharing a TV remote.

Windows helps keep peace in the family — and in the office — by requiring people to log in. The process of *logging in* (also called *signing in*) lets Windows keep track of each person's settings: You tell Windows who you are, and Windows lets you play in your own sandbox.

REMEMBER

Having personal settings that are activated whenever you log in to Windows doesn't create heavy-duty security. Unless your PC is a slave to a big Active Directory domain network, your settings can get clobbered and your files deleted, if someone else with access to your computer or your network tries hard enough. But as long as you're reasonably careful and follow the advice in this chapter, Windows security works surprisingly well.

WARNING

If someone else can put his hands on your computer, it isn't your computer anymore. That can be a real problem if someone swipes your laptop, if the cleaning staff uses your PC after hours, or if a snoop breaks into your study. Unless you use BitLocker (in Windows 10 Pro), anybody who can restart your PC can look at, modify, or delete your files or stick a virus on the PC. How? In many cases, a miscreant can bypass Windows directly and start your PC with another operating system. With Windows out of the picture, compromising a PC doesn't take much work.

Choosing Account Types

When dealing with user accounts, you bump into one existential fact of Windows life over and over again: The type of account you use puts severe limitations on what you can do.

Unless you're hooked up to a big corporate network, user accounts can generally be divided into two groups: the haves and the have-nots. (Users attached to corporate domains are assigned accounts that can exist anywhere on the have-to-have-not spectrum.) The have accounts are *administrator* accounts. The have-nots are *standard* accounts. That's it. Standard. Kinda makes your toes curl just to think about it.

What's a standard account?

A person running with a standard account can do only, uh, standard tasks:

>> Run programs installed on the computer, including programs on USB/key drives.

>> Use hardware already installed on the computer.

>> Create, view, save, modify, and use documents, pictures, and sounds in the Documents, Pictures, or Music folders as well as in the PC's Public folders.

TIP

If your computer is part of a homegroup (see Book 7, Chapter 5), a standard user can also create, view, save, modify, and use any files in the Public folders of computers that are part of your homegroup. A standard user can also access any shared folders on other computers in the homegroup.

>> Change his password or switch back and forth between requiring and not requiring a password for his account. He can also add a picture or PIN password. If your computer is sufficiently enabled, he can also use Windows Hello to set up a camera, fingerprint, or retina scan. Just like in the movies.

Controlling Users

>> Switch between a local account and a Microsoft account. I talk about both in the next section of this chapter.

>> Change the picture that appears next to his name on the Welcome screen and on the left side of the Start menu, change the desktop wallpaper, resize the Windows toolbar, add items to the old-fashioned desktop toolbar and Start menu, and make other small changes that don't affect other user accounts.

In most cases, a standard user can change systemwide settings, install programs, and the like, but only if he can provide the username and password of an administrator account.

If you're running with a standard account, you can't even change the time on the clock. It's quite limited.

There's also a special, limited version of the standard account called a *child account*. As the name implies, child accounts can be controlled and monitored by those with standard and administrator accounts. See the sidebar on child accounts.

CHILD ACCOUNTS

Microsoft provides a quick-and-dirty way to set up child accounts as part of the account creation process. Child accounts are like standard accounts, but they're automatically set up with child protection enabled — someone with an administrator account can control which websites the child accounts can access, what time of day the accounts can be used, and the total amount of time the accounts are used in a day.

It's all done on the web — the controls aren't in Windows 10 itself, they're in a website maintained by Microsoft. There's a small charge for each child account that you set up. Note that laws in various places — including COPPA in the US — require that an account for anyone under 13 has to be associated with a guardian who controls a child. There's a 44-page synopsis of the COPPA regulations at www.ftc.gov/system/files/2012-31341.pdf. Easy reading for a parent wanting to set up an account for the kids.

Full instructions for bringing a Windows 7 or 8 child account into Windows 10 are at http://windows.microsoft.com/en-us/windows-10/set-up-family-after-upgrade.

What's an administrator account?

REMEMBER

People using administrator accounts can change almost anything, anywhere, at any time. (Certain folders remain off limits, even to administrator accounts, and you have to jump through some difficult hoops to work around the restrictions.) People using administrator accounts can even change other local accounts' passwords — a good thing to remember if you ever forget your password.

If you start Windows with a standard account and you accidentally run a virus, a worm, or some other piece of bad computer code, the damage is usually limited: The malware can delete or scramble files in your Documents folder, and probably in the Public folders, but that's about the extent of the damage. Usually. Unless it's exceedingly clever, the virus can't install itself into the computer, so it can't run repeatedly, and it may not be able to replicate. Poor virus.

Someone with an administrator account can get into all the files owned by other users: If you thought that attaching a password to your account and putting a top-secret spreadsheet in your Documents folder would keep it away from prying eyes, you're in for a rude surprise. Anybody who can get into your machine with an administrator account can look at it. Standard users, on the other hand, are effectively limited to looking only at their own files.

Choosing between standard and administrator accounts

REMEMBER

The first account on a new PC is always an administrator account. If you bought your PC with Windows preinstalled, the account that you have — the one you probably set up shortly after you took the computer out of the box — is an administrator account. If you installed Windows on a PC, the account you set up during the installation is an administrator account.

When you create new accounts, on the other hand, they always start out as standard accounts. That's as it should be.

Administrator accounts and standard accounts aren't set in concrete. In fact, Windows helps you shape-shift between the two as circumstances dictated:

>> If you're using a standard account and try to do something that requires an administrator account, Windows prompts you to provide an administrator account's name and password (see Figure 4-1).

Controlling Users

FIGURE 4-1:
Windows asks
permission
before
performing
administrative
actions.

WARNING

If the person using the standard account selects an administrator account without a password, simply clicking the Yes button allows the program to run — one more reason why you need passwords on all your administrator accounts, eh?

>> Even if you're using an administrator account, Windows normally runs as though you had a standard account, in some cases adding an extra hurdle when you try to run a program that can make substantial changes to your PC — and *substantial* is quite a subjective term. You have to clear the same kind of hurdle if you try to access folders that aren't explicitly shared (see Figure 4-2). That extra hurdle helps prevent destructive programs from sneaking into your computer and running with your administrator account, doing their damage without your knowledge or permission.

FIGURE 4-2:
Windows lays
down a challenge
before you dive
in to another
user's folder.

TIP

Most experts recommend that you use a standard account for daily activities and switch to an administrator account only when you need to install software or hardware or access files outside the usual shared areas. Most experts ignore their own advice: It's the old do-as-I-say-not-as-I-do syndrome.

I used to recommend that people follow the lead of the do-as-I-say crowd and simply set up every knowledgeable user with an administrator account. Times change, and Windows has changed: It's rare that you actually need an administrator account to accomplish just about anything in "normal" day-to-day use. (One exception: You can add new users only if you're using an administrator account.) For that reason, I've come to the conclusion that you should save that one administrator account for a rainy day, and set up standard accounts for yourself and anyone else who uses the PC. Run with a standard account, and I bet you almost never notice the difference.

What's Good and Bad about Microsoft Accounts

In addition to administrator and standard accounts (and child accounts, which are a subset of standard accounts), Microsoft also has another pair of account types, *Microsoft accounts* and *local accounts.* You can have an administrator account that's a Microsoft account, or a standard account that's a Microsoft account, or an administrator account that's a local account, and so on. If you aren't confused, you obviously don't understand. Heh heh heh.

The basic differentiation goes like this:

>> **Microsoft accounts** are registered with Microsoft. Most people use their @hotmail.com or @live.com or @outlook.com email addresses, but in fact, you can register any email address at all as a Microsoft account (details in Chapter 5 of this minibook). Microsoft accounts must have a password.

When you log in to Windows 10 with a Microsoft account, Windows goes out to Microsoft's computer in the clouds and verifies your password, and then pulls down many of your major Windows settings and transfers them to the PC you just logged in to. You can control which settings get synced in the Settings app (Start, Settings, Accounts, Sync settings) — see Figure 4-3.

If you change, say, your background, the next time you log in to Windows 10 — from any machine, anywhere in the world — you see the new background. More than that, if the Microsoft account is set up to do so, you can get immediate access to all your music, email, OneDrive storage, and other Windows features without logging in again.

>> **Local accounts** are regular, old-fashioned accounts that exist only on this PC. They don't save or retrieve your settings from Microsoft's computers. Local accounts may or may not have a password.

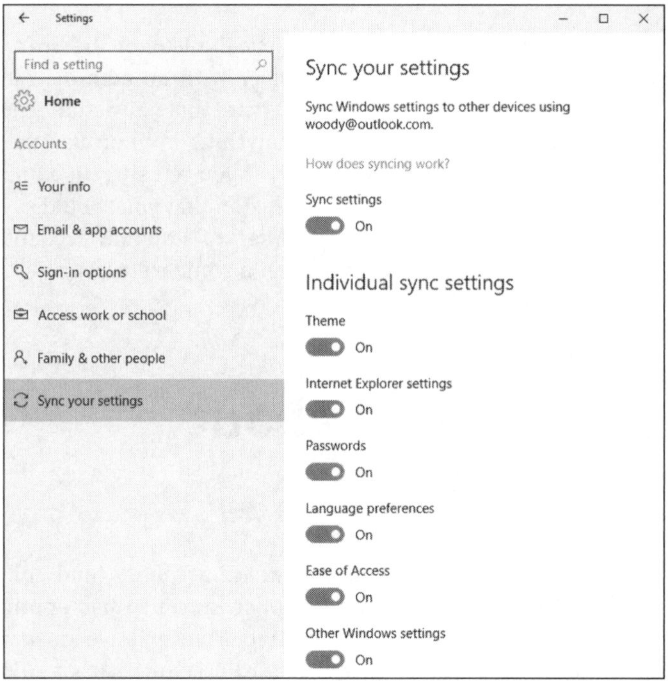

FIGURE 4-3:
Control which
Windows settings
get synced across
your Microsoft
account.

REMEMBER
On a single PC, administrator accounts can add new users, delete existing users, or change the password of any local account on the computer. They can't change the password of any Microsoft accounts.

WARNING
As you may imagine, privacy is among the several considerations for both kinds of accounts. I go into the details in Book 2, Chapter 5.

Microsoft accounts are undeniably more convenient than local accounts — sign in to Windows with your Microsoft account, and many of your apps will just realize who you are, pull in your email, sync your storage, and much more. On the other hand, using a Microsoft account means that Microsoft has a complete log of many of your interactions with your machine — when you signed in, how you used the Microsoft apps (including Edge), Bing results, and so on. Microsoft account login also lets Microsoft associate your account with a specific electronic address and IP address (see Book 2, Chapter 5).

Is the added convenience worth the erosion in privacy? Only you can decide.

Adding Users

After you log in to an administrator account, you can add more users quite easily. Here's how:

1. **Click or tap the Start icon and then the Settings icon.**

2. **On the Settings window, click or tap Accounts.**

   The Accounts screen appears, as shown in Figure 4-4.

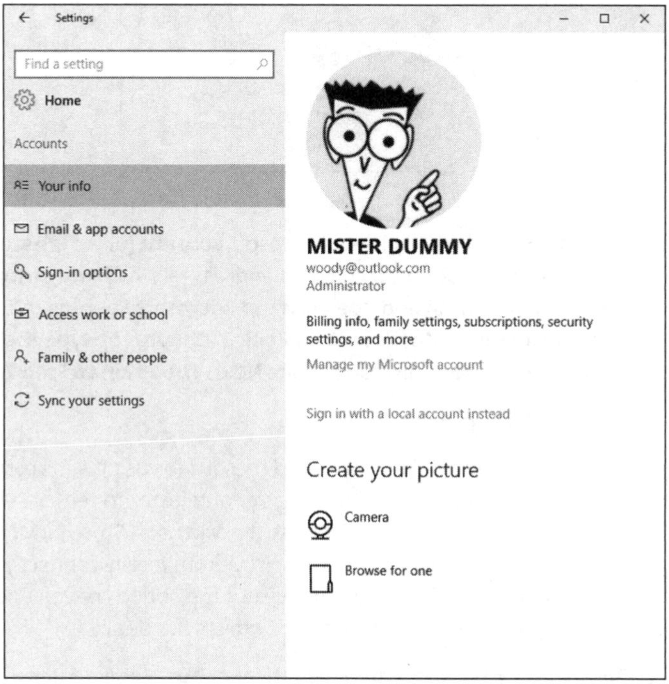

FIGURE 4-4:
The Accounts options.

3. **On the left, click or tap Family & Other People and then choose one of the following:**

   - **Add a Family Member:** Choose this if you want to control the account with Parental Controls

   - **Add Someone Else to This PC:** The someone else could well be a family member — you just don't get easy access to Parental Controls for the new account.

   You see the challenging How Will This Person Sign In? dialog box, as shown in Figure 4-5.

Controlling Users

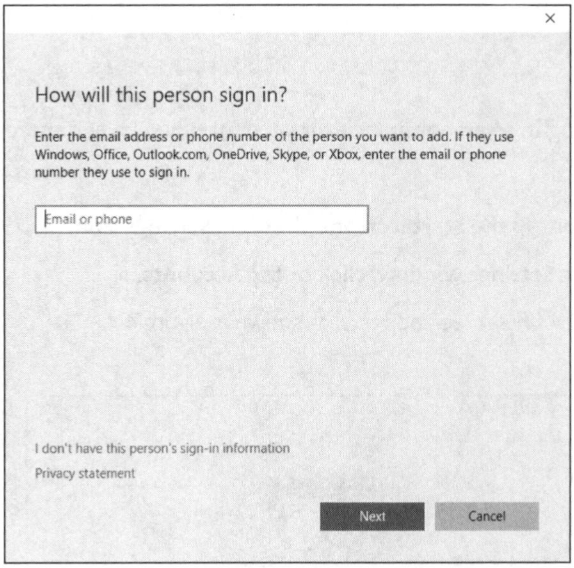

FIGURE 4-5:
Microsoft really
wants you to set
up a Microsoft
account.

4. **If the new user already has a Microsoft account (or an @hotmail.com or @live.com or @outlook.com email address — which are automatically Microsoft accounts) and doesn't mind Microsoft keeping information about when he logs in to Windows (see Book 2, Chapter 5), type the address in the box at the top and then tap or click Next. Then skip to Step 7.**

   Windows sets up your account.

   Don't get me wrong. There are good reasons for using a Microsoft account — a Microsoft account makes it much easier and faster to retrieve your mail and calendar entries, for example, or use the Microsoft Store or Music or Videos, bypassing individual account logins. It'll automatically connect you to your OneDrive account. Only you can decide if the added convenience is worth the decreased privacy. Book 2, Chapter 5 covers the details.

5. **On the other hand, if you're skeptical about using a Microsoft account, waaaaaay down at the bottom, click or tap the link that says Take Your Microsoft Account and Shove It (otherwise known as I Don't Have This Person's Sign-In Information).**

   Windows helpfully gives you yet another opportunity to set up a Microsoft account, as shown in Figure 4-6.

6. **At the bottom, click or tap Add a User without a Microsoft Account. Sheesh.**

   Windows (finally!) asks you about a local account name and password. See Figure 4-7.

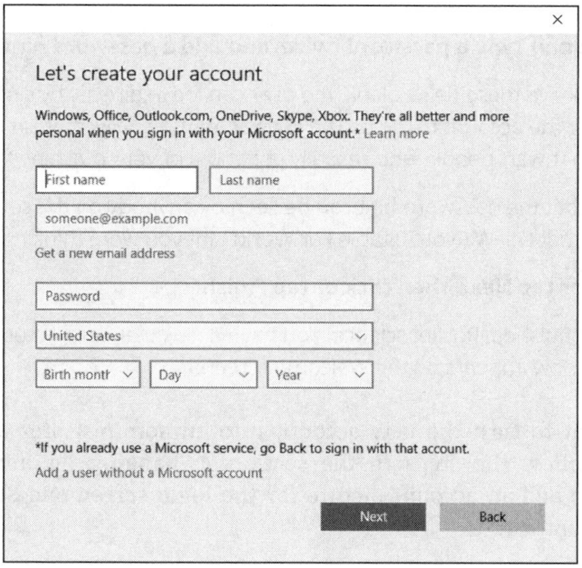

FIGURE 4-6:
Here's the second time Microsoft asks whether you want to set up a Microsoft account.

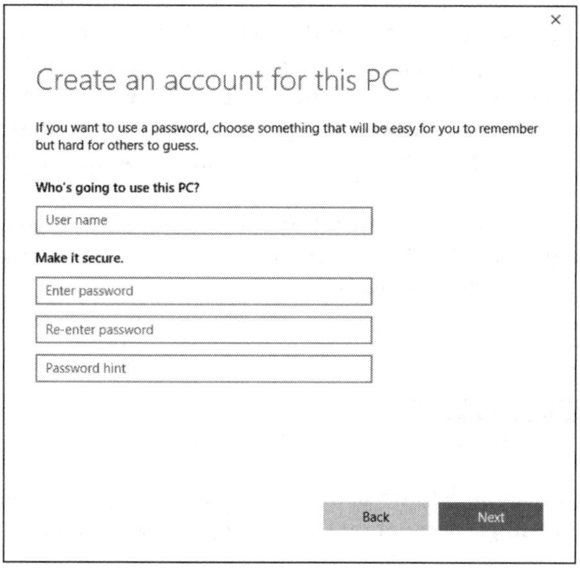

FIGURE 4-7:
Now you get to the "adding a new account" part.

7. **Type a name for the new account.**

You can give a new account just about any name you like: first name, last name, nickname, titles, abbreviations . . . No sweat, as long as you don't use the characters / \ [ ] " ; : | < > + = , ? or *.

Controlling Users

8. **(Optional) Type a password twice, and add a password hint.**

If you leave these fields blank, the user can log in directly by simply tapping or clicking the account name on the login screen. Usually, that isn't a good idea, if only to thwart people who casually get ahold of your machine for a minute.

REMEMBER

Note that the password hint can be seen by anybody on the computer, so avoid that NSFW (Not Suitable For Work) hint you were thinking about.

9. **Click or tap Next; then click or tap Finish.**

You're finished. Rocket science. You have a new standard account, and its name now appears on the Welcome screen.

If you want to turn the new account into an administrator account or a child account, follow the steps in the section, "Changing Accounts," later in this chapter. To add an account picture for the login screen and Start screen, flip to Book 3, Chapter 2.

TECHNICAL
STUFF

This topic is more than a bit confusing, but you aren't allowed to create a new account named Administrator. There's a good reason why Windows prevents you from making a new account with that name: You already have one. Even though Windows goes to great lengths to hide the account named Administrator, it's there, and you may encounter it one night when you're exploring a blind alley. For now, don't worry about the ambiguous name and the ghostly appearance. Just refrain from trying to create a new account named Administrator.

Just because you have a Microsoft account doesn't mean you can log in to any computer anywhere. Your Microsoft account has to be set up on a specific computer before you can use that computer.

Changing Accounts

If you have an administrator account, you can reach in and change almost every detail of every single account on the computer — except one.

Changing other users' settings

In general, changing other users' settings is easy if you have an administrator account. To change an account from a standard account to an administrator account:

1. **Click or tap the Start icon and then the Settings icon.**

2. **On the Settings window, click or tap Accounts. On the left, choose Family & Other People.**

   A list of all the accounts on the computer appears.

3. **Click or tap on the account you want to change.**

   For example, in Figure 4-8, I chose to change my local account called JustaLocalAccount.

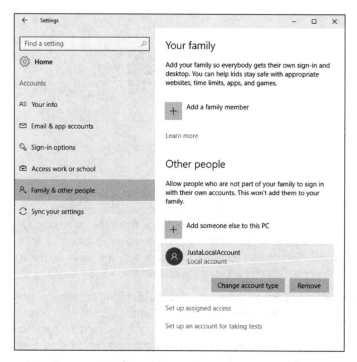

FIGURE 4-8:
Choose the account you want to change from standard to administrator, or vice versa.

4. **Select the Change Account Type option.**

   Windows responds with the option to change from standard user to administrator account and back.

5. **Click or tap OK.**

   The type changes immediately.

For other kinds of account changes, you need to venture into the old-fashioned Control Panel applet. Here's how:

1. **Press Windows key + X (or tap and hold down the Start icon) and then choose Control Panel.**

   The old-fashioned Control Panel appears.

Controlling Users

2. **Choose User Accounts, then User Accounts again. Choose Manage Another Account.**

A list of all the accounts on the computer appears.

3. **Click or tap on the account you want to change.**

Windows immediately presents you with several options (see Figure 4-9).

FIGURE 4-9:
Maintain another
user's account.

Here's what the options entail:

>> **Change the Account Name:** This option appears only for local accounts. (It'd be kind of difficult if Windows let you change someone's Microsoft account, eh?) Selecting this option modifies the name displayed on the login screen and at the top of the Start screen while leaving all other settings intact. Use this option if you want to change only the name on the account — for example, if Little Bill wants to be called Sir William.

>> **Create/Change/Remove a Password:** Again, this appears only for local accounts. If you create a password for the chosen user, Windows requires a password to crank up that user account. You can't get past the Login screen (using that account) without it. This setting is weird because you can change it for other people: You can force Bill to use a password when none was required before, you can change Bill's password, or you can even delete the password.

If you change someone's password, do her a big favor and tell her how to create a Password Reset Disk. See Book 3, Chapter 7.

Passwords are cAse SenSitive — you must enter the password, with upper-case and lowercase letters, precisely the way it was originally typed. If you can't get the computer to recognize your password, make sure that the Caps Lock setting is off. That's the number-one source of login frustration.

REMEMBER

**ASK
WOODY.COM**

Much has been written about the importance of choosing a secure password, mixing uppercase and lowercase letters with punctuation marks, ensuring that you have a long password, blah blah blah. I have only two admonitions: First, don't write your password on a yellow sticky note attached to your monitor; second, don't use the easily guessed passwords that the Conficker worm employed to crack millions of systems (see Table 4-1, at the end of this list). Good advice from a friend: Create a simple sentence you can remember, and swap out some letters for numbers (G00dGr1efTerry), or think of a sentence and use only the first letters! (toasaoutfl!) Of course, using a picture password or PIN (or even a Hello mugshot, a fingerprint, or an iris scan) makes even more sense.

TABLE 4-1   ## Most Frequently Used Passwords*

000	0000	00000	0000000	00000000	0987654321
111	1111	11111	111111	1111111	11111111
123	123123	12321	123321	1234	12345
123456	1234567	12345678	123456789	1234567890	1234abcd
1234qwer	123abc	123asd	123qwe	1q2w3e	222
2222	22222	222222	2222222	22222222	321
333	3333	33333	333333	3333333	33333333
4321	444	4444	44444	444444	4444444
44444444	54321	555	5555	55555	555555
5555555	55555555	654321	666	6666	66666
666666	6666666	66666666	7654321	777	7777
77777	777777	7777777	77777777	87654321	888
8888	88888	888888	8888888	88888888	987654321
999	9999	99999	999999	9999999	99999999
a1b2c3	aaa	aaaa	aaaaa	abc123	academia
access	account	Admin	admin	admin1	admin12
admin123	adminadmin	administrator	anything	asddsa	asdfgh
asdsa	asdzxc	backup	boss123	business	campus
changeme	cluster	codename	codeword	coffee	computer
controller	cookie	customer	database	default	desktop
domain	example	exchange	explorer	file	files
foo	foobar	foofoo	forever	freedom	f**k

(continued)

Controlling Users

TABLE 4-1 *(continued)*

games	home	home123	ihavenopass	Internet	internet
intranet	job	killer	letitbe	letmein	login
Login	lotus	love123	manager	market	money
monitor	mypass	mypassword	mypc123	nimda	nobody
nopass	nopassword	nothing	office	oracle	owner
pass	pass1	pass12	pass123	passwd	password
Password	password1	password12	password123	private	public
pw123	q1w2e3	qazwsx	qazwsxedc	qqq	qqqq
qqqqq	qwe123	qweasd	qweasdzxc	qweewq	qwerty
qwewq	root	root123	rootroot	sample	secret
secure	security	server	shadow	share	sql
student	super	superuser	supervisor	system	temp
temp123	temporary	temptemp	test	test123	testtest
unknown	web	windows	work	work123	xxx
xxxx	xxxxx	zxccxz	zxcvb	zxcvbn	zxcxz
zzz	zzzz	Zzzzz			

*From the Conficker worm, Bowdlerized with an asterisk (*) as a fig leaf

>> **Change the Account Type:** You can use this option to change accounts from administrator to standard and back again. The implications are somewhat complex; I talk about them in the section "Choosing Account Types," earlier in this chapter.

>> **Delete the Account:** Deep-six the account, if you're that bold (or mad, in all senses of the term). If you're deleting a Windows account, the account itself still lives — it just won't be permitted to log in to this computer. Windows offers to keep copies of the deleted account's Documents folder and desktop, but warns you quite sternly and correctly that if you snuff the account, you rip out all the email messages, Internet Favorites, and other settings that belong to the user — definitely not a good way to make friends. Oh, and you can't delete your own account, of course, so this option won't appear if your PC has only one account.

Changing your own settings

Changing your own account is just a little different from changing other users' accounts. Follow these steps:

1. **Bring up the Control Panel.**

   To do so, go to the old-fashioned desktop, right-click the Windows icon in the lower-left corner (or press Windows key + X) and choose Control Panel.

2. **In the upper right, choose User Accounts, then User Accounts again.**

   Windows offers you the chance to change your own account. If you want to change your password, picture, or family settings, you get bounced out to the Windows Settings app. And from there, if you have a Microsoft account, you can link into Windows Live, where your Microsoft account lives.

   Most of the options for your own account mirror those of other users' accounts, as described in the preceding section. If you have the only administrator account on the PC, you can't delete your own account and you can't turn yourself into a standard user. Makes sense: Every PC must have at least one user with an administrator account. If Windows lost all its administrators, no one would be around to add users or change existing ones, much less to install programs or hardware, right?

Switching Users

Windows allows you to have more than one person logged in to a PC simultaneously. That's convenient if, say, you're working on the family PC and checking Billy's homework when you hear the cat screaming bloody murder in the kitchen and your wife wants to put digital pictures from the family vacation on OneDrive while you run off to check the microwave.

The capability to have more than one user logged in to a PC simultaneously is *fast user switching*, and it has advantages and disadvantages:

>> **On the plus side:** Fast User Switching lets you keep all your programs going while somebody else pops on to the machine for a quick jaunt on the keyboard. When she's done, she can log off, and you can pick up precisely where you left off before you got bumped.

>> **On the minus side:** All idle programs left sitting around by the inactive (bumped) user can bog things down for the active user, although the effect isn't drastic. You can avoid the overhead by logging off before the new user logs in.

Controlling Users

To switch users, click the Start icon, click or tap your picture, and choose either the name of the user you want to switch to or Sign Out. If you choose the latter, you're taken to the sign-in screen, where you can choose from any user on the computer.

The Changing Environment

Windows Hello represents a big step forward in Windows login capabilities. Instead of one sudden "Hello, Johnny!" login experience, Microsoft is keeping all the login possibilities you've known for years, while rolling out the various pieces of Windows Hello features over time.

The initial release of Windows 10, in July 2015, included Windows Hello facial identification for the small subset of Win10 users who have special cameras. Microsoft also built some fingerprint reading smarts into Windows Hello.

The November 2015 release of Windows 10 added features for corporate machines and Passport for Work features, including an Azure AD cloud interface. The July (actually August) 2016 Anniversary Update added some basic iris scanning capabilities. The Anniversary Update also dropped the Passport terminology, but not the Passport functionality, for consumers and work.

In future versions of Win10, expect to see more features added to Windows Hello. For example, Microsoft is giving more support to the Trusted Platform Module (TPM) chip that's appearing inside all new Windows 10 machines. A thorough discussion of TPM is on the How-to-Geek site, at www.howtogeek.com/237232/what-is-a-tpm-and-why-does-windows-need-one-for-disk-encryption/.

Chapter 5

Microsoft Account: To Sync or Not to Sync?

Microsoft has been trying to get people to sign up for company-branded accounts for a long, long time.

ASK
WOODY.COM

In 1997, Microsoft bought Hotmail and took over the issuance of @hotmail.com email addresses. Even though Hotmail's gone through a bunch of name changes — MSN Hotmail, Windows Live Hotmail, and now Outlook.com, among others — the original @hotmail.com email addresses still work, and have worked, through thick and thin.

Twenty years after its inception, that old @hotmail.com ID still works the same as it ever did — except now it's called a *Microsoft account.* If you picked up an @msn.com ID, @live.com ID, Xbox ID, Skype ID, or @outlook.com ID along the way, it's now a Microsoft account as well.

ASK
WOODY.COM

In this chapter, I show you exactly what's involved with a Microsoft account, show you why it can be useful, explore the dark underbelly of Microsoft accountability, and give you a trick for acquiring a Microsoft account that won't compromise much of anything.

What, Exactly, Is a Microsoft Account?

Now that Microsoft has finally settled on a name for its ID — at least, this month — permit me to dispel some of the myths about Microsoft accounts.

An email address that ends with @hotmail.com, @msn.com, @live.com, or @outlook.com is, *ipso facto*, a Microsoft account. The same is true for Hotmail and Live and Outlook.com accounts in any country, such as @hotmail.co.uk. You don't have to use your Microsoft account. Ever. But you do have one.

REMEMBER

Many people don't realize that *any* email address can be a Microsoft account. You need only to register that email address with Microsoft; I show you how in the section "Setting Up a Microsoft Account" later in this chapter.

In the context of Windows 10, the Microsoft account takes on a new dimension. When you set up an account to log in to Windows, it can either be a Microsoft account or a *local account.* The key differences:

>> Microsoft accounts are always email addresses, and they must be registered with Microsoft. As I explain in Book 2, Chapter 4, when you log in to Windows with a Microsoft account, Windows automatically syncs some settings — Windows settings like your picture and backgrounds, Edge history and favorites, and others — so if you change something on one machine and log in with the same Microsoft account on another, the changes go with you.

In addition, a Microsoft account gives you something of a one-stop log in to Internet-based Microsoft services. For example, if you have a OneDrive account, logging in to Windows with a Microsoft account automatically hitches you up to your OneDrive files.

WARNING

>> More insidiously, if you log in to Windows 10 with a Microsoft account, and you don't modify Cortana's searching behavior, Microsoft will start tracking every search you make *on your computer.* I'm not talking about a web search. With a few exceptions (for example, www.DuckDuckGo.com), any search you perform on the Internet is tracked by the search provider, typically Google or Microsoft/Bing. I'm talking about when you search through your own documents or email messages, right there on your machine. If you turn on "Hey,

Cortana" recognition, Cortana also listens to everything you say, all the time. I talk about Cortana's search settings in Book 3, Chapter 6.

>> Local accounts can be just about any name or combination of characters. If you sign in with a local account, Microsoft doesn't try (indeed, can't) to sync anything on different machines. Sign in with a local account, and you have to sign in to your OneDrive account separately. Windows will remember your settings — your backgrounds, passwords, favorites, and the like — but they won't be moved to other PCs when you log in.

So, for example, phineasfarquahrt@hotmail.com is a Microsoft account. Because it's an @hotmail.com Hotmail email address, it's already registered with Microsoft. I can create a user on a Windows 10 machine with the name phineas-farquahrt@hotmail.com, and Windows will recognize that as a Microsoft account.

On the other hand, I can set up an account on a Windows PC that's called, oh, *Woody Leonhard.* It's a local account. Because Microsoft accounts have to be email addresses (you see why in the section "Setting Up a Microsoft Account"), the Woody Leonhard account has to be a local account.

When you set up a brand-new Windows PC, you have to enter an account, and it can be either a Windows account or a local account. Microsoft stacks the deck and makes you tap or click all over heaven's half acre to avoid using a Microsoft account. When you add a new account, Microsoft nudges you to use a Microsoft account, but will begrudgingly accept a local account (see Book 2, Chapter 4).

Deciding Whether You Want a Microsoft Account

If Microsoft tracks a Microsoft account, you may ask, why in the world would I want to sign on to Windows 10 with a Microsoft account?

Good question, grasshopper.

Signing on to Windows 10 with a Microsoft account brings a host of benefits. In particular:

>> **Most of your Windows settings will travel with you.** Your user picture, desktop, browser favorites, and other similar settings will find you no matter which PC you log in to.

I find this helpful in some ways, and annoying in others. For example, I have a big screen Windows desktop and a little Windows tablet. If I put a whole bunch of tiles on the desktop, they look horrible on the tablet.

Your tiled Universal Windows apps — the ones that came with Windows 10 or that you downloaded from the Windows Store — revert to their last state. So if you're on a killer winning streak with a Solitaire game, that'll go with you to any PC you log in to. Your Internet Explorer or Edge open tabs travel. Settings for the Windows 10 Finance app travel. Even apps *that Microsoft doesn't make* may have their settings moved from machine to machine.

>> **Sign-in credentials for programs and websites travel.** If you rely on Edge to keep sites' login credentials, those will find you if you switch machines.

>> **You will be automatically signed in to Windows 10 apps and services** that use the Microsoft account (or Windows Live ID). Universal Windows Mail, Calendar, OneDrive, Skype, and the Microsoft website all fall into that category.

Don't be overly cynical. In some sense, Microsoft dangles these carrots to convince you to sign up for, and use, a Microsoft account. But in another sense, the simple fact is that none of these features would be possible if it weren't for some sort of ID that's maintained by Microsoft.

I use a Microsoft account on my main machine, although I employ a little trick — creating a new Microsoft account and only using it to sign in to Windows — which I describe in the next section on setting up a new account.

WARNING

That's the carrot. Here's the stick. If you sign in with a Microsoft account, Microsoft has a record of every time you've signed on, to every PC you use with that account. More than that, when you crank up Edge (or Internet Explorer), you're logged in with your Microsoft account — which means that Microsoft can, at least theoretically, keep records about all your browsing (except, presumably, InPrivate browsing). Bing gets to jot down your Microsoft account every time you search through it. Microsoft gets detailed data on any music you view in the Windows 10 Music app. Your stock interests are logged in the Windows 10 Money app. Even the weather you request ends up in Microsoft's giant database. And if you use Cortana, heaven help ya, everything you search for on your computer ends up in Microsoft's big database chock full of your history.

Perhaps it's true that you have no privacy and should get over it. Fact is that most people don't care. My attitude toward data scraping and Windows snooping has changed over the years. I talk about my begrudging conversion in the first part of the next chapter, Book 2, Chapter 6.

WHAT IF MY HOTMAIL OR OUTLOOK.COM ACCOUNT IS HIJACKED?

So you set up a Hotmail account or Outlook.com for logging on to your Windows PC, and all of a sudden the account gets hijacked. Some cretin gets into the account online and changes the password. The next time you try to log in to your Windows PC, what happens?

It's not far-fetched: I get complaints almost every day from people who have been locked out of their Hotmail/Outlook.com accounts.

If you use a Hotmail ID, a Windows Live account, or an Outlook.com account for your Microsoft account and your Hotmail/Outlook.com account gets hijacked and the password changed, Windows 10 lets you log in to your PC, but when you do, you get the notice *You're signed in to this PC with your old password. Sign in again with your current password, or reset it.* If you then try to reset your password, you can't — clicking or tapping the Reset link doesn't do anything.

Until you can come up with your Hotmail/Outlook.com account's password, you're put in a reduced functionality mode that's very similar to logging on with a local account. As long as you can remember your old password — the last one you used to log in to this machine — you can continue to log in in local account mode. But ultimately you're going to want your Windows login account back!

To get your account back, you need to contact the people at Microsoft and convince them that you're the rightful owner. If you set up your Hotmail/Outlook.com account recently, chances are at least fair that you have an alternate email address or phone number designated for just such an emergency, so-called 2FA or two-factor authentication, described in a sidebar later in this chapter. Microsoft started asking for that specific information on sign-up a couple of years ago. Go to http://account.live.com/resetpassword.aspx, and have a Microsoft rep contact you.

Setting Up a Microsoft Account

Just to make life a little more complicated, shortly before Microsoft released Windows 8, it suddenly decided to kill off the name Hotmail and replace it with Outlook.com. I talk about the reasons why — basically, Hotmail was losing market share, and Microsoft needed to get it back — in Book 10, Chapter 4.

For purposes of this chapter, a Hotmail or Outlook.com account, a Live.com account, Xbox LIVE account, OneDrive account, Skype account, MSN account, Microsoft Passport account, or a Windows Phone account are all interchangeable: They're email addresses that have already been automatically signed up as Microsoft accounts. I tend to refer to them collectively as Hotmail accounts because, well, most Microsoft accounts have been Hotmail accounts for the past two decades or so. Old habits die hard.

If you don't have a Microsoft account, the way I see it, you have three choices for setting one up:

>> **You can use an existing email address.** But if you do that, Microsoft will be able to put that email address in its database, and it can cross-reference the address to many things you do with Windows 10. (Can you tell my tinfoil hat is showing?)

>> **You can use (or set up) a Hotmail/Live/Xbox/OneDrive/Skype/Windows Phone/Outlook.com account.** If you already have one, Microsoft tracks it already — Microsoft knows when you receive and send email, for example. But that's true of any online email program, including Gmail and Yahoo! Mail. Using a Hotmail/Outlook.com account to log in to Windows 10, though, means that Microsoft can track additional information and associate it with your Hotmail/Outlook.com account — the times you log in to Windows, locations, and so on — as described earlier in this section, as well as the special snooping that Cortana undertakes. You may be okay with that, or you may not want Microsoft to be able to track that kind of additional information.

>> **You can create a bogus new Hotmail/Outlook.com account and use it only to log in to Windows 10.** It's free and easy, and if you use it wisely, nobody will ever know the difference. The only downsides: If you use Hotmail/Outlook.com, you have to tell the Windows 10 Universal Mail app to look in your other inbox; your existing Hotmail/Outlook.com contacts won't get carried over into the tiled People automatically; and Skype will want to work with your new, bogus ID — although you can change it.

I love to use bogus Outlook.com accounts. I keep in mind that every time I use Edge or Internet Explorer, having signed in to Windows with a Microsoft account, that Microsoft will dump all my browsing history in its coffers.

So, of course, I use the Firefox or Chrome browser when I want to use the Internet. Google keeps Chrome data, but it doesn't have Microsoft's database of logged in Windows 10 users, and Firefox isn't beholden to anybody.

Search engines, of course, are a different story entirely. Bing/Microsoft and Google keep track of everything you send their way.

Setting up a Hotmail/Outlook.com account

Here's how to set up a new Hotmail/Outlook.com account:

1. **Using your favorite web browser, go to** `www.Outlook.com`.

The main screen asks whether you have a Microsoft account.

2. **If you aren't automatically signed in, tap or click No Account? Create One!**

You see the sign-up form, as shown in Figure 5-1.

FIGURE 5-1:
Sign up for an
anonymous
Hotmail/Outlook.
com ID.

Microsoft account

Microsoft Corporation [US] signup.**live.com**/signup?wa=

Microsoft

Create an account

You can use any email address as the user name for your new Microsoft account,
including addresses from Outlook.com, Yahoo! or Gmail. If you already sign in to a
Windows PC, tablet, or phone, Xbox Live, Outlook.com, or OneDrive, use that account
to sign in.

First name

Frumious

Last name

Bandersnatch

User name

frumiousbandersnatch3   @outlook.com

Use your email instead

frumiousbandersnatch3@outlook.com is available.

Password

••••••••

8-character minimum; case sensitive

Reenter password

••••••••

3. **Fill out the form. Be creative.**

ASK
WOODY.COM

Even though the form hints that your phone number is required, in my
experiments, it wasn't required at all — an alternate email address suffices.
You might want to give Microsoft your phone number anyway. They'll text you
anytime someone tries to log in to a new computer using your ID. See the
sidebar on two-factor authentication.

That alternate email address is useful if your Microsoft account gets hijacked. You can contact Microsoft and have it send account reset information to that address. You don't need to monitor the address constantly, but if you can retrieve email from that alternate email address, it can help get your new account back.

If you decide to tap or click the link and provide answers to security questions to make a password reset easier, make sure you keep the answers stored away some place safe.

The zip code for Microsoft's headquarters in Redmond is 98052.

4. **Type the CAPTCHA codes, if you can figure them out, deselect the Send Me Promotional Offers check box, and tap or click Create Account.**

   Hotmail/Outlook.com whirrs for a minute or so, asks for your language and time zone, and then shows you the Hotmail/Outlook.com welcome screen, as shown in Figure 5-2. That's it.

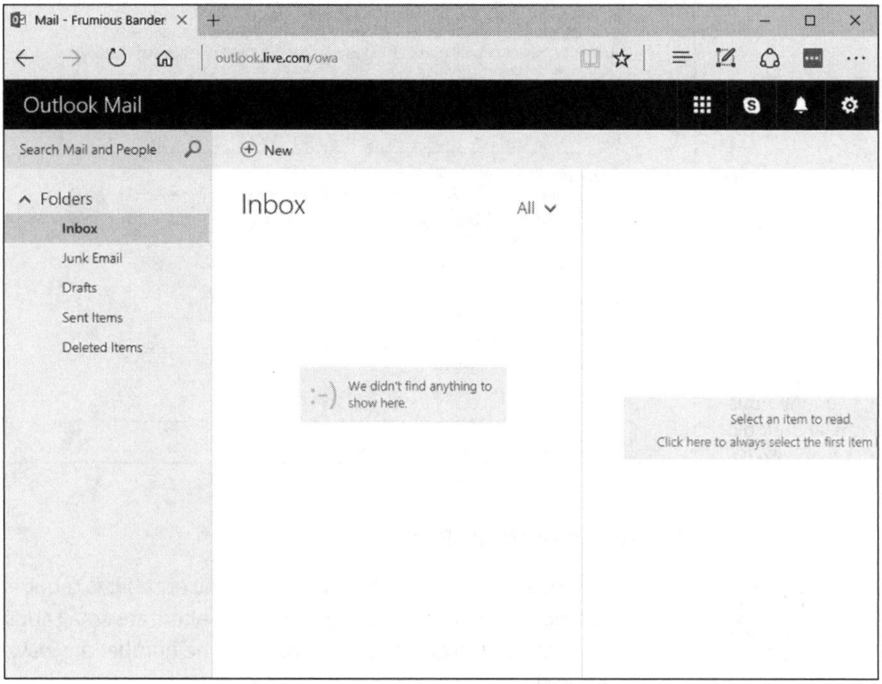

TIP

FIGURE 5-2:
Your new Microsoft account (née Windows Live ID, Hotmail account, MSN account, Outlook.com account, Xbox Live account) is alive and working.

You can now use your new Hotmail account as a Windows login ID. You can use it for email, Skype, Xbox . . . just about anything.

Making any email address a Microsoft account

You have to jump through an extra hoop to turn any email address into a Microsoft account. The procedure is simple, as long as you can retrieve email sent to the address:

1. **Use the steps in the preceding section, but in Step 3, in the User Name box, type an email address that you can access.**

It can be a Gmail address, a Yahoo! Mail address, or any other email address, no problem.

2. **Fill out the rest of the form. Fancifully, if you want.**

If you don't want to give Microsoft your smartphone number, select and answer one of its security questions. Note, though, that giving Microsoft your number allows it to SMS you a reset password, if you require one, instead of relying on a question — one that a hijacker may be able to figure out.

Note that the password you provide here is for your Microsoft account. It is *not* your email password. The password you enter here will be the password you need to use to log in to Windows 10 or any website that requires a Microsoft account. Most experts advise you to not reuse your email password as your Microsoft account password.

3. **Type the CAPTCHA code, and tap or click I Accept.**

Within a minute or two, the email address in the application form receives a message that says *This email address was used to start setting up a Windows Live ID. To finish setting it up, we need you to confirm that this email address belongs to you. Click this link to confirm your account:*

If you don't see the message, check your Junk folder.

REMEMBER

TIP

4. **Tap or click the link in the message to confirm your email address.**

You end up on a Outlook.com welcome screen (refer to Figure 5-2).

Stop Using Your Microsoft Account

So you've read about the differences between a Microsoft account and a local account, and you've decided that you just don't want to keep feeding Microsoft information. You want to move to a local account. Fortunately, that's pretty easy:

1. **Click the Start icon, the Settings icon, and then Accounts.**

   You see the account settings for your account.

2. **Click the Sign In with a Local Account Instead link.**

   Windows challenges you to retype your current account's password.

3. **Type your current password and then click Next.**

   Windows presents you with the Switch to a Local Account dialog shown in Figure 5-3.

4. **Enter the local account to use in place of your Microsoft account, and then click Next.**

   Windows warns you to make sure you've saved your work — it's about to restart — and to ensure that you know your new password. When you're ready for your machine to reboot, click Sign Out and Finish.

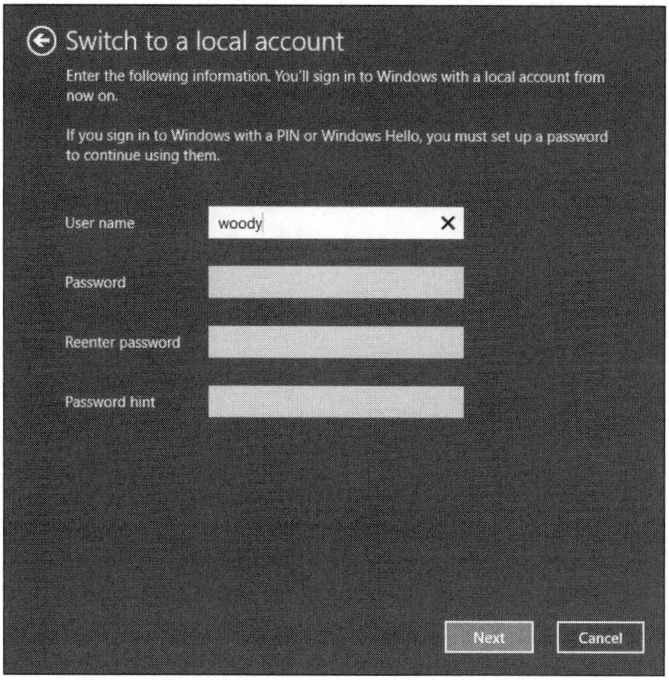

FIGURE 5-3:
Type the local
account here.

It's important to realize that your old Windows account is no longer valid for signing in to this computer. Instead, you sign in only through the local account. If you want to switch back, click the Start icon. the Settings icon, and Accounts, and click the link to Sign In with a Microsoft Account Instead. When you reboot, your old account reappears, but if you had a PIN, a picture password, or Windows Hello set up, you'll have to reset it.

Taking Care of Your Microsoft Account

If you ever want to change any of the details in your Microsoft account, it's easy — if you know where to go.

For reasons understood only by Microsoft, to maintain your Microsoft account, go to `http://account.live.com`. Sign in, and you see full account information, as shown in Figure 5-4.

To change any of the information for your account, or the password, tap or click the related link below the item you want to change.

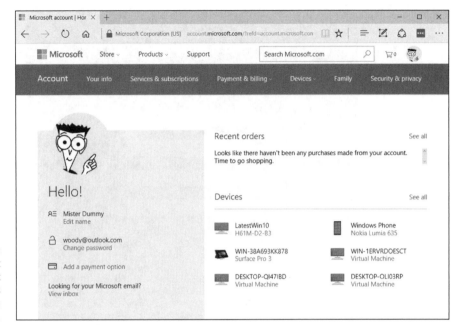

FIGURE 5-4:
Microsoft account maintenance is accessible from the Live site.

Controlling Sync

If you don't specifically change anything, logging on to Windows with a Microsoft account syncs a number of settings across all the PCs that you use.

You can tell Microsoft that you don't want to sync specific items. Here's how:

1. **Click or tap the Start icon, the Settings icon, and then Accounts.**

2. **On the left, click or tap Sync Your Settings.**

    The Sync screen appears, as shown in Figure 5-5.

3. **Following the list in Table 5-1, choose whether you want to sync specific items.**

REMEMBER

Sync happens only when you log in with the same Microsoft account on two different PCs.

You're finished. No need to tap or click OK or Apply. The changes take effect with your next login.

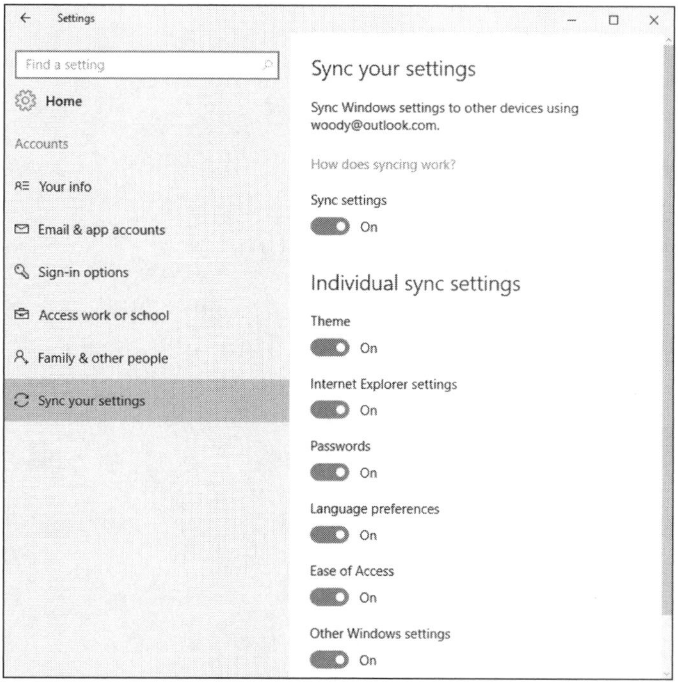

FIGURE 5-5:
Control the
way Microsoft
accounts
sync here.

TABLE 5-1 ## Sync Settings

Setting	What It Controls
Sync Settings	This is an overall off switch. If you don't want to sync anything, turn this off.
Theme	Your user picture, Start menu tiles, color, background, and old-fashioned desktop settings.
Internet Explorer Settings	Internet Explorer settings, open tabs, navigation history, and the state of File Explorer (such as whether the ribbon appears). Note that Edge setting sync is controlled in Edge itself.
Passwords	Potentially sensitive information, including login credentials for Universal apps and some website passwords.
Language preferences	The input method (language/keyboard) in effect.
Ease of Access	All ease-of-access settings.

Chapter 6
Privacy Control

"The best minds of my generation are thinking about how to make people click ads. That sucks."

— JEFF HAMMERBACHER, early Facebook employee

ASK WOODY.COM

When you work with "free" services — search engines such as Google and Bing; social networks such as Facebook, Pinterest, and LinkedIn; online storage services such as OneDrive and Google Drive; free email services such as Gmail, Hotmail/Outlook.com, and Yahoo! Mail; even the "free" versions of Windows 10 — these services may not charge you anything, but they're hardly free. You pay with your identity. Every time you go to one of those sites, or use one of those products, with a few noteworthy exceptions, you leave a trail that companies are eager to exploit, primarily for advertising.

The exceptions? Google doesn't scan activity for any paid account, or any educational account. (They've been sued up the wazoo.) Apple swears it doesn't wallow in the data grabbing cesspool. Microsoft loves to say it doesn't scan the contents of Outlook.com/Hotmail messages. There are lots of if's, and's, but's, and nuances. But by and large, if it's free, you're the product, not the customer.

There's a reason why you buy something on, say, Alibaba, and then find ads for Alibaba appearing on all sorts of websites. One of the big advertising conglomerates has your number. Maybe just your IP address. Maybe a planted cookie. But they've connected enough dots to know that, whatever site you happen to be on at the moment, you once bought something on Alibaba.

Now, even when you log in to Windows 10, if you opt to use a Microsoft account, you leave another footprint in the sand. (I talk about Microsoft accounts in Book 2, Chapter 5.)

This isn't horrible. Necessarily. It isn't illegal — although laws in different localities differ widely, and lawsuits are reshaping the picture even as we speak. In most cases, anyway. The advertisers view it as a chance to direct advertising at you that's likely to generate a response. In some respects, it's like a billboard for a cold Pepsi on a hot freeway or an ad for beer on Super Bowl Sunday.

In other respects, though, logging your activity online is something quite different.

I talk about privacy in general in Book 9, Chapter 1, and the browser Do Not Track flag (which may or may not do what you think it should do) in Book 5, Chapter 1. In this chapter, I want to give you an overview of privacy settings — and some privacy shenanigans — specifically inside Windows.

Why You Should Be Concerned

As time goes by, people are becoming more and more aware of how their privacy is being eroded by using the Internet. Some people aren't particularly concerned. Others get paranoid to the point of chopping off their clicking fingers. Chances are pretty good you're somewhere between the two poles.

Windows 10 users need to understand that this version of Windows, *much* more than any version of Windows before, pulls in data from all over the web. Every time you elect to connect to a service, you're connecting the dots for Microsoft's data-collection routines. And if you use a Microsoft account, Microsoft's dot connector gets to run into overtime.

I'm not implying that Microsoft is trying to steal your data or somehow use your identity for illegal purposes. It isn't. At this point, Microsoft mostly wants to identify your buying patterns and your interests, so it can serve you ads that you will click, for products that you will buy. The Google shtick. That's where the money is.

Although Google freely admits that it scans inbound and outbound Gmail email, on free accounts, all the better to generate ads that you will click, Microsoft insists that it doesn't — ergo, the infamous Scroogled ads, wherein the pot and kettle somehow tie it on. Don't be fooled. Microsoft *does* scan Hotmail/Outlook.com mail and Windows 10 Universal Mail app messages that you receive with Windows 10 — for spam detection, if nothing else. Whether MS will start keeping track of detailed information about your messages in the future is very hard to say.

Here's how the services stack up, when it comes to privacy (or the lack thereof):

TIP

>> **Google:** Without a doubt, Google has the largest collection of data. You leave tracks on the Google databases every time you use Google to search for a website. That's true of every search engine (except www.DuckDuckGo.com), not just Google, but Google has 70 percent or more of the search engine market. You also hand Google web-surfing information if you sign in to your Chrome browser (so it can keep track of your bookmarks for you) or if you sign in to Google itself (for example, to use Google Apps or Google Drive). The native Android browser ties into Google, too.

Google also owns *Doubleclick,* the best-known, third-party cookie generator on the web. Any time you go to a site with a Doubleclick ad — most popular sites have them — a little log about your visit finds its way into Google's database.

ASK WOODY.COM

Google's scanning policies changed significantly in late 2014. As of mid-2015, Google no longer scans email, or the contents of Google Drive files, for paid accounts, Academic accounts, or non-profit accounts. If you have a free Google account, you should expect that Google will sift through your mail and files, looking for information that can convince you to click on an ad.

>> **Facebook:** Although Facebook may not have the largest collection of data, it's the most detailed. People who sign up for Facebook tend to give away lots of information. When you connect your Microsoft account in Windows 10 to Facebook — for example, add your Facebook Friends to your Ultimate People app list (unless Facebook has shut Microsoft out this week, which happens from time to time) — some data that you allow to be shared on Facebook is accessible to Microsoft. That's why it's important to lock down your Facebook account (see Book 6, Chapter 2).

REMEMBER

Every time you go to a website with a Facebook Like icon, that fact is tucked away in Facebook's databases. If you're logged in to Facebook at the time you hit a site with a Like icon, your Facebook ID is transmitted, along with an indication of which site you're looking at, to the Facebook databases. As of this writing, Microsoft can't get into the Facebook database — which is truly one of the crown jewels of the Facebook empire — although it can pull a list of your Friends, if you allow it.

>> **Microsoft:** Microsoft's Internet access database may not be as big as Google's, or as detailed as Facebook's, but the 'Softies are trying to get there fast. One of the ways they're catching up is by encouraging you to use a Microsoft account. The other is to create all these connections to other data-collecting agencies

inside Windows 10. Then there's Bing, which logs what you're looking at just like a Google search does.

Windows 10 is light-years ahead of earlier versions of Windows when it comes to harvesting your data. Or perhaps I should say it's light-years behind earlier versions of Windows when it comes to protecting your privacy. Same, same.

WARNING

The single biggest leaker in Windows 10 is Cortana's Smart Search feature — which is certainly smart for Microsoft's data collection efforts. Unless you go to great lengths to trim back Cortana's snooping, Microsoft (through Bing) keeps a list of all the terms you search for *on your computer.* Because Cortana's Smart Search is enabled by default when you install Windows 10, chances are pretty good that Microsoft's collecting information about every single search you make for your documents, pictures, email, and so on. I talk about Cortana's wayward ways — and, most importantly, show you how to turn the leak off, or at least clip its wings — in Book 3, Chapter 6.

For an ongoing, authoritative discussion of privacy issues, look at the Electronic Frontier Foundation's Defending Your Rights in the Digital World page at `www.eff.org/issues/privacy`.

Privacy Manifesto

Privacy has become such a huge issue with Windows 10 that many folks won't install it, just because they figure Win10 is sending all their private information to Microsoft. In one sense, that's true – Windows 10 snoops in ways no previous version of Windows ever dared. In another sense, though, increased snooping is a sign of changing times. And I'm convinced that Microsoft is no worse than most of the alternatives.

The important point is that you, the Win10 user, need to understand what's going on — and you need to make decisions accordingly.

**ASK
WOODY.COM**

Like it or not, times have changed, and attitudes toward snooping have changed along with them.

The past: Watson to WER

Back in the distant past, the Windows 3.0 beta (in 1989-1990) included a program called Dr. Watson, which responded to Windows crashes by gathering all the data it could find and packaging it as a text file (drwtsn32.log). Dr. Watson was also smart enough to generate a core dump, which could be fed into a debugger on a diagnostic machine.

Dr. Watson worked offline. If you wanted to send your text log file or core dump to somebody, that was up to you. Dr. Watson was highly successful, leading to the identification and eradication of thousands of bugs (most, it must be said, in non-Microsoft drivers).

Around the time of Windows XP, Dr. Watson turned into the Problem Reports and Solutions program, which became part of the larger Windows Error Reporting (WER) system built into XP and then enhanced for Vista, Win7, and Win8. WER differs from Dr. Watson in many respects, not the least of which is an optional automated upload to Microsoft's servers.

The folks who wrote WER, and those who poured through the dumps, knew full well that sensitive information might be transmitted as part of the WER collection. That's why the good doctor asked for permission before sending the info on to Microsoft's servers.

WER was a resounding success. Steve Ballmer says that WER let the Windows team fix 29 percent of all WinXP errors in WinXP Service Pack 1. More than half of all Office XP bugs were squashed in Office XP SP1, thanks to WER. WER became the envy of the operating system software class, propelling many doctoral theses.

Frighteningly, WER data wasn't encrypted prior to transmission until March 2014. If you had a crash before then and WER kicked in and delivered it to Microsoft, anybody snooping on your Internet connection could see the contents of the report. There have also been allegations that the NSA hooked into WER reports.

Customer Experience Improvement Program

While Watson and WER concentrated on crash reports, an independent force arose in the Windows camp. Borrowing on the Business School buzz phrase "customer experience," Microsoft's Customer Experience Improvement Program (CEIP) gathers a wide array of information about your computer and how you use it, and then shuttles it all off to Microsoft. Historically, when Microsofties used the term *telemetry,* they were referring specifically to CEIP data. That's changing as more telemetry becomes accessible.

CEIP (known internally in Microsoft as SQM, or Software Quality Management) started with MSN Messenger, moving rapidly to Office 2003, and then to Windows Vista and Windows Media Player. It's been part of Windows and Office ever since.

When you install any of those programs, Microsoft activates CEIP by default, although you can opt out.

Nobody knows what data is collected under the rubric CEIP. A CEIP privacy policy was posted on the web (www.microsoft.com/products/ceip/en-us/privacypolicy.mspx) but as best I can tell it was pulled down in November 2015. That policy said:

CEIP reports generally include information about:

- *Configuration, such as how many processors are in your computer, how many network connections you use, the operating system that your computer is currently running, screen resolutions for display devices, the strength of the wireless signal between your computer and a media player device, and if some features such as Bluetooth wireless technology or high-speed USB connections are turned on.*

- *Performance and reliability, such as how quickly a program responds when you click a button, how many problems you experience with a program or a device, and how quickly information is sent or received over a network connection.*

- *Program use, such as the features that you use the most often, how frequently you launch programs, and how many folders you typically create on your desktop.*

  Microsoft uses CEIP information to improve our software. We may share CEIP information with partners, but the information cannot be used to identify you.

There's no indication as to why the policy was pulled. Internal links now point to a general privacy policy statement at https://privacy.microsoft.com/en-us/privacystatement, which has no details about CEIP.

Feedback & Diagnostics tab and DiagTrack

One part WER, one part CEIP, Windows 10 brings all the snooping together under the Feedback & Diagnostics tab. Telemetry in Win10 includes data uploaded by the Connected User Experience and Telemetry component, also known as Universal Telemetry Client, with a service application name of DiagTrack.

Microsoft has a detailed description of its telemetry collection policy in a TechNet post by Brian Lich at `https://technet.microsoft.com/en-us/itpro/windows/manage/configure-windows-telemetry-in-your-organization`. Lich includes an informative diagram that explains Microsoft's conceptual levels of telemetry. See Figure 6-1.

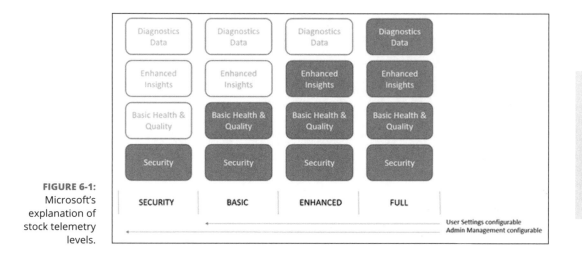

FIGURE 6-1: Microsoft's explanation of stock telemetry levels.

It's far from a definitive list of what data gets sent to Microsoft, but at least the diagram should give you a basic understanding.

To see what you're up against, click the Start icon, the Settings icon, and then Privacy. On the left, choose Feedback & Diagnostics. You see the Feedback Frequency dialog shown in Figure 6-2.

The Diagnostic and Usage Data setting is one of the key methods you have to reduce — but not eliminate — the Win10 telemetry sent from your PC to Microsoft. If you're concerned about sending Microsoft your usage information, set the drop-down list at the bottom of Figure 6-1 to Basic. Then work through the detailed list in "Minimizing Privacy Intrusion" at the end of this chapter.

As with CEIP (and WER, for that matter), I've never seen a definitive list of what Microsoft collects. Lots and lots of descriptions of Microsoft's privacy policy are available (start at `https://privacy.microsoft.com/en-us/privacystatement` for an, uh, immersive experience), but they have few solid details.

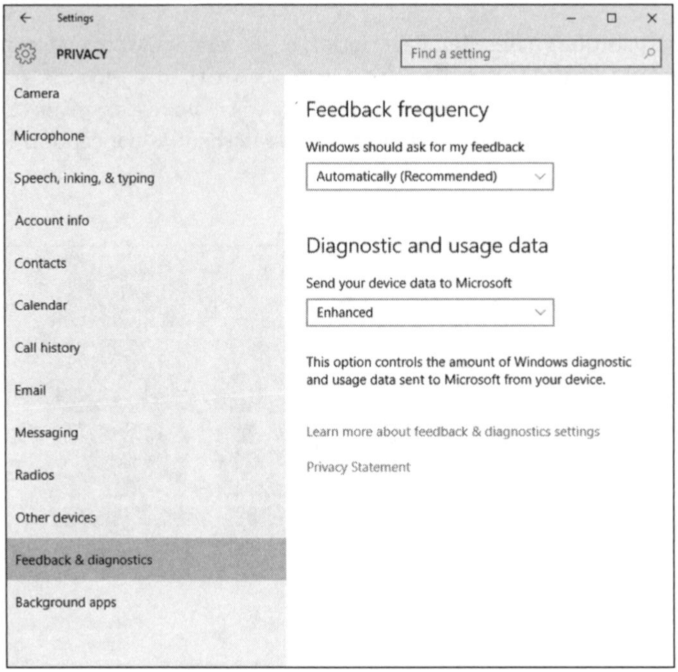

FIGURE 6-2:
The old crash reporting and CEIP settings have a new guise.

Denial ain't nuthin' but a river

Here's what I know:

>> Microsoft collects telemetry — data about your use of Windows — no matter what. You can minimize the amount of data collected (as described at the end of this chapter), but you can't stop the flow unless you're connected to a corporate domain.

>> No list is being made available of what's being collected, exactly, nor are there details of how it's being used.

>> The data being sent to Microsoft is encrypted. That means anyone who's snooping on your connection won't be able to pull out any useful information. It also means that people trying to figure out exactly what's going out don't have any chance of deciphering the stream.

There's a larger picture. Windows, like the rest of the industry, is evolving. I've seen no indication that Microsoft is any worse than, say, Google — and it's likely that Apple undertakes similar data stockpiling. So do Facebook and dozens, if not thousands, of lesser snoopers.

If you want to minimize the identifiable data harvested from you and don't feel comfortable with the fact that Microsoft collects data about you, best to switch to Linux, avoid Chrome (use Firefox), don't use Google Search (use DuckDuckGo), and always run a VPN (see Book 9, Chapter 4).

'Course, you'd also have to avoid using a mobile phone — or even a landline for that matter — and pay with cash or bitcoin only. You'd also need to avoid walking in public, given the current state of facial recognition, and hope you never end up in a hospital!

The question is how comfortable you feel entrusting all these companies — not just Microsoft — with your data. And heaven help ya if you live in a house that has a smart electric meter.

I think that data privacy will be one of the foremost legal questions of the next decade. We already have some data protection regulations in place for health records and credit records, but they don't apply in this case. Unless people give up — which may be a reasonable reaction — I predict large-scale problems.

Knowing What Connections Windows Prefers

If you use Windows, you're not on a level playing field. Microsoft plays favorites with some online companies and shuns others as much as it possibly can. Cases in point:

>> **Microsoft owns part of Facebook.** You see Facebook here and there in Windows. There's a reason why: Microsoft owns a 1.6-percent share of Facebook (at the time of this writing, anyway). Facebook is ambivalent about Microsoft, at best, and as of mid-2015 some open warfare had started. Hard to say how it will play out.

It isn't clear whether Microsoft and Facebook share any data about individual users. But that's certainly a possibility, if not now, at some point in the undefined future.

>> **Microsoft doesn't play well with Google.** Windows has some hooks into Google, but invariably they exist in order to pull your personal information out of Google (for example, Contacts) and put it in Microsoft's databases. When you see a ready-made connector in Windows 10's Universal Mail app to add a

Gmail account — so you can retrieve your Gmail messages in Microsoft's tiled Mail app — there's an ulterior motive.

» **Microsoft gives lip service to Apple.** There's no love lost between the companies. Microsoft makes software for Mac and iPad platforms (for example, Office for iPad is a treat, OneNote runs on the iPad, and Office has been on the Mac for longer than it's been on Windows!). Apple still makes software for Windows (such as iTunes, Safari, and QuickTime). But they're both fiercely guarding their own turf. Don't expect to see any sharing of user information.

» **Microsoft once tried to buy Yahoo!, which owns Flickr.** Although that possibility seems less likely now than it did in 2008 and again in 2011, it comes up from time to time. Microsoft has hired a boatload of talented people from Yahoo!. Microsoft also still has strong contractual ties to Yahoo!, particularly for running advertising on its search engine, although that could change.

And of course, you know that Microsoft also owns Skype, Hotmail/Outlook.com, and OneDrive, right?

Your information — aggregated, personally identifiable, vaguely anonymous, or whatever — can be drawn from any of those sources and mashed up with the data that Microsoft has in its databases. No wonder data mining is a big topic on the Redmond campus.

Controlling Location Tracking

Just as in Windows 8 of yore, Windows 10 has *location tracking.* You have to tell Windows and specific applications that it's okay to track your location, but if you do, those apps — and Windows itself — know where you are.

ASK
WOODY.COM

Location tracking isn't a bad technology. Like any technology, it can be used for good or not-so-good purposes, and your opinion about what's good may differ from others'. That's what makes a horse race. And a lawsuit or two.

Location tracking isn't just one technology. It's several.

If your PC has a *GPS* (Global Positioning System) chip (see Figure 6-3) — they're common in tablets, but unusual in notebooks and rare in desktops — and the GPS is turned on, and you've authorized a Windows app to see your location, the app can identify your PC's location within a few feet.

HOW APPLE'S LOCATION TRACKING RANKLED

In April 2011, two researchers — Alasdair Allan and Pete Warden — found that iPads and iPhones with GPS systems were keeping track of location and time data, inside the devices, even if the user explicitly disallowed location tracking. They discovered a log file inside every iPad and iPhone running iOS 4 that included detailed information about location and time since 2010.

They also found that the file was being backed up when the iPhone or iPad was backed up, and the data inside the file wasn't encrypted or protected in any way, and a copy was kept on any computer you synced with the iPhone or iPad.

When confronted with the discovery, Apple at first denied it, and then said that "Apple is not tracking the location of your iPhone. Apple has never done so and has no plans to ever do so" — effectively confirming the researchers' discoveries. As details emerged, Apple claimed it was storing the information to make the location programs work better, but it wasn't being used in, or passed to, any location tracking programs.

In May 2011, Apple released iOS 4.3.3, which no longer kept the data. But by then a series of lawsuits and a class action suit followed in the United States. In Korea, the Communications Commission fined Apple about $3,000 for its transgressions. As I write this, the US case is making its way through the courts.

Location tracking in tablets is a relatively new phenomenon, and it's bound to have some bugs. With a little luck, the bugs — and gaffes — won't be as bad as Apple's.

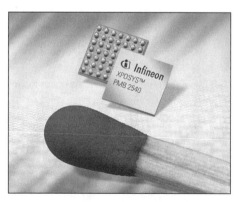

FIGURE 6-3: GPS chips turn tiny.

Source: Infineon press release

GPS is a satellite-based method for pinpointing your location. Currently, two commercial satellite clusters are commonly used — GPS (United States, two dozen satellites) and GLONASS (Russia, three dozen satellites). They travel in specific orbits around the earth (see Figure 6-4); the orbits aren't geosynchronous, but they're good enough to cover every patch of land on earth. The GPS chip locates four or more satellites and calculates your location based on the distance to each.

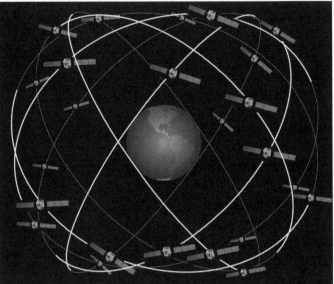

FIGURE 6-4:
Carefully crafted orbits ensure that a GPS chip can almost always find four satellites.

Source: HEPL, Stanford University

TRACKING YOUR SHOTS

Any time you put a GPS system and a camera together, you have the potential for lots of embarrassment. Why? Many GPS-enabled cameras — including notably the ones in many phones and tablets — brand the photo with a very precise location. If you snap a shot from your tablet and upload it to Facebook, Flickr, or any of a thousand photo-friendly sites, the photo may have your exact location embedded in the file, for anyone to see.

Law enforcement has used this approach to find suspects. The US military warns active duty personnel to turn off their GPSs to avoid disclosing locations. Even some anonymous celebrities have been outed by their cameras and phones. Be careful.

If your Windows PC doesn't have a GPS chip, or it isn't turned on, but you do allow Windows apps to track your location, the best Windows can do is to approximate where your Internet connection is coming from, based on your IP address (a number that uniquely identifies your computer's connection to the Internet). And in many cases, that can be miles away from where you're actually sitting.

When you start a Windows 10 app that wants to use your location you may see a message asking for your permission to track your location, as in the Maps app shown in Figure 6-5.

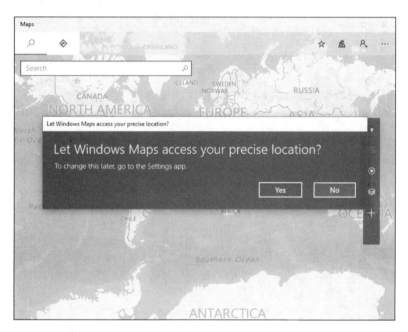

FIGURE 6-5:
Windows 10's Maps app wants you to reveal your location.

If you've already turned on location services, each time you add another app that wants to use your location, you see a notification that says, "Let Windows 10 app access your precise location?" You can respond either Yes or No. The following sections explain how you can control location tracking in Windows 10.

Blocking all location tracking

To keep Windows from using your location in *any* app — even if you've already turned on location use in some apps — follow these steps:

1. **Click or tap the Start icon and then the Settings icon.**

2. **Click or tap Privacy. On the left, choose Location.**

   The Location Privacy screen appears, as shown in Figure 6-6.

3. **To turn off location tracking — even if you've already given your permission to various and sundry applications to track your location — set Location to Off.**

   That's all it takes.

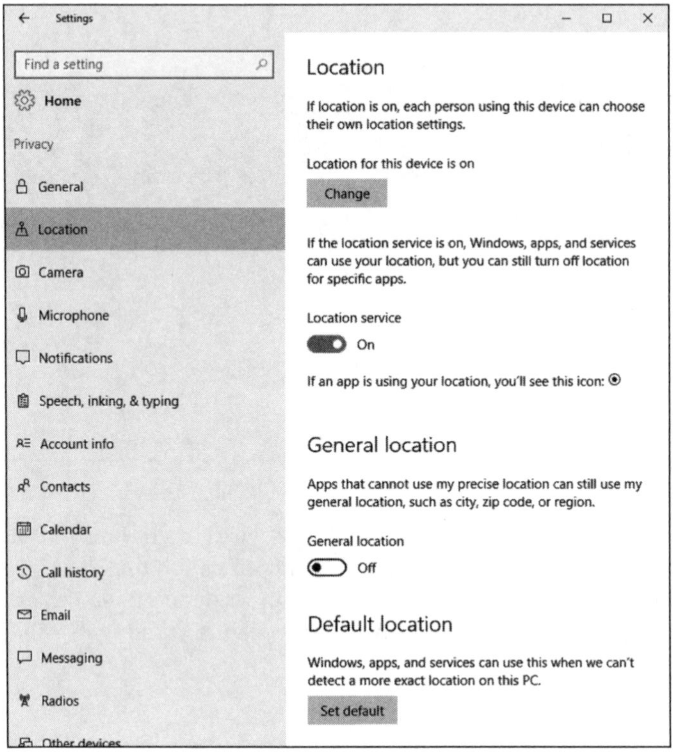

FIGURE 6-6:
The master shut-off switch for location tracking is at the top.

Blocking location tracking in an app

If you've given an app permission to use your location, but want to turn it off, without throwing the big Off switch described in the preceding steps, here's how to do it:

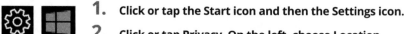

1. **Click or tap the Start icon and then the Settings icon.**

2. **Click or tap Privacy. On the left, choose Location.**

3. **Scroll down until you find the app you want to cut off.**

    In Figure 6-7, I looked for the Weather app.

4. **On the right, slide the Location slider to Off.**

    The app loses its permission.

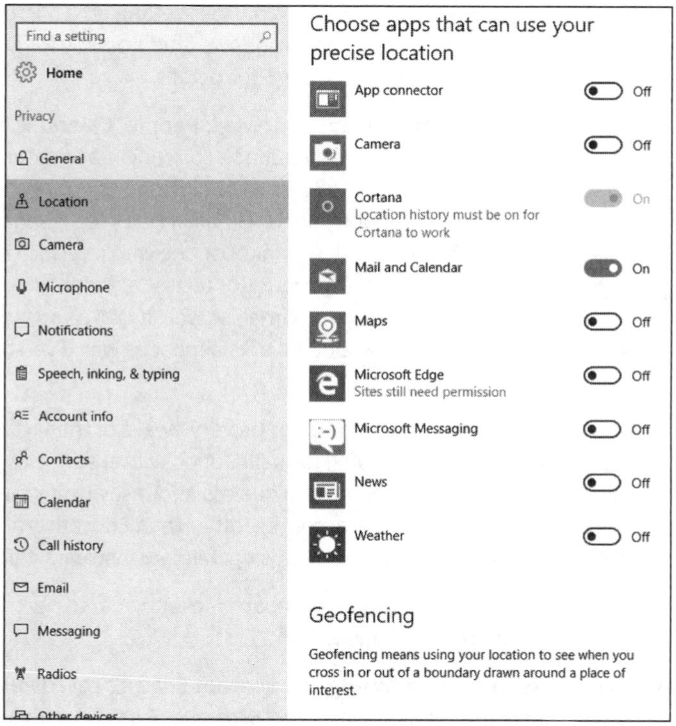

FIGURE 6-7:
You can turn off location tracking for individual apps, as well.

Find a setting

🏠 Home

Privacy

🔒 General

📍 Location

📷 Camera

🎤 Microphone

🗨 Notifications

📋 Speech, inking, & typing

≅ Account info

👥 Contacts

📅 Calendar

🕓 Call history

✉ Email

💬 Messaging

📡 Radios

📲 Other devices

Choose apps that can use your precise location

	App connector	Off
	Camera	Off
	Cortana — Location history must be on for Cortana to work	On
	Mail and Calendar	On
	Maps	Off
	Microsoft Edge — Sites still need permission	Off
	Microsoft Messaging	Off
	News	Off
	Weather	Off

Geofencing

Geofencing means using your location to see when you cross in or out of a boundary drawn around a place of interest.

Privacy Control

Some apps keep a history of your locations or searches that may pertain to your location. If you want to verify that's been deleted, too, bring up the app, click or tap the hamburger icon in the upper-left corner (and shown in the margin) and choose Settings. The Settings pane appears on the right. In most cases, you can choose Options and then click the link that says Clear Searches.

Minimizing Privacy Intrusion

Although it's true that using Windows 10 exposes you to many more privacy concerns than any previous version of Windows, you can reduce the amount of data kept about you by following a few simple rules:

>> If you want to log in to Windows using a Microsoft account — and there are many good reasons for doing so — consider setting up a Microsoft account that you use only for logging in to Windows (and possibly for OneDrive, Xbox, and/or Skype). See Book 2, Chapter 5 for details.

>> **Don't use the Windows 10 apps for Mail, People, Calendar, Skype, or OneDrive.** If you have a Hotmail/Outlook.com or Gmail account, don't access them through Windows 10's Universal Mail app; go to your browser (Firefox?), and log in to Hotmail/Outlook.com or Gmail. If you keep a separate Microsoft account for logging in to Windows only, use the web interface for OneDrive — by going through OneDrive. Run your Contacts, Calendar, and Messaging through Hotmail/Outlook.com or Gmail as well. It isn't as snazzy as using the Windows 10 Universal apps, but it works almost as well. Even better, in many cases.

Also, as noted earlier in this chapter, be very aware of the fact that both Google (Gmail) and Microsoft (Hotmail/Outlook.com) scan every inbound and outbound message. Google has no qualms about saying it scans inbound and outbound messages on free accounts (other than Education accounts) for text that will improve its aim with advertising. Microsoft swears it doesn't.

I use Gmail. If Google wants to bombard me with ads, so be it: I don't buy anything from the ads anyway.

ASK
WOODY.COM

>> **Always use private browsing.** In Microsoft Edge it's called *InPrivate;* Firefox calls it *Incognito;* Chrome says *Private Browsing.* Turning on this mode keeps your browser from leaving cookies around, and it wipes out download lists, caches, browser history, forms, and passwords.

Realize, though, that your browser still leaves crumbs wherever it goes: If you use Google to look up something, for example, Google still has a record of your IP address and what you typed.

Private browsing isn't the same thing as Do Not Track. In fact, as of this writing, Do Not Track is a largely futile request that you make to the websites you visit, asking them to refrain from keeping track of you and your information. For details, see Book 5, Chapter 1.

» **If you use Office, turn off telemetry in it.** In any Office 2016 program, choose File ➪ Options ➪ Trust Center. Select the Trust Center Settings option, and then on the left choose Privacy Options. Deselect the box marked "Send us information about your use and performance of Office software to help improve your Microsoft experience."

In addition to rolling the Feedback & Diagnostics setting to Basic, as described at the beginning of this chapter, you can clamp down further on your privacy settings by going through the lengthy list compiled by Matt Klein on How-To Geek, at www.howtogeek.com/221864/digging-into-and-understanding-windows-10s-privacy-settings/. You can find lots of anti-Windows-10-snooping advice on the web, but only some of it is reputable. Klein has compiled the most thorough list of safe settings that I've seen.

3

Working on the Desktop

Contents at a Glance

Chapter 1

Running Your Desktop from Start to Finish

This chapter explains how to find your way around the Windows windows. If you're an old hand at Windows, you know most of this stuff — such as mousing and interacting with dialog boxes — but I bet some of it will come as a surprise, particularly if you've never taken advantage of Windows libraries or if Windows 8/8.1's Metro side tied you in knots. You know who you are.

Most of all, you need to understand that you don't have to accept all the default settings. Windows 10 was designed to sell more copies of Windows 10. Much of that folderol just gets in the way. What's best for Microsoft isn't necessarily best for you, and a few quick clicks can help make your PC more usable, and more . . . yours.

TIP

If you're looking for information on customizing the Windows 10 Start menu and the taskbar, skip ahead to Book 3, Chapter 2. To look at personalizing the desktop (and thus tablet mode), read Book 3, Chapter 3.

Tripping through Win10's Three Personas

As soon as you *log in* to the computer (that's what it's called when you click your name), you're greeted with an enormous expanse of near-nothingness, cleverly painted with a pretty picture. Your computer manufacturer might have chosen the picture for you, or you might see the default Microsoft screen.

Your Windows destiny, such as it is, unfolds on the computer's screen.

When you crank up Windows 10, it can take on one of three personas. They're pretty easy to discern, if you follow these guidelines:

>> **Windows desktop:** Almost everybody starts with the Windows desktop. It has a Start icon in the lower-left corner, more icons along the taskbar at the bottom, and larger icons (possibly just the Recycle Bin) on top of the desktop. The picture on the desktop could look like just about anything.

If you click the Start icon in the lower-left corner (and shown in the margin), you see a Start menu on the left and a whole bunch of tiles on the right, as in Figure 1-1. That's what I think of as regular Windows. Your background picture will no doubt differ, as will the contents of the Start menu on the left and probably the Start tiles on the right.

FIGURE 1-1:
This is the traditional Windows 10 desktop — the default view on a Dell XPS-15.

If you look at the row of little icons on the far left, the most important one that to remember is the one shaped like a gear (and shown in the margin). It's just about the on-off switch icon. Others have used the gear for Settings for decades, and Microsoft has finally caught on. You now find Settings in many parts of Windows behind an eight-spoked icon.

» **Full-screen start:** If you've been playing around with your computer, or someone else has done it for you, you may arrive in full-screen start, shown in Figure 1-2.

FIGURE 1-2:
The full-screen start. If you see this, drop back to regular Start before you try to change anything.

If you're in full-screen start, I recommend that you get out of it for now, while you're still getting your bearings. To do so, click the hamburger icon, the Settings icon (both shown in the margin), Personalization, Start. Under Start Behaviors, slide the switch marked Use Start Full Screen to Off. That will put you back in Figure 1-1, the "real" Start screen.

» **Tablet mode:** The third possibility is that you started in tablet mode, shown in Figure 1-3. The differences between full-screen start and tablet mode are subtle, but you can see major differences in the taskbar at the bottom. Full-screen start has a big search box to the right of the Start icon, but tablet mode has a back arrow.

If you're going to use Windows primarily with your pinkies, instead of a mouse, tablet mode is a good way to, uh, start. I talk about tablet mode extensively in its own section of this chapter. If you find yourself in tablet mode and want to get back to a mouse-happy desktop, click the Action Center icon, waaaaaay down in the lower-right corner, to the right of the time, and then deselect the Tablet Mode tile (refer to Figure 1-3).

Working with the Traditional Desktop

So your main starting screen looks like Figure 1-1, yes? Good. This is where you should start.

The screen that Windows shows you every time you start your computer is the *desktop,* although it doesn't bear much resemblance to a real desktop. Try putting a pencil on it.

ASK
WOODY.COM

I talk about changing and organizing your desktop in Book 3, Chapter 3, but every new Windows 10 user will want to make a few quick changes. That's what you do in this chapter.

TECHNICAL
STUFF

The Windows desktop looks simple enough, but don't fool yourself: Under that calm exterior sits the most sophisticated computer program ever created. Hundreds of millions of dollars went into creating the illusion of simplicity — something to remember the next time you feel like kicking your computer and screaming at the 10 gods.

Changing the background

Start taking your destiny into your own hands by changing the wallpaper (er, the *desktop background*). If you bought a new computer with Windows 10 installed, your background text probably says *Dell* or *Vaio* or *Billy Joe Bob's Computer Emporium,* or *Dial 555-3106 for a good time.* Bah. Change your wallpaper by following these steps:

1. **Right-click an empty part of the desktop, or tap and hold down, and then choose Personalize.**

   Windows hops to the Settings app's Background pane, shown in Figure 1-4.

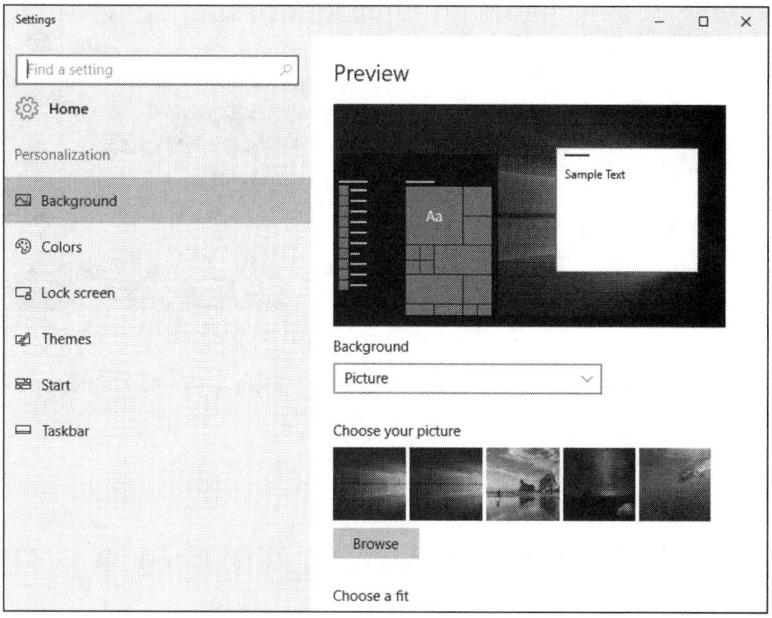

FIGURE 1-4:
Choose your desktop background (even a slideshow) here.

2. **Play with the Background drop-down box, and see if you find a background that you like.**

   You can choose one of the pictures that Windows offers, a solid color, or a slideshow.

3. **If you don't see a background that tickles your fancy, or if you want to roll your own backgrounds, click Browse.**

   Windows responds by going into your machine and letting you pick a pic, any pic.

4. **If you find a picture that you like but it looks like a smashed watermelon on your screen or is too small to be visible, in the Choose a Fit drop-down list, tell Windows how to use the picture.**

   These are your options:

   - Stretched to fill the screen
   - Centered in the middle of the desktop
   - Tiled over the desktop (as in Figure 1-5)

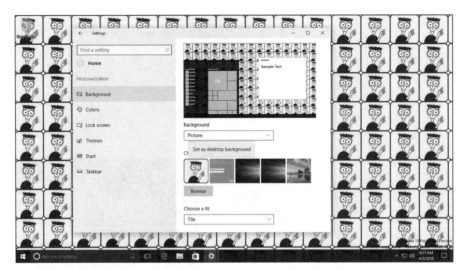

FIGURE 1-5:
Tiling can be
a bit excessive.

5. **Tap or click the Close (X) button to close the Settings app's Background pane.**

   Your new wallpaper settings take effect immediately.

Cleaning up useless icons and programs

If you haven't yet taken control and zapped those obnoxious programs that your PC vendor probably stuck on your machine, now is the time to do it.

TIP

You might think that your brand-spanking-new Windows 10 computer wouldn't have any junk on it. Ha. The people who make and sell computers — all the big-name manufacturers — sell chunks of real estate on your computer, just to turn a profit. Hate to break it to you, but the AOLs and Nortons of the world pay Dell and HP and Sony and Asus and all the others for space. The manufacturers want you to think that they've installed this lovely software for your convenience. Bah. Humbug.

Even Microsoft has taken a dip in the ad-dispersing sewer by cluttering your desktop and Start menu with all sorts of must-have Windows-enhancing products, such as Candy Crush Saga and World of Tanks. Ka-ching! Ka-ching!

» **To get rid of most icons,** simply right-click them and choose Delete.

» **To get rid of the icons' associated programs,** try to remove them the Settings app way first: Click or tap the Start icon, the Settings icon, System, Apps and Features. See if the program is listed. If so, click or tap it and click Uninstall. If you can't find the program in the Settings app, right-click or tap and hold down the Start icon, choose Control Panel, and under Programs, choose Uninstall a Program. When the Uninstall or Change a Program dialog box opens, double-click a program to remove it.

ASK
WOODY.COM

Unfortunately, many scummy programs don't play by the rules: Either they don't have uninstallers or the uninstaller that appears in the Change a Program dialog box doesn't get rid of the program entirely. (I won't mention Norton Internet Security by name.) To get rid of the scummy stuff, look in Book 1, Chapter 4 for information about PC Decrapifier, a program from Jason York. It's at www.pcdecrapifier.com/download.

Mousing with Your Mouse

For almost everybody, the computer's mouse (or the lowly touchpad) serves as the primary way of interacting with Windows. But you already knew that. You can click the left mouse button or the right mouse button, or you can roll the wheel in the middle (if you have one), and the mouse will do different things, depending on where you click or roll. But you already knew that, too.

ASK
WOODY.COM

The Windows 10 Multi-Touch technology and those ever-fancier 11-simultaneous-finger screens let you act like Tom Cruise in *Minority Report,* if you have the bucks for the multiple-finger stuff, the right application software, and the horsepower to drive it. But for those of us who put our gloves on one hand at a time, the mouse remains the input device of choice.

The best way to get the feel for a new mouse? Play one of the games that ships with Windows. Choose the Start icon, Microsoft Solitaire Collection, and take it away — just realize that Microsoft will charge you for ad-free versions of the programs. Or hop over to the Windows Store for amazing new versions of Minesweeper, Chess Titans, and many others for mouse orienteering. In Figure 1-6, I'm playing a rousing game of traditional Klondike, the program you probably think of when you think "Solitaire."

Try clicking in unlikely places, double-clicking, or right-clicking in new and different ways. Bet you'll discover several wrinkles, even if you're an old hand at the games. (See Book 5, Chapter 5 for more on Windows games.)

TECHNICAL
STUFF

Inside the computer, programmers measure the movement of mice in units called *mickeys.* Nope, I'm not making this up. Move your mouse a short distance, and it travels a few mickeys. Move it to Anaheim, and it puts on lots of mickeys.

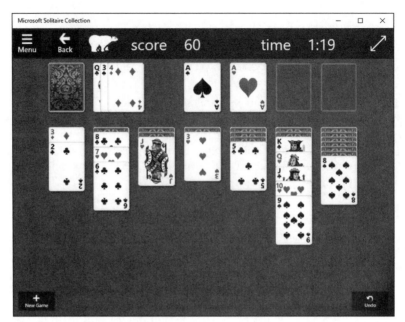

FIGURE 1-6:
The Microsoft
Solitaire
Collection is
great for mouse
practice.

What's up, dock?

Windows 10 includes several gesture features that can save you lots of time. Foremost among them: a quarter- and half-window docking capability called *snap.*

REMEMBER

If you click the title bar of a window and drag the window a-a-all the way to the left side of the screen, as soon as the mouse hits the edge of the screen, Windows 10 resizes the window so that it occupies the left half of the screen and the docks the window on the far left side. Similarly, *mutatis mutandis,* for the right side. That makes it two-drag easy to put a Word document and a spreadsheet side by side, or an email message and a list of files from File Explorer, as shown in Figure 1-7.

A new feature in Windows 10 called Snap Assist makes snapping easier than ever. If you snap one window to an edge, Windows brings up thumbnails of all the other programs that are running at the time. Click or tap the program, and it occupies the vacant part of the screen, as shown in Figure 1-8.

You can also drag into the corners of the screen and snap four programs into the four corners. (If you're curious, these all are controlled in the Settings app. Tap or click the Start icon, the Settings icon, System, Multitasking; the relevant settings are at the top of the pane.)

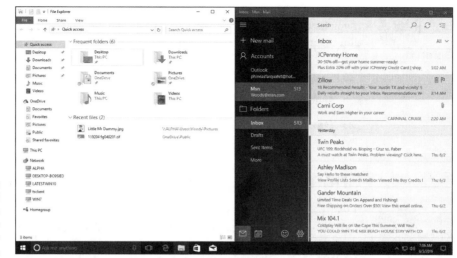

FIGURE 1-7:
Two drags and you can have Windows arrange two programs side by side.

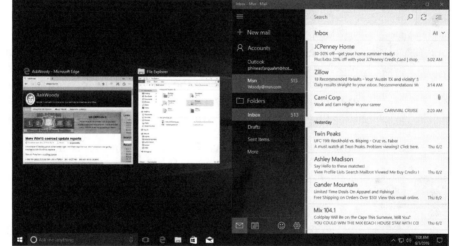

FIGURE 1-8:
Snap Assist helps you put two programs side by side by offering to snap the other running programs.

Those aren't the only navigation tricks. If you drag a window to the top of the screen, it's *maximized*, so it occupies the whole screen. (Yeah, I know: You always did that by double-clicking the title bar.) And, if you click a window's title bar and shake it, all other windows on the screen move out of the way: They *minimize* themselves on the toolbar.

ASK
WOODY.COM

If you have rodentophobia, you can also do the mouse tricks explained in this section by pressing the following key combinations:

>> **Snap left:** Windows key+left arrow

>> **Snap right:** Windows key+right arrow

>> **Maximize:** Windows key+up arrow

Changing the mouse

TIP

If you're left-handed, you can interchange the actions of the left and right mouse buttons — that is, you can tell Windows 10 that it should treat the left mouse button as though it were the right button and treat the right button as though it were the left. The swap comes in handy for some left-handers, but most southpaws I know (including both of my sons) prefer to keep the buttons as is because it's easier to use other computers if your fingers are trained for the standard setting.

TIP

The Windows ClickLock feature can come in handy if you have trouble holding down the left mouse button and moving the mouse at the same time — a common problem for notebook users who have fewer than three hands. When Windows uses ClickLock, you hold down the mouse button for a while (you can tell Windows exactly how long) and Windows locks the mouse button so that you can concentrate on moving the mouse without having to hold down the button.

To switch left and right mouse buttons or turn on ClickLock, follow these steps:

REMEMBER

1. **Click or tap the Start icon, the Settings icon, Devices, Mouse & Touchpad.**

   Settings is the icon that looks like a gear.

   Windows opens the Mouse & Touchpad dialog box, shown in Figure 1-9.

2. **If you want to switch the functions of the left and right mouse buttons, change the entry in the Select Your Primary Button box.**

3. **If you want to turn on ClickLock, tap or click the Additional Mouse Options link, at the bottom.**

   You get an old-fashioned Control Panel dialog box called Mouse Properties, which you can see in Figure 1-10.

4. **At the bottom of the Mouse Properties dialog box, select the Turn on ClickLock box, and then click OK.**

   Although changes made in the Settings app take effect immediately, changes in the old-fashioned Control Panel don't go into effect until you click Apply or OK.

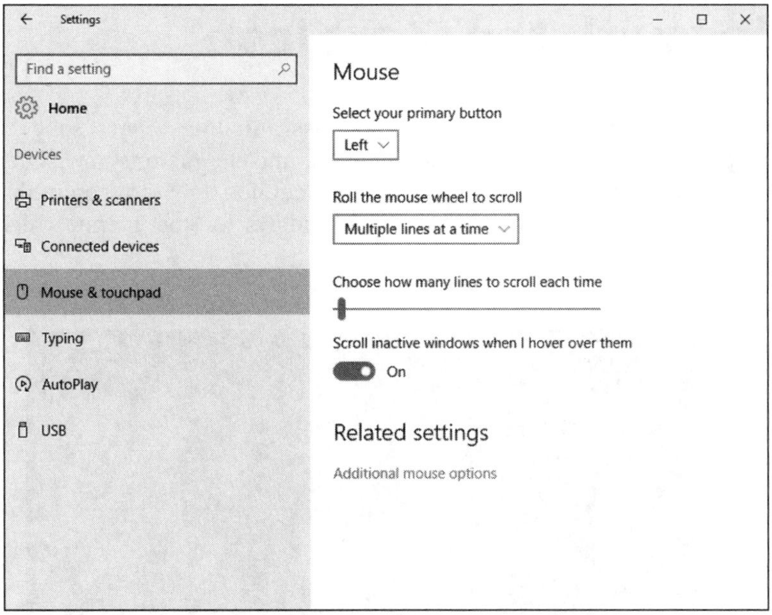

FIGURE 1-9:
Reverse the left and right mouse buttons with one click in the Settings app.

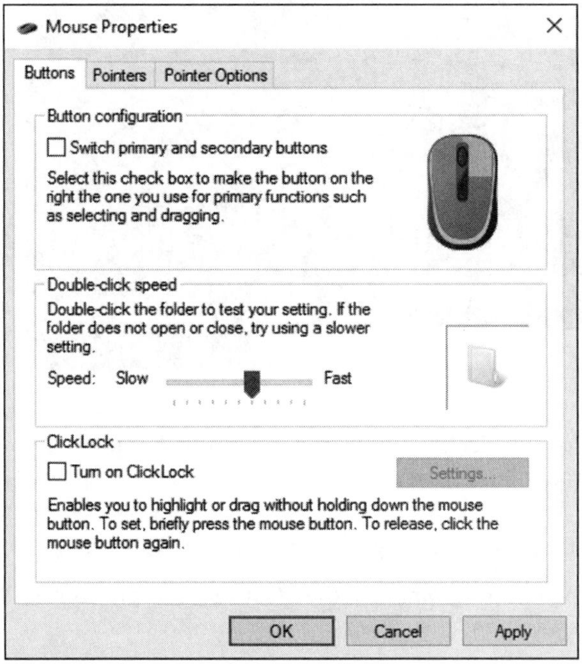

FIGURE 1-10:
This old-fashioned Control Panel dialog box offers the setting for ClickLock.

Starting with the Start Icon

 Microsoft's subverting of the classic Rolling Stones song "Start Me Up" for Windows 95 advertising might be ancient history now, but the royal road to Windows still starts at the Start icon. Click the Start icon in the lower-left corner of the screen to open the new Windows 10 Start menu, which looks something like the one shown in Figure 1-11.

FIGURE 1-11: The Windows Start menu can be customized a little bit.

The Start menu looks like it's etched in granite, but it isn't. You can change three pieces without digging deep:

>> **To change the name or picture of the current user,** see Book 2, Chapter 2.

>> **To remove a program from the Most Used programs list,** right-click it, choose More, and then select Don't Show in This List.

>> **To move a tile on the right or resize one,** just click and drag the tile. You also can right-click (or click and hold down), choose Resize, and then pick a new size — see Book 3, Chapter 2 for details.

TIP

If you bought a new computer with Windows 10 preinstalled, the people who make the computer may have sold one or two or three of the spots on the Start menu. Think of it as an electronic billboard on your desktop. Nope, I'm not exaggerating. I keep expecting to bump into a Windows machine with fly-out Start menu entries that read, oh, "Statistics prove/Near and far/That folks who drive/Like crazy are/Burma Shave." (See `Burma-shave.org/jingles`.)

UNIVERSAL WINDOWS APPS

Microsoft has always had a hard time with branding — making its technical achievements sparkle and fizz, and convey meaning with a name. I think *Windows RT* was the all-time low in Microsoft marketing nomenclature — *Windows Live* sure gave it a run for the money — but that's a bygone.

Near the top of the list (or the bottom, depending on how you stand) of bad branding is the new term *Universal Windows app*. At least in theory, Universal Windows apps (sometimes called, confusingly, just *Windows apps* or just *Universal apps* or even *Universal Windows Platform apps*) are computer programs that can, in theory, run on any Windows 10 device, whether it's a desktop, a laptop, a tablet, a phone, an Xbox gaming console, a HoloLens headset, or a hearing aid. I wonder what a Blue Screen sounds like.

They can, in theory, run on any device because they make use of a new set of Windows programming interfaces, called the WinRT API. The WinRT API is very different from the old Windows programming interfaces, generally called the Win32 API. The programs you've used on Windows for years run on the Win32 API, and they work on the Windows 10 desktop, much as they always have. But the new Universal Windows apps run inside their own little boxes — yep, they look just like Windows windows — and the boxes sit on the desktop.

When you think of Windows versions, the new Universal Windows apps run only on Windows 10. In general, they won't run on Windows 8 or 8.1. They definitely can't run on Windows 7 or earlier, because those versions of Windows didn't include the WinRT API.

The WinRT API has all sorts of advantages over the old Win32 API — security, for one, because it's harder to hack a system from inside a WinRT app, but there are lots of additional capabilities that have become more important as we've turned more mobile. The WinRT API reduces battery demand, makes programming easier for touch input and for resizing screens. It keeps programs from clobbering each other. And on and on.

In the ripe old days (circa Windows 8), the programs that used the WinRT API were called Metro apps. When, according to legend, the German supermarket chain Metro

(continued)

Running Your Desktop from Start to Finish

(continued)

threatened to take Microsoft to task (Who is Microsoft to complain? They trademarked *windows*), Microsoft stopped calling Metro apps *Metro* and the result has been pandemonium.

The names used in the interim include Metro, Metro Style, Windows 8 application, Windows Store app, Windows 8–style user interface app (that really sizzles, doesn't it?), new user interface app, Modern app, and a handful of additional names that aren't entirely printable. Just ask the developers.

Microsoft seems to have dropped the name *program* entirely, no doubt because Apple and Google have apps, not (sniff) programs.

No matter what you call them, Universal Windows apps are clearly the way of the future. The WinRT API has the Win32 API beat in all sorts of ways, except compatibility: Win32 programmers have to learn a completely new way of programming and a new way of thinking, and transferring those tens of billions of lines of code from Win32 to WinRT will take decades. By which time WinRT will be obsolete, no doubt.

In the interim, we have Windows 10, which tries — nobly and somewhat successfully — to bridge the gap between the two worlds. Welcome to the future.

The right side of the Start menu contains a plethora of tiles. At the beginning, the built-in tiles are all for Universal Windows apps (see the nearby sidebar) from Microsoft itself, plus a peppering of tiles from companies that have emerged on Microsoft's good side. Your computer vendor may have stuck in a couple extras. Ka-ching. And in the normal course of using your computer, you may well put some tiles over there, too.

Here's what you find on the Right Side of the Start Force:

>> The **productivity apps from Microsoft** (Calendar and Mail) are marginally useful, but not likely to draw you away from your current email or calendar program, especially if you use email or a calendar on your phone or tablet. Win10 used to have a People app here, but it was so bad the powers-that-be got rid of it. See Book 4, Chapters 1 and 2.

>> **Microsoft Edge** may be the most complex Universal Windows app ever written. Microsoft is serious about getting rid of Internet Explorer, and getting people moved over to a modern browser. See Book 5, Chapter 1.

>> The **Cortana** tile just duplicates the search box at the bottom. I talk about Search and Hey, Cortana! in Book 3, Chapter 6.

>> **OneNote** is a useful note-taking and clipping app from Microsoft. I use Evernote, but they're directed at two different audiences. See Book 4, Chapter 4.

Also included are a whole bunch of **shovelware apps**, including Groove Music, Movies & TV (Book 5, Chapter 3), Photos (Book 4, Chapter 3), Skype Preview (the "real" app still doesn't work), and Weather, plus an enormous number of apps that invite you to spend more money.

You can modify most of the right side of the Start menu by dragging and dropping tiles, and right-clicking (or tapping and holding down) a tile to resize. There's much more about working with Universal Windows app tiles in Book 3, Chapter 2.

Touching on the Taskbar

Windows 10 sports a highly customizable taskbar at the bottom of the screen (see Figure 1-12). I go into detail in Book 3, Chapter 3.

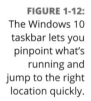

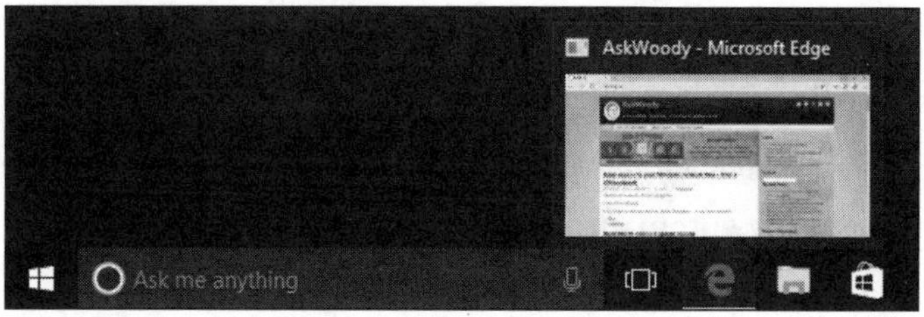

FIGURE 1-12: The Windows 10 taskbar lets you pinpoint what's running and jump to the right location quickly.

The taskbar's a wonderfully capable locus for most of the things you want to do, most of the time. For example:

>> **Hover your mouse cursor over an icon to see what the program is running.** In Figure 1-12, I hovered my mouse cursor over the Edge icon and see that www.AskWoody.com is open.

TECHNICAL STUFF

Some applications, such as File Explorer, show each tab or open document in a separate thumbnail. Clicking a thumbnail brings up the application, along with the chosen tab or document. This nascent feature is implemented unevenly at this point.

>> **Right-click an icon, and you see the application's jump list.** The jump list MAY show an application's most recently opened documents and, for many programs, a list of common tasks and activities. It may show a browser's

history list. We're just starting to see how program writers will exploit this new capability, too.

If you click an icon, the program opens, as you would expect. But if you want to open a second copy of a program — say, another copy of Firefox — you can't just click the icon. You have to right-click and choose the application's name.

You can move most of the icons around on the taskbar by simply clicking and dragging. (You can't move the Start, Cortana, or the Task View icons.)

If you want to see all the icons on your desktop and relegate all open windows to shadows of their former selves, click the far right edge of the taskbar.

The Windows taskbar has many tricks up its sleeve, but it has one capability that you may need, if screen real estate is at a premium. (Hey, you folks with 30-inch monitors need not apply, okay?)

Auto-Hide lets the taskbar shrink to a thin line until you bump the mouse pointer way down at the bottom of the screen. As soon as the mouse pointer hits bottom, the taskbar pops up. Here's how to teach the taskbar to auto-hide:

1. **Right-click an empty part of the taskbar.**

2. **Choose Settings.**

   The Taskbar tab should be visible.

3. **Slide the Automatically Hide the Taskbar setting to On.**

   The taskbar holds many surprises. See Book 3, Chapter 3.

Working with Files and Folders

"What's a file?" Man, I wish I had a nickel for every time I've been asked that question.

A file is a, uh, thing. Yeah, that's it. A thing. A thing that has stuff inside it. Why don't you ask me an easier question, like "What is a paragraph?" or "What is the meaning of life, the universe, and everything?"

A *file* is a fundamental chunk of stuff. Like most fundamental chunks of stuff (say, protons, Congressional districts, or ear wax), any attempt at a definitive definition gets in the way of understanding the thing itself. Suffice it to say that a Word document is a file. An Excel workbook is a file. That photograph your cousin emailed you the other day is a file. Every track on the latest Coldplay album is a file, but so is every track on every audio CD ever made. Chris Martin isn't that special.

WARNING

Filenames and folder names can be very long, but they can't contain the following characters:

/ \ : * ? " < > |

Files can be huge. They can be tiny. They can even be empty, but don't short-circuit any gray cells on that observation.

KEEPING FOLDERS ORGANIZED

If you set folders up correctly, they can help you keep track of things. If you toss your files around higgledy-piggledy, no system of folders in the world can help. Unfortunately, folders have a fundamental problem. Permit me to illustrate.

Suppose you own a sandwich shop. You take a photograph of the shop. Where do you stick the photo? Which folder should you use? The answer: There's no good answer. You could put the photo in with all your other shop stuff — documents and invoices and payroll records and menus. You could stick the photo in the Pictures folder, or in your OneDrive Pictures folder, which Windows 10 automatically provides. You could put it in the Public or Public Documents or Public Pictures folder so other people using your PC, or other folks connected to your network, can see the photo of the shop. You could create a folder named Photos and file away the picture chronologically (that's what I do), or you could even create a folder named Shop inside the Photos folder and stick the picture in \Photos\Shop.

I stick my photos in the Google Photos app (see Book 4, Chapter 3) and rely on a Google search to find them, but you see the point.

This where-to-file-it-and-where-to-find-it conundrum stands as one of the hairiest problems in all of Windows, and until Windows 7, you had only piecemeal help in keeping things organized. Now, using the Windows 10 libraries, and a Search function that (finally!) works the way you would expect, you stand a fighting chance of finding that long-lost file, especially if you're diligent in assigning tags to pictures and videos. For more info on that, see the sidebar "Creating libraries," later in this chapter.

But if you stick the photo in OneDrive, ay, that's another story entirely. See Book 6, Chapter 1 for the sad story (and sidebar) of smart files.

Running Your Desktop
from Start to Finish

Folders hold files and other folders. Folders can be empty. A single folder can hold millions — yes, quite literally millions — of files and other folders.

 To look at the files and folders on your machine that you probably use every day, click or tap the File Explorer icon down in the taskbar (and shown in the margin). A program named File Explorer appears, and it shows you the contents of your frequently used folders (see Figure 1-13).

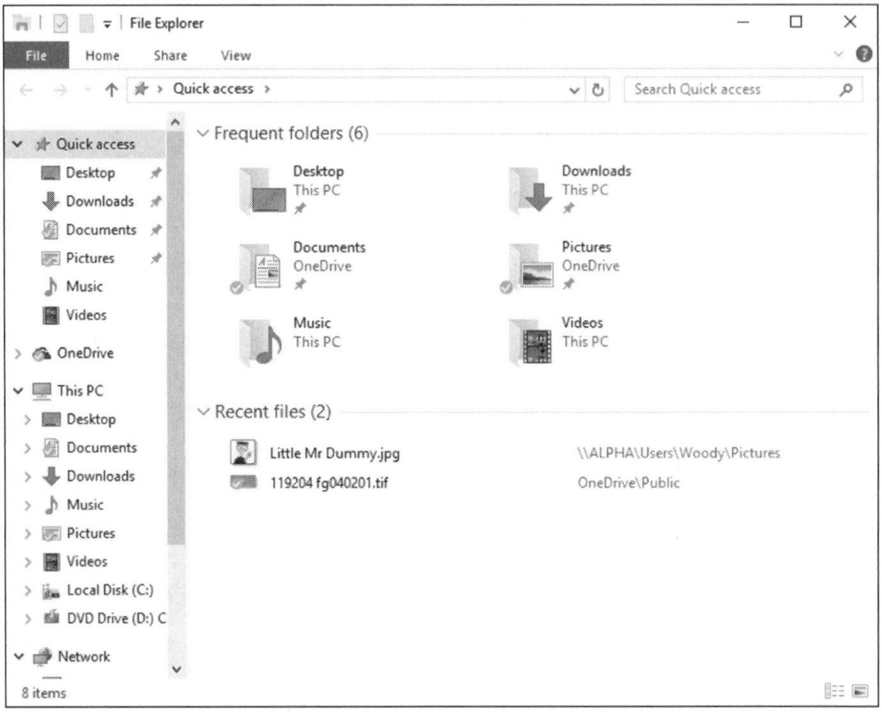

FIGURE 1-13:
The most
frequently used
folders and
recently accessed
files, shown by
File Explorer.

File Explorer can show you the contents of a hard drive — folders and files — or a thumbdrive or a CD/DVD drive. File Explorer can also help you look at other computers on your network, if you have a network.

Using File Explorer

Your PC is a big place, and you can get lost easily. Microsoft has spent hundreds of millions of dollars to make sure that Windows 10 points you in the right direction and keeps you on track through all sorts of activities.

Amazingly, some of it actually works.

CREATING LIBRARIES

Windows 7 brought a powerful new concept to the table: libraries. Think of them as easy ways to mash together the contents of many folders: You can work with a collection of folders as easily as you work with just one folder, no matter where the folders live. You can pull together pictures in ten of the folders on your desktop plus the ones in your computer's \Public folder plus the ones on that external 4 terabyte drive and the \Public folder on another computer connected to your network, and treat them all as though they were in the same folder.

Unfortunately, as Microsoft pushed deeper into the cloud and brought OneDrive to the fore, libraries got left behind. In Windows 8 and 8.1, it's hard to find the vestiges and make them work right. Windows 10 continues in the Windows 8/8.1 tradition. Microsoft wants you to stick your data in its cloud — on its computers — not on your piddlin' little PC.

Many people find libraries too difficult. I find working *without* libraries is too difficult.

I refer to libraries occasionally in this chapter, but if you want the whole story, check out Book 7, Chapter 3. Unless you want to put all your data in OneDrive (which isn't a bad idea, really) or Google Drive or Dropbox (my choice for most of my online storage), drop by Book 7, Chapter 3 to find a better way to organize your data here on earth.

If you're going to get any work done, you must interact with Windows. If Windows is going to get any work done, it must interact with you. Fair 'nuff.

Microsoft refers to the way Windows interacts with people as the *user experience*. Gad. File Explorer lies at the center of the, er, user experience. When you want to work with Windows 10 — ask it where it stuck your wedding pictures, show it how to mangle your files, or tell it (literally) where to go — you usually use File Explorer.

Navigating

File Explorer helps you get around in the following ways:

>> **Click a folder to see the files you want.** On the left side of the File Explorer window (refer to Figure 1-13), you can click a real folder (such as Desktop or Downloads), a shortcut you dragged to the Quick access list on the left, other computers in your homegroup (see the "What is a homegroup" sidebar), other drives on your computer, or other computers on the network. You can also reach into your OneDrive account, in the sky, as you can see in Figure 1-14.

FIGURE 1-14:
File Explorer
helps you move
around, even
into the sky, with
OneDrive.

>> **Use the "cookie crumb" navigation bar to move around**. At the top of the File Explorer window (refer to Figure 1-14), you can click the wedges to select from available folders. So, in Figure 1-14, if you click Pictures up at the top, you end up in the OneDrive Pictures folder.

>> **Details appear below.** If you click a file or folder once, details for it (number of items, Sharing state) appear in the Details box at the bottom of the File Explorer window. If you double-click a folder, it becomes the current folder. If you double-click a document, it opens. (For example, if you double-click a Word document, Windows fires up Word, if you have it installed, and has it start with that document open and ready for work.)

>> **Many of the actions you might want to perform on files or folders show up in the command bar at the top.** Most of the other actions you might want to perform are accessible by right-clicking the file or folder.

TIP

>> **To see all options, press Alt.** Depending on how you have it configured, File Explorer may show you an old-fashioned command bar (File, Edit, View, Tools, Help) with dozens of functions tucked away. It will also show you keyboard shortcuts (single letters in small boxes) that you can use to get to the commands from the keyboard. (For example, Ctrl+V displays the View tab.)

>> **Open as many copies of File Explorer as you like.** That can be very helpful if you're scatterbrained like I am — er, if you like to multitask and you want to look in several places at once. Simply right-click the File Explorer icon in the taskbar (and shown in the margin) and choose File Explorer. An independent copy of File Explorer appears, ready for your finagling.

Viewing

Extra-large icons view (refer to Figure 1-14) is, at once, visually impressive and cumbersome. If you grow tired of scrolling (and scrolling and scrolling) through those icons, click the View menu and choose Details. You see the succinct list shown in Figure 1-15.

Windows 10 offers several picturesque views — dubbed extra-large icons, large icons, medium icons, small icons, and infinitesimal eye-straining icons (okay, I got carried away a bit) — that can come in handy if you're looking through a bunch of pictures. In most other cases, though, the icons only get in the way.

TIP

In details view, you can sort the list of files by clicking a column headings — Name or Date, for example. You can right-click one of the column headings and choose More to change what the view shows (get rid of Type, for example, and replace it with Date Taken).

WHAT IS A HOMEGROUP?

Homegroups make it easier to set up sharing among Windows 7, 8/8.1, and 10 computers on a network. I cover the details in Book 7, Chapter 5, but here's the one-minute version.

When your PC joins a homegroup, Windows strips away much of the hassle and mind-numbing details generally associated with sharing folders and printers and replaces the mumbo jumbo with a cookie-cutter method of sharing that works quite well, in almost all home and many small-business networks.

All the computers in a homegroup share their printers and some other peripherals. When individuals sign up for the homegroup, their Pictures, Music, and Videos libraries are shared by default. An extra click adds the Documents library to the list.

Other accounts on the computer — ones that haven't been explicitly logged into the homegroup — share only their printers. In other words, you must specifically log in to the homegroup to have your folders shared.

Every File Explorer window can show a Preview pane — a strip along the right side of the window that, in many cases, shows a preview of the file you selected.

Some people love the preview feature. Others hate it. A definite speed hit is associated with previewing — you may find yourself twiddling your thumbs as Windows 10 gets its previews going. The best solution is to turn off the preview unless you absolutely need it. And use the right tool for the job — if you're previewing lots of picture files, fire up a Photo app (not necessarily the one in Windows 10; see Book 4, Chapter 3).

You can set the preview pane, and all other File Explorer panes, by clicking the View tab, and on the left, choosing Preview Pane.

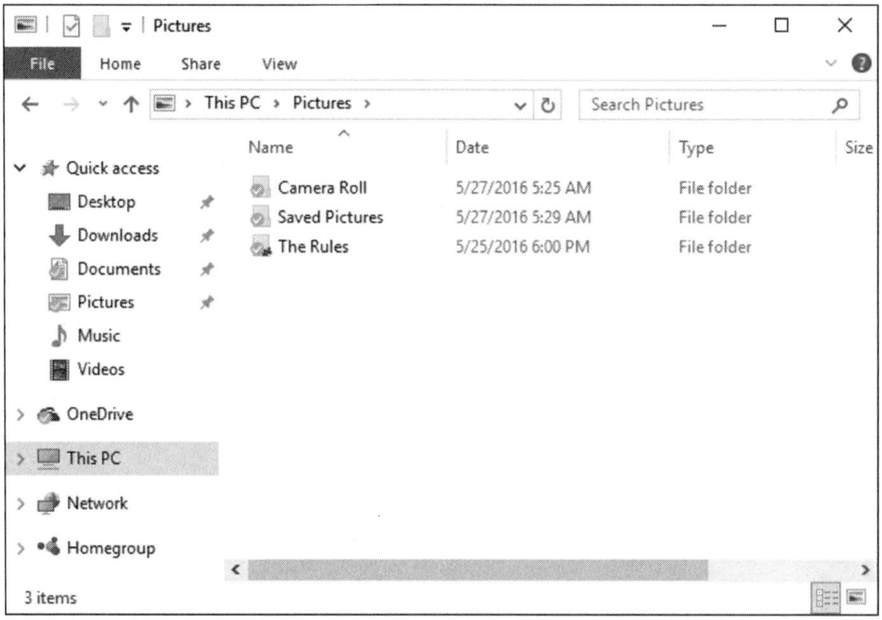

FIGURE 1-15:
Details view
has more meat,
less sizzle.

Creating files and folders

Usually, you create new files and folders when you're using a program. You make new Word documents when you're using Word, say, or come up with a new folder to hold all your offshore banking spreadsheets when you're using Excel. Programs usually have the tools for making new files and folders tucked away in the File, Save and File, Save As dialog boxes. Click around a bit and you'll find them.

But you can also create a new file or folder directly in an existing folder quite easily, without going through the hassle of cranking up a 900-pound gorilla of a program. Follow these steps:

1. **Move to the location where you want to put the new file or folder.**

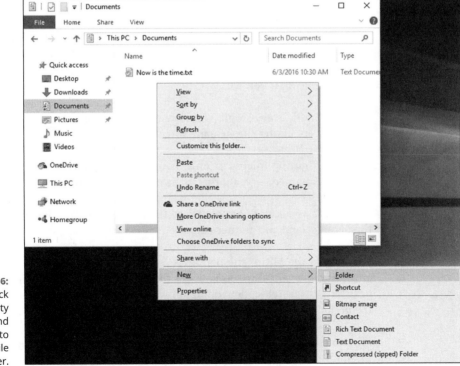

   For example, if you want to stick the new folder Revisionist Techno Grunge in your Documents folder, click the File Explorer icon in the taskbar (and shown in the margin), and on the left, under Quick Access, click Documents.

2. **Right-click a blank spot in your chosen location.**

   By "right-click a blank spot," I mean "don't right-click an existing file or folder," okay? If you want the new folder or file to appear on the desktop, right-click an empty spot on the desktop.

3. **Choose New (see Figure 1-16), and pick the kind of file you want to create.**

   If you want a new folder, choose Folder. Windows creates the new file or folder and leaves it with the name highlighted so that you can rename it by simply typing.

FIGURE 1-16:
Right-click an empty location, and choose New to create a file or folder.

Modifying files and folders

REMEMBER

As long as you have permission (see the section "Sharing folders," later in this chapter), modifying files and folders is easy — rename, delete, move, or copy them — if you remember the trick: right-click (or, for the painfully tap addicted, tap and hold down).

To copy or move more than one file (or folder) at a time, select all the files (or folders) before right-clicking. You can select more than one file using any of these methods:

>> Hold down Ctrl while clicking.

>> Click and drag around the outside of the files and folders to lasso them.

>> Use the Shift key if you want to choose a bunch of contiguous files and folders — ones that are next to each other. Click the first file or folder, hold down Shift, and click the last file or folder.

Showing filename extensions

If you're looking at the Recent files on your computer and you can't see the period and three-letter suffixes of the filenames (such as .txt and .tif and .jpg) that are visible in Figures 1-13, 1-14, 1-15, 1-16, and most of the rest of this book, don't panic! You need to tell Windows to show them — electronically knock Windows upside the head, if you will.

ASK WOODY.COM

In my opinion, every single Windows 10 user should force Windows to show full filenames, including the (usually three-letter) extension at the end of the name.

I've been fighting Microsoft on this topic for many years. Forgive me if I get a little, uh, steamed — yeah, that's the polite way to put it — in the retelling.

Every file has a name. Almost every file has a name that looks more or less like this: Some Name or Another.ext.

The part to the left of the period — Some Name or Another, in this example — generally tells you something about the file, although it can be quite nonsensical or utterly inscrutable, depending on who named the file. The part to the right of the period — ext, in this case — is a filename *extension*, the subject of my diatribe.

Filename extensions have been around since the first PC emerged from the primordial ooze. They were a part of the PC's legacy before anybody ever talked about legacy. Somebody, somewhere decided that Windows wouldn't show filename extensions anymore. (My guess is that Bill Gates himself made the decision, about 20 years ago, but it's only a guess.) Filename extensions were considered danger-ous: too complicated for the typical user, a bit of technical arcana that novices shouldn't have to sweat.

WARNING

No filename extensions? That's garbage. Pure, unadulterated garbage.

The fact is that nearly all files have names such as Letter to Mom.docx, Financial Projections.xlsx, or ILOVEYOU.vbs. But Windows, with rare exception, shows you only the first part of the filename. It cuts off the filename extension. So you see Letter to Mom, without the .docx (which brands the file as a Word document), Financial Projections, without the .xlsx (a dead giveaway for an Excel spread-sheet), and ILOVEYOU, without the .vbs (which is the filename extension for Visual Basic programs).

I really hate it when Windows hides filename extensions, for four big reasons:

>> **If you can see the filename extension, you can usually figure out which kind of file you have at hand and which program will open it.** People who use Word 2003, for example, may be perplexed to see a .docx filename extension — which is generated by Word 2010 and can't be opened by bone-stock Word 2003.

ASK WOODY.COM

Legend has it that former Microsoft CEO (and current largest individual stockholder) Steve Ballmer once infected former CEO (and current philanthro-pist extraordinaire) Bill Gates's Windows PC using a bad email attachment, ILOVEYOU.VBS. If Ballmer had seen the .VBS on the end of the filename, no doubt he would've guessed it was a program — and might've been disinclined to double-click it.

>> **It's almost impossible to get Windows to change filename extensions if you can't see them.** Try it.

>> **Many email programs and spam fighters forbid you from sending or receiving specific kinds of files, based solely on their filename exten-sions.** That's one of the reasons why your friends might not be able to email certain files to you. Just try emailing an .exe file, no matter what's inside.

>> **You bump into filename extensions anyway.** No matter how hard Microsoft wants to hide filename extensions, they show up everywhere — from the Readme.txt files mentioned repeatedly in the official Microsoft documentation to discussions of .jpg file sizes on Microsoft web pages and a gazillion places in between.

Take off the training wheels, okay? To make Windows show you filename extensions the easy way, follow these steps:

1. **In the taskbar, click the File Explorer icon.**

   File Explorer appears (refer to Figure 1-13).

2. **Click or tap View.**

   You see File Explorer's View ribbon, shown in Figure 1-17.

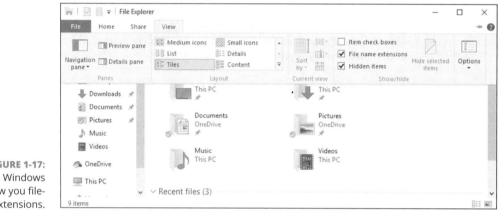

FIGURE 1-17:
Make Windows show you file-name extensions.

3. **Select the File Name Extensions box.**

ASK
WOODY.COM

   While you're here, you may want to change another setting. If you can avoid the temptation to delete or rename files you don't understand, select the Hidden Items box. That way, Windows will show you all files on your computer, including ones that have been marked as hidden, typically by Microsoft. Sometimes, you need to see all your files, even if Windows wants to hide them from you.

4. **Your changes take place immediately.**

   Look at your unveiled filename extensions.

Sharing folders

Sharing is good, right? Your mom taught you to share, didn't she? Everything you need to know about sharing you learned in kindergarten — like how you can share your favorite crayon with your best friend and get back a gnarled blob of stunted wax, covered in mysterious goo.

SHARING AND ONEDRIVE

Microsoft wants you to put all your files in OneDrive. No, they aren't trying to snoop the contents. Microsoft gives away lots of "free" cloud storage in OneDrive because they want you to use (and pay for) other Microsoft products. Microsoft's cost for 7 or 25 GB of "free" cloud space is measured in pennies, and it's getting cheaper. Microsoft's income from keeping you in the Microsoft fold — maybe buying a subscription to Office 365, say, or clicking an ad in Bing — pays for the free storage and then some.

That's why Windows 10 doesn't put a big emphasis on file sharing, here on earth. This book shows you many ways to share files — libraries, public folders, homegroups — that Microsoft isn't particularly interested in proliferating. They don't make money and don't lock you into their ecosystem when your files are all down here, out of the cloud.

In some cases, OneDrive is your best choice for storing and sharing files. I use it all the time, although I tend to put my most important files (including all the files used in preparing this book) in Dropbox. For many people who get nosebleeds in the cloud, for a wide variety of reasons, though, keeping your sharing out of Microsoft's cloud makes good sense.

It's your data. You can choose. You can even change your mind if you want. This book has an extensive discussion of OneDrive and sharing in Book 6, Chapter 1. But if you want to keep your data out of Microsoft's cloud and off Microsoft's computers, follow along here to see how it's done the Windows way.

You can put your files in the cloud, and use the features built into all the cloud services for sharing files or folders. OneDrive (see the "Sharing and OneDrive" sidebar), Dropbox, Google Drive, Box, Mega, and the others have different rules. If you want to share from a Windows 10 computer, though, you have to follow the Win10 rules.

Windows 10 supports two very different ways for sharing files and folders:

>> **Move the files or folders you want to share into the \Public folder.** The \ Public folder is kind of a big cookie jar for everybody who uses your PC: Put a file or folder in the \Public folder so all the other people who use your computer can get at it. The \Public folder is available to other people in your homegroup (see the nearby sidebar), if you have one, but you have little control over who, specifically, can get at the files and folders.

>> **Share individual files or folders, without moving them anywhere.** When you share a file or folder, you can tell Windows 10 to share the folder with everyone in your homegroup, or you can specify exactly who can access the file or folder and whether they can just look at it or change it or delete it.

Using the \Public folder

You might think that simply moving a file or folder to the \Public folder would make it, well, public. At least to a first approximation, that's exactly how things work.

Any file or folder you put in the \Public folder, or any folder inside the \Public folder, can be viewed, changed, or deleted by all the people who are using your computer, regardless of which kind of account they may have and whether they're required to log in to your computer. In addition, anybody who can get into your computer through the network will have unlimited access. The \Public folder is (if you'll pardon a rather stretched analogy) a big cookie jar, open to everybody who is in the kitchen.

(For more details, and important information about Public networks and big-company domains, check out *Networking All-in-One For Dummies*, 6th Edition, by Doug Lowe [Wiley].)

TIP

Follow these easy steps to move a file or folder from one of the built-in personal folders (Desktop, Documents, Downloads, Music, Pictures, or Videos) into its corresponding location in one of the \Public folders:

1. **Tap or click the File Explorer icon in the taskbar.**

2. **Navigate to the file or folder that you want to move into the \Public folder.**

   In Figure 1-18, I double-clicked the Quick Access Pictures folder to get to my Pictures.

3. **Right-click the folder or file you want to move, and choose Cut.**

   In this case, I wanted to move the _Leonhard Family Photos folder, so I cut it.

4. **Navigate to the \Public folder where you want to move the folder or file.**

   This is more difficult than you might think. In general, on the left of File Explorer, double-click This PC, then scroll way down and double-click or tap Local Disk (C:). Then double-click Users, then Public. You see the list of Public folders shown in Figure 1-19.

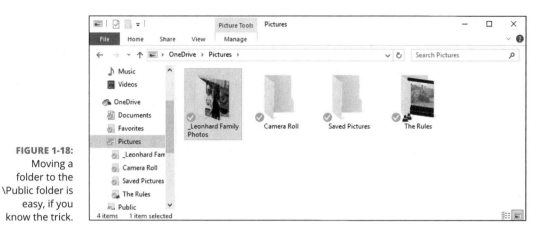

FIGURE 1-18:
Moving a
folder to the
\Public folder is
easy, if you
know the trick.

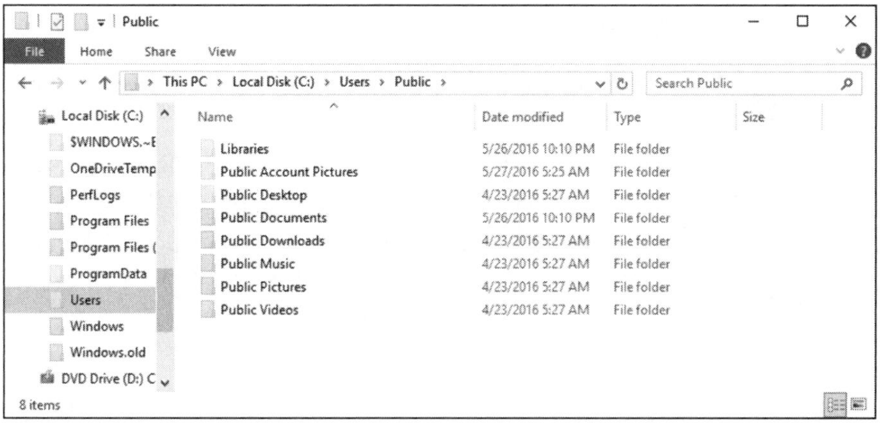

FIGURE 1-19:
Your \Public
folders live here.

Running Your Desktop
from Start to Finish

5. **Double-click the \Public folder you want to use. Then right-click inside the folder, and choose Paste.**

In this case, I double-clicked Public Pictures and pasted the _Leonhard Family Photos into the Public Pictures folder. From that point on, the photos are available to anybody who uses my computer and to people who connect to my computer using homegroups. (It may also be available to other computers connected to your network, workgroup, or domain, depending on various network settings. See *Networking All-in-One For Dummies* for specific examples.)

Recycling

When you delete a file, it doesn't go to that Big Bit Bucket in the Sky. An intermediate step exists between deletion and the Big Bit Bucket. It's called purgatory — oops. Wait a sec. Wrong book. (*Existentialism For Dummies*, anybody?) Let me try that again. Ahem.

The step between deletion and the Big Bit Bucket is the Recycle Bin.

When you delete a file or folder from your hard drive — whether by selecting the file or folder in File Explorer and pressing Delete or by right-clicking and choosing Delete — Windows doesn't actually delete anything. It marks the file or folder as being deleted but, other than that, doesn't touch it.

WARNING

Files and folders on USB key drives, SD cards, and network drives don't go into limbo when they're deleted. The Recycle Bin doesn't work on USB key drives, SD cards, or drives attached to other computers on your network. That said, if you accidentally wipe out the data on your key drive or camera memory card, there is hope. See the discussion of the Recuva program in Book 10, Chapter 5.

To rummage around in the Recycle Bin, and possibly bring a file back to life, follow these steps:

1. **Double-click the Recycle Bin icon on the Windows desktop (and shown in the margin).**

   File Explorer opens the Recycle Bin, shown in Figure 1-20. You may have to click the Recycle Bin's Tools tab at the top to bring up the ribbon.

2. **To restore a file or folder (sometimes Windows calls it *undeleting*), click the file or folder and then click Restore the Selected Items in the ribbon.**

   You can select a bunch of files or folders by holding down Ctrl as you click.

TIP

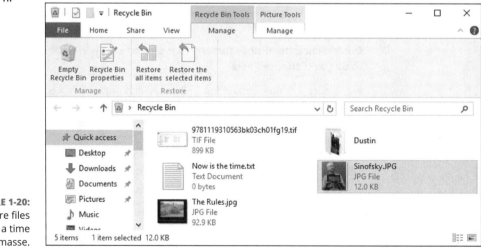

FIGURE 1-20: Restore files one at a time or en masse.

If you set things up properly, Windows 10 maintains shadow copies of previous versions of many kinds of files. If you can't find what you want in the Recycle Bin, follow the steps in Book 8, Chapter 1 to see whether you can dig something out of the Windows Time Machine.

To reclaim the space that the files and folders in the Recycle Bin are using, click the Empty the Recycle Bin icon. Windows asks whether you really, truly want to get rid of those files permanently. If you say Yes, they're gone.

Creating Shortcuts

Sometimes, life is easier with shortcuts. (As long as the shortcuts work, anyway.) So, too, in the world of Windows, where shortcuts point to things that can be started. You may set up a shortcut to a Word document and put it on your desktop. Double-click the shortcut and Word starts with the document loaded, as if you double-clicked the document in File Explorer.

You can set up shortcuts that point to the following items:

>> Old-fashioned Windows programs (er, apps), of any kind (I haven't yet found a way to put a shortcut for a Universal Windows app on the desktop, but for that you have tiles.)

>> Web addresses, such as www.dummies.com

>> Documents, spreadsheets, databases, PowerPoint presentations, and anything else that can be started in File Explorer by double-clicking it

>> Specific chunks of text (called *scraps*) inside documents, spreadsheets, databases, and presentations, for example

>> Folders (including the weird folders inside digital cameras, the Fonts folder, and others that you may not think of)

>> Drives (hard drives, CD drives, and key drives, for example)

>> Other computers on your network, and drives and folders on those computers, as long they're shared

>> Printers (including printers attached to other computers on your network), scanners, cameras, and other pieces of hardware

>> Network connections, interface cards, and the like

You have many different ways to create shortcuts. In many cases, you can go into File Explorer, right-click a file, drag it to the desktop, and choose Create Link here.

Here's a more general-purpose method that works for, say, websites:

1. **Right-click a blank area on the desktop, and choose New ⇨ Shortcut.**

   The Create Shortcut wizard appears, as shown in Figure 1-21.

2. **In the top box, type the name or location of the program (not Universal Windows app), file, folder, drive, computer, or Internet address. Click Next.**

   Windows asks you for a name for the shortcut.

3. **Give the shortcut a memorable name, and click Finish.**

   Windows places an icon for the program, file, folder, drive, computer, website, document . . . whatever . . . on the desktop.

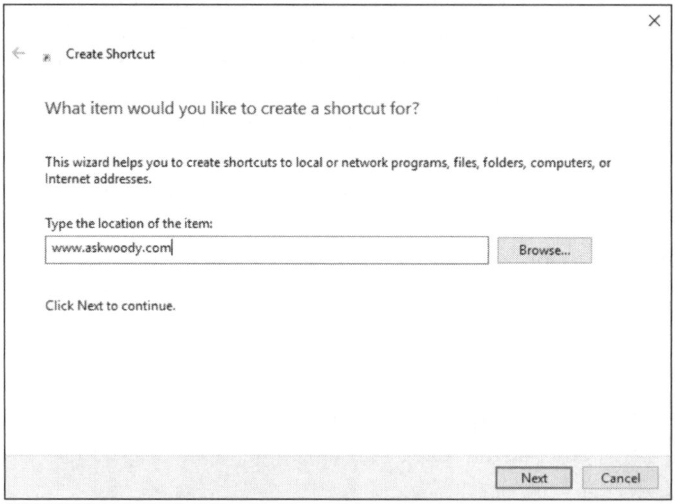

✕

← 🔲 Create Shortcut

What item would you like to create a shortcut for?

This wizard helps you to create shortcuts to local or network programs, files, folders, computers, or Internet addresses.

Type the location of the item:

| www.askwoody.com| | Browse... |

Click Next to continue.

| Next | Cancel |

FIGURE 1-21: Create shortcuts the old-fashioned manual way.

Anytime I double-click the AskWoody icon on my desktop, the default browser pops up and puts me on the www.AskWoody.com main page.

You can use a similar procedure for setting up shortcuts to any file, folder, program, or document on your computer or on any networked computer.

TECHNICAL STUFF

Believe it or not, Windows thrives on shortcuts. They're everywhere, lurking just beneath the surface. For example, every single entry on the Start menu is a (cleverly disguised) shortcut. The icons on the taskbar are all shortcuts. Most of File Explorer is based on shortcuts — although they're hidden where you can't reach them. Even the Universal Windows app icons work with shortcuts; they're just hard to find. So don't be afraid to experiment with shortcuts. In the worst-case scenario, you can always delete them. Doing so gets rid of the shortcut; it doesn't touch the original file.

Keying Keyboard Shortcuts

As I mention in Book 2, Chapter 1, Windows 10 has loads of keyboard shortcuts, but I don't use very many of them.

REMEMBER

Here are the keyboard shortcuts that everyone should know. They've been around for a long, long time:

- **Ctrl+C** copies whatever you've selected and puts it on the Clipboard. On a touchscreen, you can do the same thing in most applications by tapping and holding down, and then choosing Copy.

- **Ctrl+X** does the same thing but removes the selected items — a cut. Again, you can tap and hold down, and Cut should appear in the menu.

- **Ctrl+V** pastes whatever is in the Clipboard to the current cursor location. Tap and hold down usually works.

- **Ctrl+A** selects everything, although sometimes it's hard to tell what "everything" means — different applications handle Ctrl+A differently. Tap and hold down usually works here, too.

- **Ctrl+Z** usually undoes whatever you just did. Few touch-enabled apps have a tap-and-hold-down alternative; you usually have to find Undo on a ribbon or menu.

- When you're typing, **Ctrl+B**, **Ctrl+I**, and **Ctrl+U** usually flip your text over to Bold, Italic, or Underline, respectively. Hit the same key combination again, and you flip back to normal.

Sleep: Perchance to Dream

Aye, there's the rub.

Windows 10 has been designed so that it doesn't need to be turned off.

TECHNICAL STUFF

Okay, that's a bit of an overstatement. Sometimes, you have to restart your computer to let patches kick in. Sometimes, you plan to be gone for a week and need to give the beast a blissful rest. But by and large, you don't need to shut off a Windows 10 computer — the power management schemes are very green.

Laptops and tablets are a different story altogether. Most laptops, when they're working properly, will shut themselves off shortly after you fold them together. Many tablets will power off, too. If yours doesn't, you should take the initiative and shut the machine down before stashing it away.

The only power setting most people need to fiddle with is the length of time Windows allows before it turns the screen black. Here's the easy way to adjust your screen blackout time:

1. **Click or tap the Start icon and then the Settings icon.**

2. **Choose System and then Power & Sleep.**

   Windows brings up the Power & Sleep dialog box shown in Figure 1-22.

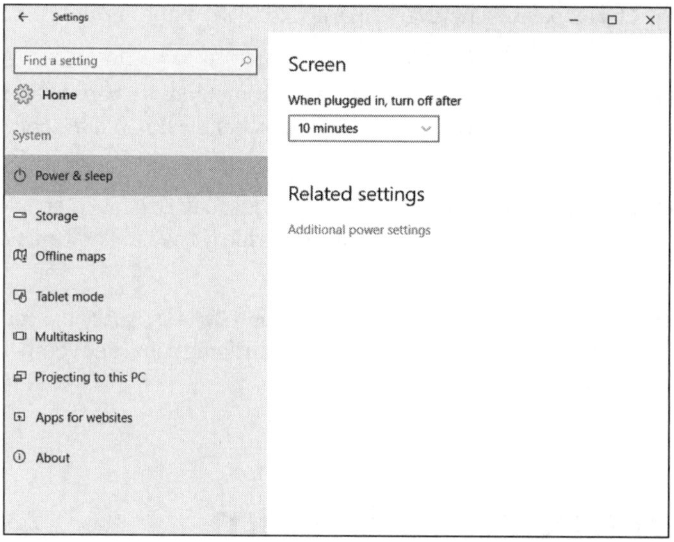

FIGURE 1-22:
Tell your machine how long to run off to never-never-land.

3. **In the drop-down box at the top, choose whatever time you like.**

   Your changes take effect immediately.

You can click the Additional Power Settings link, if you want to open up the old-fashioned Control Panel pane for power settings.

Although Microsoft has published voluminous details about the power down and power up sequences, I haven't seen any details about how long it takes before your PC actually goes to sleep. In theory, that shouldn't matter too much because the wake-ups are so fast.

ASK WOODY.COM

Microsoft recently published some recommendations that I found fascinating. To truly conserve energy with a desktop computer, be aggressive with the monitor idle time (no longer than two minutes), and make sure that you don't have a screen saver enabled. If you want to conserve energy with a notebook or netbook, your top priority is to reduce the screen brightness!

Chapter 2

Personalizing the Start Menu

I f you're an experienced Windows user, chances are good that the first time you saw the Windows 8 Start screen, you wondered who put an iPad on it. However, if you're an experienced iPad user, chances are good that the first time you worked with the Win8 Start screen, you went screaming for your iPad.

Windows 10 has, I'm convinced, improved upon the Windows 8 experience greatly. If you have a mouse, the Windows 10 Start menu — the screen that almost everybody sees when he or she clicks the Start icon, and the screen you'll come back to over and over again — defines and anchors Windows. Like it or not. See Figure 2-1.

If you don't have a mouse or touchpad — if your machine is touch-only, and Windows 10 recognized that fact — you're acquainted with, and probably live in, the tablet mode screen shown in Figure 2-2.

My advice, if you don't like those newfangled Start tiles, is to give it a real workout for a month or two. I don't expect that you'll end up singing hosannas about the tiles. But I do expect that you'll warm up to it a little bit — and, like me, you may even miss it when you go back to Windows 7. That goes double if you can use Windows 10 on a touch-friendly tablet.

FIGURE 2-1:
The normal
mouse-and-
keyboard
version of the
Start menu,
as seen on a
Dell XPS-15.

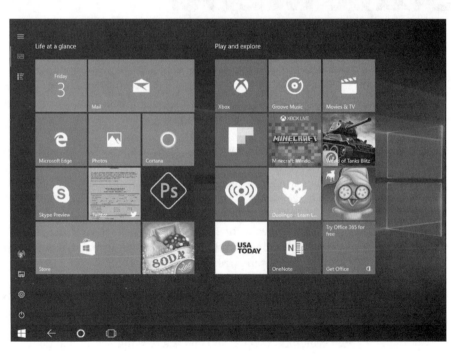

FIGURE 2-2:
The tablet mode
Start screen.

TIP

In this chapter, I take you through the Start menu, from beginning to end. It's a bit confusing because changes in the desktop's Start menu (refer to Figure 2-1) affects the appearance of the tablet mode Start screen (refer to Figure 2-2).

Hey, if you can get your thumb and all your pinkies on the screen simultaneously, touch has the mouse beat five to one. Sorta.

Touring the Start Menu

The very first screen you see when you click or tap the Start icon, the Start menu (refer to Figure 2-1), is designed to be at the center of your Windows universe. Don't let the fact that the right side's intentionally made to look like a smartphone screen deter you in the least.

You've probably sworn at the Start menu a few times already, but if you can keep a civil tongue, permit me to expound a bit:

>> The left side of the Start menu (refer to Figure 2-1) consists of a handful of icons that you're likely to use all the time.

If you're in tablet mode — identifiable because you don't see a list of program names (refer to Figure 2-2) — click or tap the three-line (hamburger) icon in the upper-left corner (and shown in the margin). The full left side of the Start menu unfolds, as shown in Figure 2-3.

A third mode, called full-screen start, looks and acts much like tablet mode. It also has a hamburger menu that brings up the left side. See Book 3, Chapter 1 for details.

>> Tiles (the squares on the right side of the screen) appear in four sizes: large, wide, medium, and small (rocket science). In Figure 2-4, I changed my tiles around a bit to make most advertising tiles small (Flipboard, iHeartRadio, DuoLingo, Farmville, World of Tanks, Try Office, Candy Crush Crapola, Adobe Photoshop Express, and a come-on for Skype because the Universal Windows version doesn't work yet). Comparing sizes, the Calendar tile is medium, Mail is wide, and Weather looms large. Many tiles that come from Microsoft are live tiles, with active content (latest news, stock prices, date, temperature, email messages) that changes the face of the tile.

>> Tiles are bunched into groups, which may or may not have group names. Figures 2-1 through 2-4 show two groups: one marked Life at a Glance, the other marked Play and Explore. Don't shoot me. Those are the names Microsoft gave them.

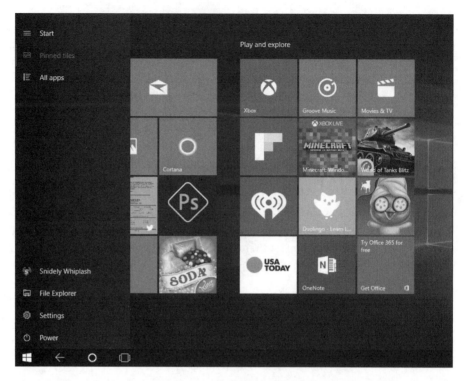

FIGURE 2-3:
In tablet mode, the left side of Start sits under the hamburger icon.

FIGURE 2-4:
After a few swift changes, your Start menu can look like this.

>> Somewhere near the middle of the far-left bar, you see your picture. Hover your mouse cursor over the picture and you see either your Windows username or (if you're logged in with a Microsoft account) your full name. For a description of the Microsoft account and the pros and cons of using one, see Book 2, Chapter 5.

Modifying the Start Menu

Windows 7 has a marvelously malleable Start menu. You can click and drag and poke and rearrange it every which way but loose. I particularly enjoyed setting up nested folders and having them show up as cascading items on the Start menu. But that was then.

The left side of Windows 10's Start menu, by comparison, has a very rigid format that can be changed only in a few specific, preprogrammed ways (see Figure 2-4). Customizing the Start menu in Win10 is nothing like customizing Start in Win7. (And, of course, Windows 8/8.1 didn't *have* a Start menu.)

Changing your picture

I start with an easy change to the Start screen: changing the picture on the far left edge.

Here's how to change your picture:

1. **Tap or click your picture, and select Change Account Settings.**

   Windows takes you to a familiar-looking place in the PC Settings hierarchy, as shown in Figure 2-5.

2. **If you already have a picture in mind, follow these steps (if you'd rather take a picture, continue to Step 3):**

   a. At the bottom, choose Browse for One, and navigate to the picture.

   b. When you find the picture you want, select it, and tap or click Choose Image.

   You return to the PC Settings location shown in Figure 2-5, with your new picture in place.

3. **If you'd rather take a picture with your computer's webcam, comb your hair, pluck your eyebrows, and tap or click Webcam (in that order).**

   In any case, however you create your new picture, it takes effect immediately — no need to click OK or anything of the sort.

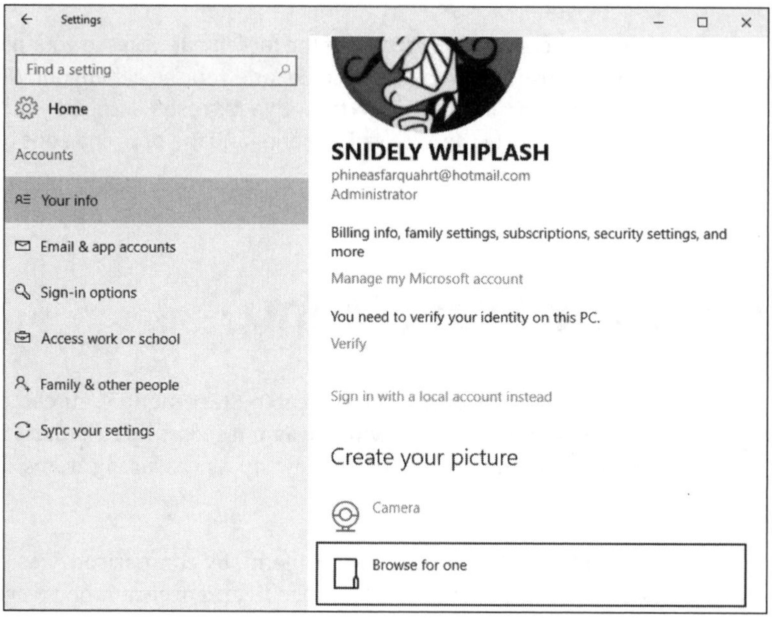

Settings

Find a setting

⚙ Home

Accounts

≈ Your info

✉ Email & app accounts

🔑 Sign-in options

✉ Access work or school

👤 Family & other people

🔄 Sync your settings

SNIDELY WHIPLASH
phineasfarquahrt@hotmail.com
Administrator

Billing info, family settings, subscriptions, security settings, and more

Manage my Microsoft account

You need to verify your identity on this PC.

Verify

Sign in with a local account instead

Create your picture

◎ Camera

▢ Browse for one

FIGURE 2-5:
Change your
picture in the
Settings app.

ASK
WOODY.COM

Want a weird picture? Any picture you can find on the Internet and download to your computer is fair game — as long as you aren't violating any copyrights.

Manipulating the Most Used section

You would think that the next part of the Start menu — Most Used — would contain links to the apps and locations that you use most often. Ha. Silly mortal.

Microsoft (and, likely, your hardware manufacturer) salts the list: They put items in there that don't deserve to be there, and they keep items on the list long after they should've disappeared. I've experimented with it for ages, and the list of which items appear on the list, and how rapidly they fall off, seems to be controlled by some sort of counter — a counter that isn't updated correctly all the time.

**TECHNICAL
STUFF**

At this point, the only action I can find that you can perform on the list is to remove a link you don't like. Just right-click (or tap and hold) an entry you don't like, and choose Don't Show in This List.

Alternatively, you can get rid of the list entirely. See the next section.

Controlling the left-side lists

Although you can't pin individual programs on the left side of Start, as you could in Win7, you do have some high-level say in what appears on the left.

To see the choices on offer, choose the Start icon and then the Settings icon (both shown in the margin). Choose Personalization, and then, on the left, choose Start. (Yeah, the sequence starts and ends with Start.) You see the Start menu options shown in Figure 2-6.

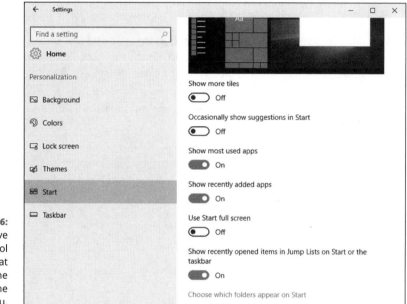

FIGURE 2-6:
You do have some control over what appears on the left side of the Start menu.

Some of those choices are obscure. Here's what they mean:

>> **Show More Tiles:** Normally, the tiled area on the right of the Start screen displays columns that are three normal-sized tiles wide. Slide this setting On and the area becomes four columns wide. It takes a little more real estate off your screen, but most people with most monitors can handle four readily.

>> **Occasionally Show Suggestions on Start:** One of Microsoft's big advertising "features" in Windows 10 sticks a purposefully chosen app on the left side, in the list of apps. If you ever wondered why Microsoft keeps track of what you do in Win10, here's one of the reasons. Microsoft may make money when you click the suggested app, they may put specific apps there to fulfill contractual obligations, or they may use it to nudge you once again to install a Microsoft app. On by default (I wonder why), you can safely turn it off.

>> **Show Most Used Apps:** That's the salted most-recently-used set that I talked about in the preceding section. I find it useful — you may not.

>> **Show Recently Added Apps:** When you install a new program, er, app, Start notifies you by putting at the top of the Start apps list a new entry labelled Recently Added. See Pandora in Figure 2-4. The word *New* also appears under Recently Added apps, in the main apps list. It's an innocuous setting that saves some time, if you can't remember or figure out where your new app falls alphabetically.

>> **Use Start Full Screen:** Full-screen start is a compromise between the regular Start menu and the tablet mode Start screen. It's unlikely you'll want to use it, but I discuss the effect in Book 3, Chapter 1.

>> **Show Recently Opened Items in Jump Lists on Start or the Taskbar:** This option lets you, for example, jump directly to a specific document when you click the Word link or play a specific video when starting VLC.

Click the Choose Which Folders Appear on Start link, and another set of options appears, as shown in Figure 2-7.

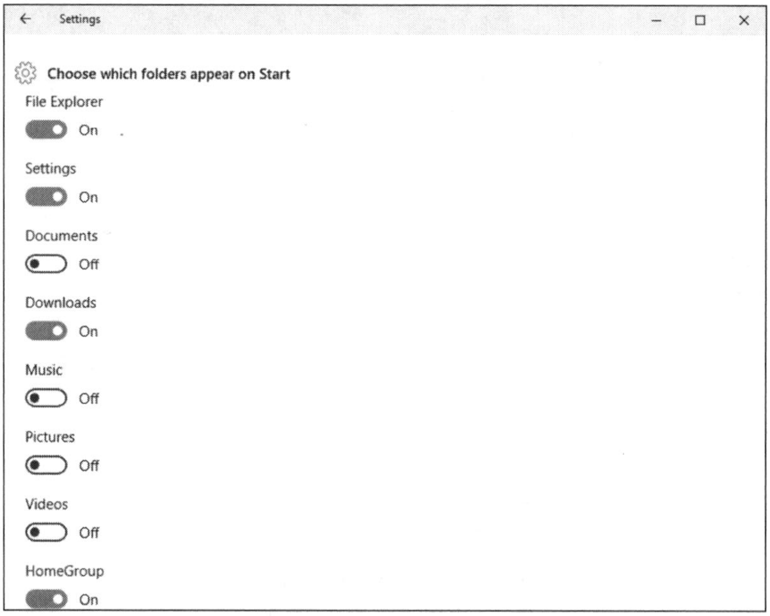

FIGURE 2-7:
You can add a long list of icons to the far left of the Start menu.

Table 2-1 shows you what each of the settings means.

TABLE 2-1   **Start Menu Customizing**

Choose This	And the Start Menu Starts
File Explorer	File Explorer as usual
Settings	The Settings app
Documents	File Explorer with your Documents folder (not your Documents library) open
Downloads	File Explorer at your personal Downloads folder
Music	File Explorer in your Music folder (not your Music library)
Pictures	File Explorer in your Pictures folder
Videos	File Explorer in your Videos folder
Homegroup	File Explorer with homegroup selected on the left
Network	File Explorer with Network selected on the left
Personal folder	File Explorer at \Users\<*yourname*>

Circumnavigating the Start apps list

After the Most Used list, the advertising (oops, the "occasionally show suggestions" entry), and the Recently Added list, Windows starts listing all the programs/apps installed on your computer. I call it the *Start apps list* — an alphabetized list of programs installed on your computer. In some cases, the programs are arranged in logical groups (apparently corresponding to instructions in the programs' installer). Most of the time, though, you may spend a while trying to find what you seek.

In Figure 2-8, for example, you can see how the old Control Panel doesn't appear under *C*; it's under *W* for *Windows System.*

Count on all sorts of oddities. With my copy of Office 2016, the link for Word appears under *M* for *Microsoft Office.* If you have Office 365, you'll probably find Word under *W.*

WARNING

There doesn't appear to be any way to rearrange the entries in the Start apps list — another Windows 7 feature that's sorely missed. You can uninstall some of the programs by right-clicking and choosing Uninstall, but there's no way to move the entries around, create new groups or coalesce old ones, rename, or shuffle in any way.

You can, however, click one of the alphabetic headers in the list — such as the *W* in Figure 2-8 — to bring up an unintelligent phone book that lets you skip to a specific letter. See Figure 2-9.

FIGURE 2-8:
Looking for
Internet Explorer?
Check under Win-
dows Accessories.

FIGURE 2-9:
This is all the
organizing the
Start apps list
can give.

If you right-click (or tap and hold down) one of the apps in the Start apps list, you're usually given two choices:

>> **Pin to Start:** Creates a new tile on the right side of the Start menu that runs the program. (Yeah, I know it's confusing: *Start,* to me, means the left side of the Start menu, and I bet it does to you, too. Still, that's the terminology Microsoft uses.)

>> **Pin to Taskbar:** You have to click More first. This option creates an icon on the bottom of the taskbar, which also runs the program.

In some cases, right-clicking a program gives you the option to uninstall the program or run it as if you were an administrator (see Book 2, Chapter 4), or both.

WARNING

Also in some cases, you can click an app in the Start apps list and drag it over to the right, tiled part of the Start menu. I've had problems with that in the past, where the app disappears from the Start apps list and it won't come back. Beware.

Resizing the Start Menu

The Start menu can be resized, either taller and shorter (vertically) or wider and skinnier (horizontally). If you click the upper edge of the Start screen in Figure 2-4 and slide it down, you see the screen shown in Figure 2-10.

FIGURE 2-10:
Adjust the Start
menu vertically.

In general, you can shorten the Start menu only so most of the most used apps show. Beyond that, it won't shrink. There's also a limit to the height of the Start menu, which varies according to screen size.

Similarly, you can widen the Start menu to the width of two (sometimes more) columns of tiles, or squish it to one column, as you can see in Figure 2-11.

FIGURE 2-11:
Widen or squish
the Start menu
by dragging
the edges.

That appears to be the extent of the Start menu shrinking-expanding range. Remember that you can adjust the number of tiles in each column from three to four, using the Show More Tiles setting described earlier in this chapter under "Controlling the left side lists."

Changing Tiles on the Start Menu

You can click and drag tiles anyplace you like on the right side of the Start menu. Drag a tile way down to the bottom, and you start a new group. Pin a new program to the Start screen (see the preceding section), and its tile magically appears, probably in a new group made just for that tile.

You can change every tile, too. The actions available depend on what the creator of the tile permits. Here's how to mangle a tile:

1. **Right-click (or tap and hold down) the tile you want to change.**

In Figure 2-12, I right-clicked the Weather tile. A list of actions appears.

FIGURE 2-12:
You can control
tiles individually.

2. **See Table 2-2 to determine which action you want to take, and select the desired action.**

You can easily delete any tile, and you can resize many of them.

TABLE 2-2 **Tile Actions**

Tile Action Name	What the Action Does
Unpin from Start	Removes the tile from the right side of the Start menu. Doesn't affect the app itself. If you later change your mind, you can right-click the app in the Start apps list and choose Pin to Start.
Uninstall	Removes all vestiges of the program, using the Control Panel's Remove Programs option. This option isn't available for programs that come with Windows, nor is it available for advertising tiles that point to apps you haven't installed yet.
Resize	Makes the tile icon large (four times the size of a normal tile, such as the Weather tile in the figure), wide (the size of the Mail tile), medium (the size of the Calendar tile), or small (one-quarter the size of a medium tile).
Pin to Taskbar	Puts an icon for the app on the desktop's taskbar (see Book 3, Chapter 3).
Turn Live Tile Off/On	Stops or starts the animation displayed on the tile. Stopping the active content can help reduce battery drain, but the big benefit is stifling obnoxious flickering tiles — of which there are many.

3. **If you would like to put a name above any of the groups of tiles, simply type it in the indicated spot.**

For example, you can change Life at a Glance (at the top of the left column of tiles) to Another Sticky Day in Paradise by clicking (or tapping) Life at a Glance and typing. The changes you make take effect immediately, and they carry through on both the traditional Start menu and over in tablet mode.

Organizing Your Start Menu Tiles

The beauty of the Start menu tiles is that, within strictly defined limits, you can customize them like crazy. As long as you're happy working with the basic building blocks — four sizes of tiles, and groups — you can slice and dice till the cows come home.

ASK
WOODY.COM

The hard part about corralling the Start menu is figuring out what works best for you.

Add, add, add your tiles

Some people never use the Start menu's tiles. But if you do use them, it's easier to get organized if you put all of them on the table, as it were, before trying to sort them out.

TIP

You don't really need to have *any* tiles in the Start menu. You can right-click and choose Unpin from Start and get rid of every single one. Unfortunately, having done that, you can't make the Start screen narrower, but such is life.

The process for sticking tiles in the Start menu couldn't be simpler, although it may take an hour or two. Click the Start icon (shown in the margin), and go through your apps one by one. Right-click any apps that amuse you, and choose Pin to Start. The tile appears on the right.

At the same time, you can also right-click (or tap and hold) and choose to put the app on the taskbar. Or, in most cases, you can drag the app onto the desktop and create a link to the app on the desktop.

The only significant decision you need to make is whether you want a specific app among the tiles on the Start menu, on the desktop, on the taskbar (see Book 3 Chapter 3), or on all three. As a general rule, I put my most-used apps on the task-bar, put tiles that convey useful information (such as Weather, News, and even Photos — for bringing back memories) on the Start menu, and only rarely stick anything on the desktop.

Before you start working with the tiles on your Start menu, it'll behoove you to go through your Start apps list and pull out the tiles you want or need.

Forming and naming your groups

After you have all your tiles on the right side of the Start menu, it's easy to get the menagerie organized. Try this:

1. **Tap (or click) and drag your tiles so similar tiles are in the same group.**

For example, if you use Mail, Messaging, People, and Calendar all day long, put them in the same group. If you have Office installed, go through the procedure described in the preceding section to move the tiles you want over to the right side of the Start screen.

Don't worry just yet if the groups are in the wrong sequence: There are easy ways to move entire groups. Just concentrate on getting your similar tiles into the same group.

If you have programs that you look at constantly because they have important information — stock market results, your music playlist, Skype notifications, or new mail — keep them in one or two groups.

If you need to create a new group, drag a tile all the way to the bottom. You see a faint vertical bar, which indicates that a new group has just been formed. Drop the tile below the bar.

2. **To give your groups names, click or tap the existing name (which may be Name Group) and type over the name.**

In Figure 2-13, I put together all the tiles I like to glance at to see how things are going, and gave the group the name The Important Stuff.

Personalizing the
Start Menu

FIGURE 2-13:
Here's my
homemade
collection of tiles
that I use to keep
up-to-date at
a glance.

3. **To move the group, click or tap the two-thirds-of-a-hamburger icon in the upper right of the group, and drag it anywhere you like on the right side of the Start menu.**

I put this group in the upper-left corner. Then I put together another group of the tools I use most often and called the group Tools.

4. **Click or tap and drag, and resize the Start menu if you like.**

Move tiles around any way you like. Don't be bashful! It's your machine. And if you find that you don't like something, change it around a bit and see if you like an alternative.

IN THIS CHAPTER

**Putting shortcuts on the desktop —
the advanced course**

Changing desktop colors and pictures

**Customizing the taskbar in
unexpected, and useful, ways**

Chapter 3

Personalizing the Desktop and Taskbar

t's your desktop. Do with it what you will.

In Book 3, Chapter 2, I talk about gussying up your Start menu — the left side, with icons, the middle, with links, and the right side, with tiles. This chapter looks at the rest of your desktop, what you can do about it, and how you can grab Windows 10 by the throat and shake it up a bit. Player's gotta play, play, play, play, and tweakers gotta tweak, tweak, tweak, tweak.

Shake it up.

With Windows 10's tiles now basically replacing (and improving upon) Windows 7's gadgets, there are fewer reasons to use the desktop now than ever before. Still, many installers put links for their own programs on the desktop, avoiding Start menu tiles like the plague, and you may have your own reasons for using Desktop shortcuts.

No matter what your bias, the taskbar remains an excellent place to put your most heavily used icons.

Decking out the Desktop

The Windows 10 desktop may look simple, but it isn't. In Figure 3-1, for example, you can see the Start menu and the taskbar at the bottom, with an icon for the Recycle Bin, a picture file inside a running Universal Windows app, and the action/notification center on the right.

FIGURE 3-1:
The desktop is
a complicated
place.

Underneath everything is a background picture (the Windows window, in this case). And there is subtle blurring between the windows.

Windows lays down the desktop in layers — and paints the mouse cursor on top of all of them.

You have a handful of options when it comes to making the desktop your kind of place. Let me step you through them.

1. **Click or tap the Start icon, the Settings icon, Personalization. On the left, select Background.**

   Windows shows you the Background personalization page.

2. **If you're going to use a picture that stretches all the way across the screen as your background (what we used to call wallpaper), skip to Step 5.**

   If your background doesn't fill up the entire screen, you should first set a background color.

3. **In the Background drop-down box, choose Solid Color.**

   The dialog box shown in Figure 3-2 appears.

4. **Pick a color.**

   At this point you're limited to just the colors that appears in the standard colors box. After you've picked a new color, it should appear in the Preview box and on the screen itself.

5. **If you want to use a picture as your background, in the Background box, choose Picture.**

   That sets up everything to not only pick a pic but also to center it, as shown in Figure 3-3.

   If you'd rather use a whole bunch of pictures as a slideshow on your Start screen, in the Background box, choose Slideshow. You must have all the pictures in one album or folder; see Book 4, Chapter 3 for a discussion of albums.

TIP

6. **Choose a picture from the ones on offer, or click Browse and go out (using File Explorer) to find one you like better.**

   You can use a picture in any common picture file format.

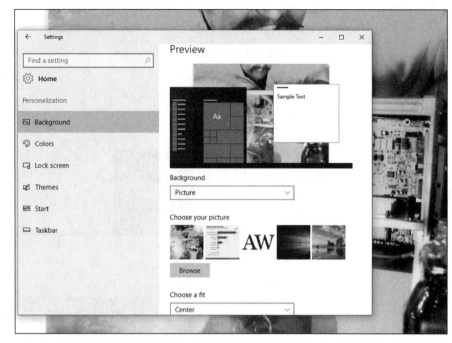

FIGURE 3-3:
Use a picture as
your background.

7. **If your picture is too big or too small to fit on the screen, you can tell Windows how to shoehorn it into the available space.**

    Use the Choose a Fit drop-down list at the bottom of the Desktop Background dialog box. Details are in Table 3-1.

8. **Click X in the upper-right corner of the Desktop Background dialog box.**

    Your changes take effect immediately.

TABLE 3-1 Picture Position Settings

Setting	What It Means
Fill	Windows expands the picture to fit the entire screen and then crops the edges. The picture doesn't appear distorted, but the sides or top and bottom may get cut off.
Fit	The screen is letterboxed. Windows makes the picture as big as possible within the confines of the screen and then shows the base color in stripes along the top and bottom (or left and right). No distortion occurs, and you see the entire picture, but you also see ugly strips on two edges.
Stretch	The picture is stretched to fit the screen. Expect distortions.
Tile	The picture is repeated as many times as necessary to fill the screen. If it's too large to fit on the screen, you see the Fill options.
Center	This one is the same as the Fit setting except that the letterboxing goes on all four sides.
Span	Expand the picture to fit as many monitors as are active, left to right.

Windows lets you right-click a picture — a JPG or GIF file — using File Explorer, and choose Set as Desktop Background. When you do so, Windows makes a copy of the picture and puts it in the C:\Users\<username>\AppData\Roaming\Microsoft\Windows\Recent Items folder and then sets the picture as your background.

You can also control a few aspects of the colors on your desktop, although the pickings are meager, compared to earlier versions of Windows. Here's how to colorize your life:

1. **Click or tap the Start icon, the Settings icon, Personalization. On the left, choose Colors.**

   The Desktop Colors dialog box shown in Figure 3-4 appears.

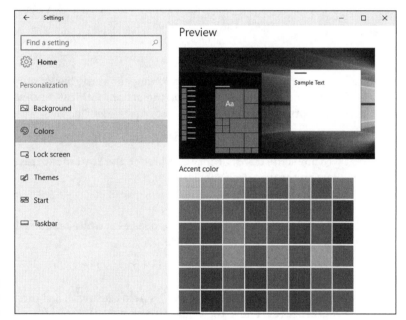

FIGURE 3-4:
Choose a second-
ary color here.

2. **Do one of the following:**

   ● **If you want to let Windows choose an accent color for you:** Select the Automatically Pick an Accent Color from My Background option. The accent color will be used sporadically to highlight choices in menus, the background for navigational arrows, and other odd spots.

   ● **If you want to choose your own accent color:** Deselect the Automatically Pick an Accent Color from My Background option, and choose from a limited selection of colors.

WHAT HAPPENED TO DESKTOP THEMES?

Windows 10 still has a vestigial link to old-fashioned desktop themes: You can see the option in Figure 3-2, on the left. Themes are collections of the Windows desktop background, window color, sound scheme, and screen saver; you can simply choose among the offered themes.

At this moment, Themes don't sit front-and-center like they did in Windows 7. From Figure 3-2, click or tap Themes, and you're transported to the Control Panel's Themes applet. Although you can still save your current theme or bring up new ones, the old controls for individual parts of the theme are gone. In particular, there's no screen saver in Windows 10, and the color selections in Windows 10 are very limited.

It's unlikely to be a high priority, but at some point Microsoft may bring back Themes. Look for them in later versions of Windows 10.

3. **To have your chosen accent color appear as the background color on the Start menu, on the taskbar, on the action/notification center pane, and the battery charge indicator, turn that slider On.**

   Usually, Windows uses varying shades of gray for those colors.

4. **To put some transparency and blur on the Start menu, taskbar, and action center, turn that slider On.**

   I rather like the blurring effect.

5. **To make (almost) all the apps appear with white text on a black background, choose Dark app mode.**

   I prefer black-on-white, so I leave the option set on Light.

ASK
WOODY.COM

Of course, I'm still a fan of Windows 7's Aero Glass with its blurred edges and striking contrasts. Yes, I have the visual discernment of a cow. I can live with that. Moo.

Resolving Desktop Resolution

The best, biggest monitor in the world "don't mean jack" if you can't see the text on the screen. Windows contains a handful of utilities and settings that can help you whump your monitor upside the head and improve its appearance.

With apologies to Billy Crystal, sometimes it *is* more important to look good than to feel good.

Setting the screen resolution

I don't know how many people ask me how to fix this new monitor they just bought. The screen doesn't look right. Must be that %$#@! Windows, yes? The old monitor looked just fine.

Nine times out of ten, when somebody tells me that a new monitor doesn't look right, I ask whether the person adjusted the screen resolution. Invariably, the answer is no. So here's the quick answer to one of the questions I hear most.

REMEMBER

If you plug in a new monitor (or put together a new computer) and the screen looks fuzzy, the most likely culprit entails a mismatch between the resolution your computer expects and the resolution your monitor wants. To a first approximation, a screen resolution is just the number of dots that appear on the screen, usually expressed as two numbers: 1920x1080, for example. Every flat-panel screen has exactly one resolution that looks right and a zillion other resolutions that make things look like you fused your monitor with the end of a Coke bottle.

Setting the screen resolution is easy:

1. **Right-click any empty place on the desktop, and choose Display Settings.**

You see the Customize Your Display dialog box shown in Figure 3-5. (If you have more than one monitor or certain kinds of video cards, you may see multiple monitors in the top box.) You come back to this bunch of settings in Step 5. For now, zero in on the resolution.

2. **Click or tap the Advanced Display Settings link, at the bottom.**

You see the resolution setting part of Customizing, shown in Figure 3-6.

3. **Click the Resolution drop-down box, and choose the resolution you want to try.**

If there's a resolution marked (Recommended), that's the resolution your monitor manufacturer recommends. Nine times out of ten, it's your best choice. That's the easy part.

The hard part? If you don't see a (Recommended) resolution, you must figure out which resolution your monitor likes — its *native resolution.* Some monitors have the resolution printed on a sticker that may still adhere to the front. (Goo Gone works wonders.) All monitors have their native resolutions listed in the manual. (You do have your monitor's manual, yes? No, I don't either.)

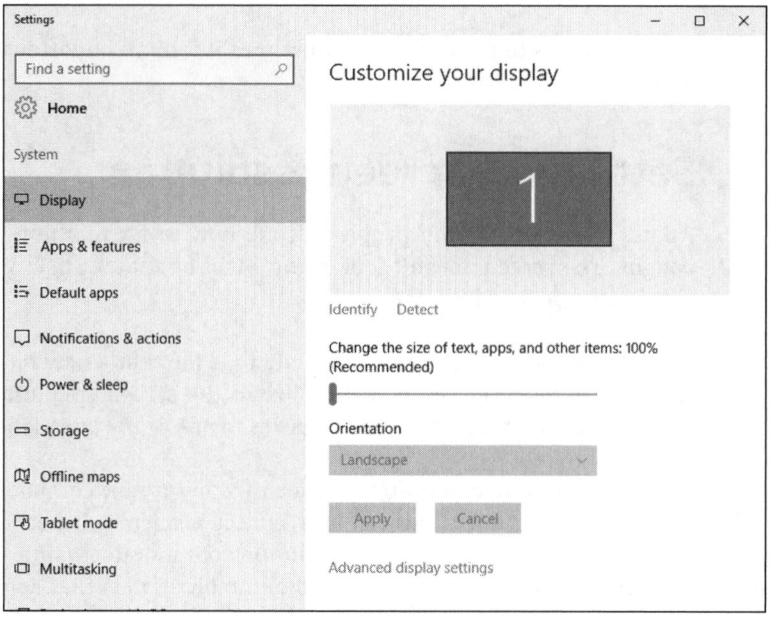

Settings   — □ ✕

Find a setting   🔍

⚙️ **Home**

System

🖵 **Display**

🗐 Apps & features

🖇 Default apps

🖵 Notifications & actions

⏻ Power & sleep

🖴 Storage

🏬 Offline maps

🖵 Tablet mode

🗗 Multitasking

Customize your display

Identify   Detect

Change the size of text, apps, and other items: 100%
(Recommended)

Orientation

Landscape   ⌄

Apply   Cancel

Advanced display settings

FIGURE 3-5:
Seeking clarity
the Windows way.

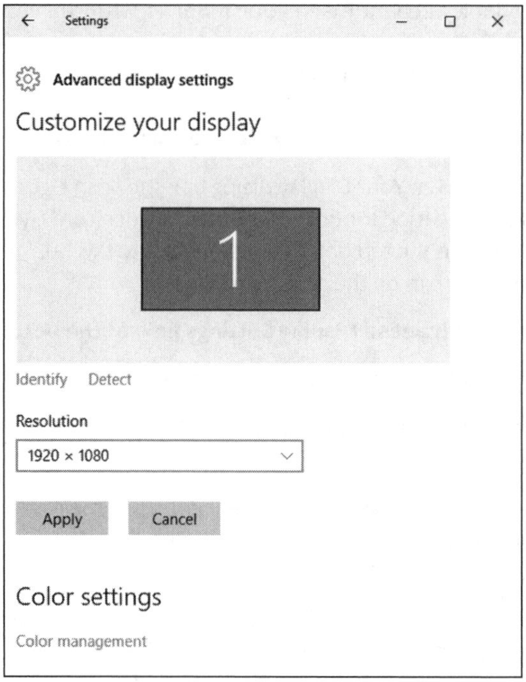

←   **Settings**   — □ ✕

⚙️ **Advanced display settings**

Customize your display

Identify   Detect

Resolution

1920 × 1080   ⌄

Apply   Cancel

Color settings

Color management

FIGURE 3-6:
Set the
resolution here.

TIP

If you don't know your monitor's native resolution, Google is your friend. Go to www.google.com and type *native resolution* followed by your monitor's model number, which you can (almost) always find engraved in the bezel or stuck on the side. For example, typing *native resolution U3011* immediately finds the native resolution for a Dell U3011 monitor.

If you have, uh, mature eyesight, you may find it helpful to ignore recommendations on tablets and bump up the resolution to make everything larger anyway.

4. **In the upper-left corner, click or tap the back arrow.**

    You return to Figure 3-5. I had you check the resolution first, because if you change it, everything else in this dialog box changes, too.

5. **If you find it difficult to read text on the monitor, you can move the slider to make everything bigger or smaller.**

**ASK
WOODY.COM**

If your eyes aren't what they used to be (mine never were), you may want to tell Windows to increase the size of text and other items on the screen. It's just enough boost to help, particularly if you're at an Internet cafe and forgot your glasses.

I strongly recommend that you use this setting with caution. Changing the magnification can cause older programs, in particular, to go bananas. The overall effect can be chilling. So take it slowly, test often, and go back to your default if things don't look or act right.

6. **If you want to lock the orientation of the display — make it portrait all the time, or landscape — change the Orientation drop-down box to Portrait.**

    It's unusual that you want to lock the orientation, but sometimes it happens — like when you're trying to read the news while skinning the cat. I mean the acrobatic maneuver, of course.

    That's all it takes. Your changes take effect immediately.

Using magnification

If you need more zoom than the font enlarger can offer, you can always use the Ease of Access tool called the Magnifier. As you can see in Figure 3-7, the Magnifier can make everything very big.

The Magnifier lets you zoom the entire screen by a factor of 200, 300, or 400 — or as high as you like.

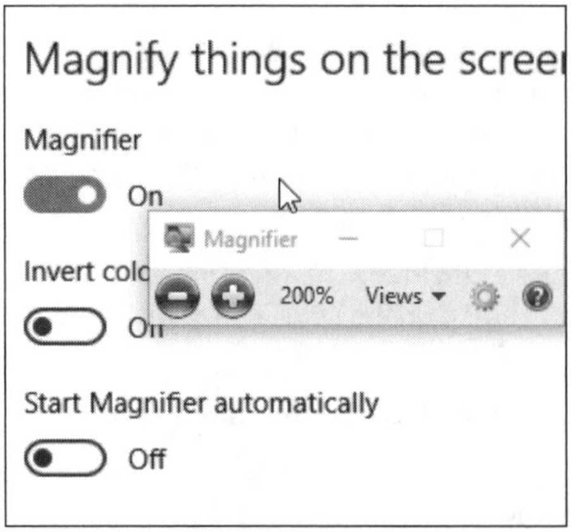

FIGURE 3-7:
The Magnifier
can help make
everything
onscreen
reeeeeeeeally big.

Note that magnifying doesn't increase the quality or resolution of text or pictures. It makes them bigger not finer. That *CSI* "David, can you make the picture sharper?" thing doesn't work with Windows. Sorry, Grissom.

REMEMBER

To use the Magnifier, do this:

1. **Click or tap the Start icon, the Settings icon, Ease of Access. On the left, choose Magnifier.**

2. **Slide the Magnifier setting to On.**

Everything immediately displays at twice its normal size — 200% in the parlance.

3. **Experiment with moving around. It's odd.**

Slide your mouse cursor all the way to the left or right to move the screen to the left or right. Same with up and down. This is one situation where a touchscreen really does help.

A small control shows up with buttons to increase and decrease magnification. (It turns into a magnifying glass icon if you don't use it immediately.)

4. **Click or tap the Views drop-down box on the controller, and choose Lens.**

The lens view, shown in Figure 3-8, lets you drag a viewing window across a regular-size screen and magnify what's under the window.

5. **Play with the settings to get the right combination for your eyesight.**

The settings are sticky, so when you come back to the Magnifier, it'll remember what settings you like best.

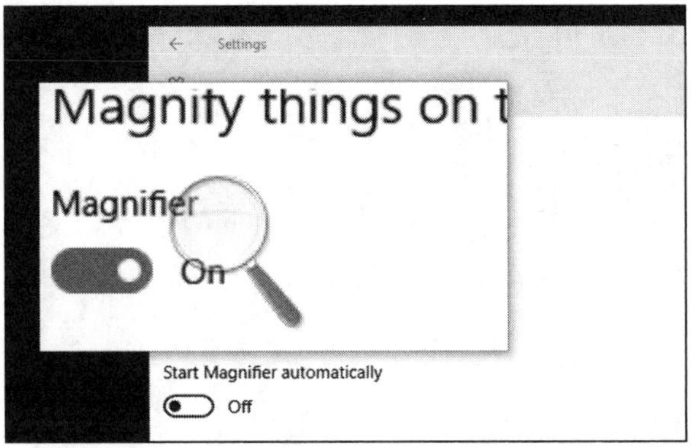

FIGURE 3-8:
The lens slides
across the
top of a normal-
sized view.

6. **To reduce the magnification, press the Windows key and – (minus) repeatedly.**

    That steps you down the magnification levels, until you reach the normal 100% magnification. To turn off magnification, go back to Step 1 and set the Magnifier slider to Off.

If these nostrums don't do the job, you should take advantage of the Windows high-contrast themes. They use color to make text, in particular, stand out. High-contrast themes are available from the Ease of Access dialog box on the left side.

WARNING

If you accidentally hit the Windows key and the + or − key, and your magnification changes mysteriously, now you know the culprit. Go to Ease of Access and turn off Magnifier.

Putting Icons and Shortcuts on the Desktop

Back in the day, if you wanted to get at a program (er, app) quickly, you put a shortcut for it on your desktop. Nowadays, life isn't quite so straightforward. Your choices are many — and that's a good thing.

To access a program/app quickly in Windows 10, you can do any of these:

TIP

>> **Stick a tile on the right side of the Start menu.** This is almost always pretty easy: You find the program (usually by going into the Start ⇨ All Apps menu, but also possibly through File Explorer, or maybe there's already a shortcut on your desktop that was put there when the app was installed). Right-click the program, and choose Pin to Start. See Figure 3-9.

FIGURE 3-9:
It's usually easy to put a program on the right side of the Start menu.

>> **Put a link to it in the taskbar.** Using the same technique as with Pin to Start, instead choose More, then Pin to Taskbar. That puts a link to the program in the taskbar, where it's generally available (although, in odd situations — such as tablet mode — it may not be).

>> **Use Cortana to search for the program.** I talk about Cortana in Book 3, Chapter 6. This is my least favorite way because it's not nearly as precise as having a tile on the right side of the Start menu, a link on the taskbar, or a shortcut on the desktop.

If you've considered adding the program to the Start menu's tiles and putting it on the taskbar, and both approaches leave you a little bit cold, then it's not hard to stick a shortcut to the program on your desktop.

The wonder of desktop shortcuts: You can put many things on the desktop that you just can't get hornswaggled into the Start menu or the taskbar.

Creating shortcuts

Back in Book 3, Chapter 1, I showed you how to put a shortcut to a website on your desktop. Now it's time for the advanced course.

You can set up shortcuts that point to the following items:

>> Old-fashioned Windows programs (er, apps), of any kind

>> Web addresses, such as www.dummies.com

>> Documents, spreadsheets, databases, PowerPoint presentations, pictures, PDF files, and anything else that can be started by double-clicking it

>> Folders (including the weird folders inside digital cameras, the Fonts folder, and others that you may not think of)

>> Drives (hard drives, CD drives, and key drives, for example)

>> Other computers on your network, and drives and folders on those computers, as long they're shared

>> Printers (including printers attached to other computers on your network), scanners, cameras, and other pieces of hardware

>> Network connections, interface cards, and the like

Here's a whirlwind tour of many different desktop shortcut techniques:

1. **To pin a Universal Windows app to the desktop, find the app in the Start ⇨ All Apps list, click the link, and drag it to the desktop.**

   That creates a shortcut to the Universal app, as shown with the Calculator app in Figure 3-10.

2. **To create a shortcut to a document (such as a Word file you open over and over):**

   a. Use File Explorer to go to the document.

   b. Right-click the document and drag it to the desktop.

   c. Release the mouse, and choose Create Shortcut Here.

3. **To create a desktop shortcut for a folder, a drive, or another computer on your network (even in a homegroup):**

   a. Use File Explorer to navigate to the folder or drive.

   b. Right-click the folder or drive and drag it to the desktop.

   c. Release the mouse button, and choose Create Shortcut Here.

   In Figure 3-11, I have shortcuts to Calculator, a document on OneDrive, my Music folder, my C: drive, and a program, all set up and ready to click.

FIGURE 3-10:
Drag a Universal
Windows app
to the desktop
to create a short-
cut there.

FIGURE 3-11:
Shortcuts are
easy to set up, if
you work through
File Explorer.

4. **To create a shortcut to a network connection:**

   *a. Right-click the Start icon (or press Windows key+X) and choose Network
   Connections.*

b. *Right-click the connection and drag it to the desktop.*

c. *Release the mouse button, and choose Create Shortcut Here.*

That will give you a quick view of whether the connection's working, how long it's been up, and how much data has been going in each direction, as shown in Figure 3-12.

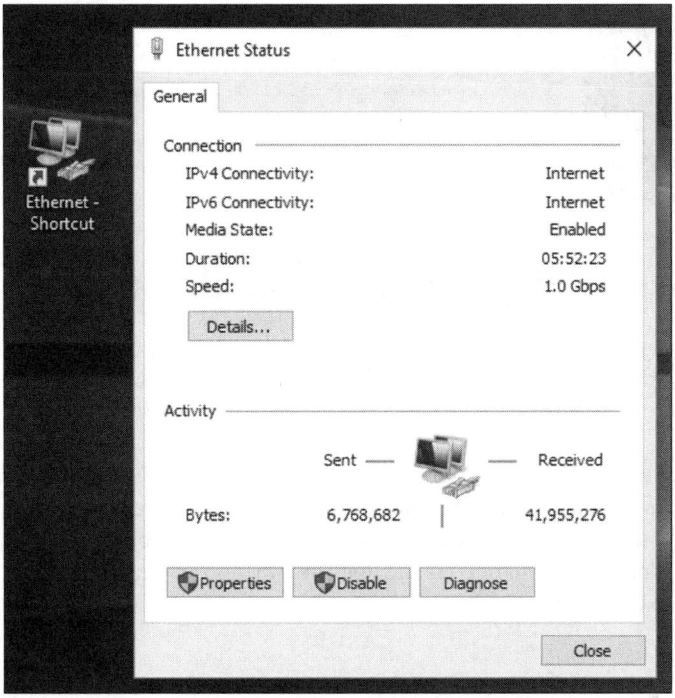

FIGURE 3-12: A shortcut to a network connection quickly brings up this information.

5. **To create a shortcut to a printer or other attached device (such as a mouse or a keyboard):**

   a. *Right-click the Start icon or press Win+X, and choose Control Panel.*

   b. *Click Hardware and Sound, then Devices and Printers.*

   c. *Right-click the printer or other device, and drag it to the desktop.*

   d. *Release the mouse button, and choose Create Shortcut Here.*

   That makes it easy to see, for example, a printer queue or your current printer settings, as shown in Figure 3-13.

FIGURE 3-13:
This HP printer status panes make status reports a click away.

Arranging icons on the desktop

If you bought a PC with Windows preloaded, you probably have so many icons on the desktop that you can't see straight. That desktop real estate is expensive, and the manufacturers receive a pretty penny for dangling the right icons in your face.

**ASK
WOODY.COM**

Know what? You can delete all of them, without feeling the least bit guilty. The worst you'll do is delete a shortcut to a manufacturer's tech support program, and if you need to get to the program, the tech support rep can tell you how to find it. The only icon you need is the Recycle Bin, and you can bring that back pretty easily (see the nearby sidebar).

RESTORING THE RECYCLE BIN ICON

Sooner or later, it happens to almost everyone. You delete the Recycle Bin icon, and you're not sure how to get it back.

Relax. It isn't that hard . . . if you know the trick.

Bring up the Control Panel (Win+X will do it). In the search box in the upper-right corner, type (precisely) **desktop icon setting**. Under Personalization, click or tap Show or Hide Common Icons on the Desktop. Follow that link, and you can reselect the box to show the Recycle Bin.

You're welcome.

Windows gives you several simple tools for arranging icons on your desktop. If you right-click any empty part of the desktop, you see that you can do the following:

>> **Sort:** Choose Sort By, and then choose an option to sort icons by name, size, type (folders, documents, and shortcuts, for example), or the date on which the icon was last modified. See Figure 3-14.

FIGURE 3-14:
Sort all the icons
on your desktop
with a few clicks.

View	>
Sort by	>
Refresh	
Paste	
Paste shortcut	
New	>
🖥 Display settings	
📷 Personalize	

Name
Size
Item type
Date modified

>> **Arrange:** Right-click an empty place on the desktop, and choose View, Auto Arrange Icons. That is, have Windows arrange them in an orderly fashion, with the first icon in the upper-left corner, the second one directly below the first one, the third one below it, and so on.

>> **Align to a grid:** Choose View, Align Icons to Grid. If you don't want to have icons arranged automatically, at least you can choose Align Icons to Grid so that you can see all the icons without one appearing directly on top of the other.

>> **Hide:** You can even choose View, Show Desktop Icons to deselect the Show Desktop Icons option. Your icons disappear — but that kinda defeats the purpose of icons, doesn't it?

TIP

>> **Delete:** In general, you can remove an icon from the Windows desktop by right-clicking it and choosing Delete or by clicking it once and pressing the Delete key.

The appearance of some icons is hard wired: If you put a Word document on your desktop, for example, the document inherits the icon — the picture — of its associated application, Word. The same goes for Excel worksheets, text documents, and recorded audio files. Icons for pictures look like the picture, more or less, if you squint hard.

Icons for shortcuts, however, you can change at will. Follow these steps to change an icon — that is, the picture — on a shortcut:

1. **Right-click the shortcut, and choose Properties.**

2. **In the Properties dialog box, click the Change Icon button.**

3. **Pick an icon from the offered list, or click the Browse button and go looking for icons.**

   Windows abounds with icons. See Table 3-2 for some likely hunting grounds.

4. **Click the OK button twice.**

   Windows changes the icon permanently (or at least until you change it again).

TABLE 3-2   ## Where to Find Icons

Contents	File
Windows 10, 8.1, 8, 7, and Vista icons	C:\Windows\system32\imageres.dll
Everything	C:\Windows\System32\shell32.dll
Computers	C:\Windows\explorer.exe
Household	C:\Windows\System32\pifmgr.dll
Folders	C:\Windows\System32\syncui.dll
Old programs (Quattro Pro, anybody?)	C:\Windows\System32\moricons.dll

TIP

Lots and lots of icons are available on the Internet. Use your favorite search engine to search for the term *free Windows icons*. If you go out looking for icons, be painfully aware that many of them come with *crapware wrappers* — programs that install themselves on your machine when all you wanted was an icon. Be careful.

Tricking out the Taskbar

Microsoft developers working on the Windows 7 taskbar gave it a secret internal project name: the Superbar. Although one might debate how much of the Super in the bar arrived compliments of Mac OS, there's no doubt that the Windows 10 taskbar is a key tool for anyone who uses the desktop. Now that you can pin Universal Windows apps on the taskbar, it's become productivity central for many of us.

The Windows Super, uh, taskbar appears at the bottom of the screen, as in Figure 3-15.

FIGURE 3-15:
The taskbar
juggles many
different tasks.

If you hover your mouse cursor over an icon, and the icon is associated with a program that's running, you see a thumbnail of what it's doing. For example, in Figure 3-15, Edge is running, and the thumbnail gives you a preview of what's on offer.

Anatomy of the taskbar

The taskbar consists of two kinds of icons:

>> **Pinned icons:** Windows ships with six icons on the taskbar, one for Start, one for Cortana (and Search), one for task view (multiple desktops), and one each for Edge, File Explorer, and the Store. You can see them at the bottom in Figure 3-15. If you install a program and tell the installer to put an icon on the taskbar, an icon for the program appears on the taskbar. You can also pin programs of your choice on the taskbar.

TECHNICAL
STUFF

Some older programs have installers that offer to attach themselves to the Quick Launch toolbar. It's a Windows XP–era thing. If you agree to put the icon on the Quick Launch toolbar, the icon for the program gets put on the far-more-upscale taskbar.

>> **Icons associated with running desktop programs:** Every time a program starts, an icon for the program appears on the taskbar. If you run three copies of the program, only one icon shows up. When the program stops, the icon disappears.

You can tell which icons represent running programs: Windows puts an almost imperceptible line under the icon for any running program. If you have more than one copy of the program running, you see more than one line underneath. It's subtle. In Figure 3-15, Edge has a line under the icon.

Jumping

If you right-click any icon in the taskbar or tap and hold down, whether or not the icon is pinned, you see a bunch of links called a *jump list,* as shown in Figure 3-16.

The contents of the jump list vary depending on the program that's running, but the bottom pane of every jump list contains the name of the program and the entry Unpin This Program from Taskbar (or conversely, Pin This Program to Taskbar, if the program is running but hasn't been pinned).

Jump lists were new in Windows 7, and they haven't taken off universally. Implementation of jump lists ranges from downright obsessive (such as Edge) to completely lackadaisical (including most applications that aren't made by Microsoft).

Here are the jump list basics:

>> **Jump lists may show your recently opened file history.** For example, the Paint jump list (shown in Figure 3-17) shows you the same Recent Documents list that appears inside Paint. The currently open document(s) appear at the top of the list.

>> **It's generally easy to pin an item to the jump list.** When you pin an item, it sticks to a program's jump list whether or not that item is open. To pin an item, run your mouse out to the right of the item you want to pin and click the stick pin. That puts the item in a separate pane at the top of the jump list.

FIGURE 3-17:
Lowly Paint's
jump list shows
recently opened
documents.

ASK
WOODY.COM

The jump list has one not-so-obvious use. It lets you open a second copy of the same program. Suppose you want to copy a handful of albums from the music library to your thumbdrive on F:. You start by clicking the File Explorer icon in the taskbar, and on the left, click Music Library. Cool.

You can do the copy-and-paste thang — select an album, press Ctrl+C to copy, use the list on the left of File Explorer to navigate to F:, and then press Ctrl+V to paste. But if you're going to copy many albums, it's much faster and easier to open a second copy of File Explorer and navigate to F: in that second window. Then you can click and drag albums from the Music folder to the F: folder.

To open a second copy of a running program (File Explorer, in this example), you have two choices:

● Hold down the Shift key, and click the icon.

● Right-click the icon (or tap and hold down, perhaps with a nudge upward), and choose the program's name.

In either case, Windows starts a fresh copy of the program.

Changing the taskbar

The taskbar rates as one of the few parts of Windows that are highly malleable. You can modify it till the cows come home:

>> **Pin any program** on the taskbar by right-clicking the program and choosing Pin This Program to Taskbar. Yes, you can right-click the icon of a running program on the taskbar.

>> **Move a pinned icon** by clicking and dragging it. Easy. You know, the way it's supposed to be. You can even drag an icon that isn't pinned into the middle of the pinned icons. When the program associated with the icon stops, the icon disappears, and all pinned icons move back into place.

>> **Unpin any pinned program** by right-clicking it and choosing Unpin This Program from Taskbar. Rocket science.

Unfortunately, with a few exceptions, you can't turn individual documents or folders into icons on the taskbar. But you can pin a folder to the File Explorer jump list, and you can pin a document to the jump list for whichever application is associated with the document. For example, you can pin a song to the jump list for Windows Media Player.

Here's how to pin a folder or document to its associated icon on the taskbar:

1. **Navigate to the folder or document that you want to pin.**

   You can use File Explorer to go to the file or folder or you can make a shortcut to the file or folder.

2. **Drag the folder or document (or shortcut) to the taskbar.**

   Windows tells you where it will pin the folder, document, or shortcut, as shown in Figure 3-18. For example, if you are dragging a .docx file, Windows will let you pin it to WordPad, Word, File Explorer, or any program that can open a .docx file.

3. **Release the mouse button.**

   That's all it takes.

TIP

A little-known side effect: If you pin a file to a program on the taskbar, the program itself also gets pinned to the taskbar, if it wasn't already.

Working with the taskbar

I've discovered a few tricks with the taskbar that you may find worthwhile:

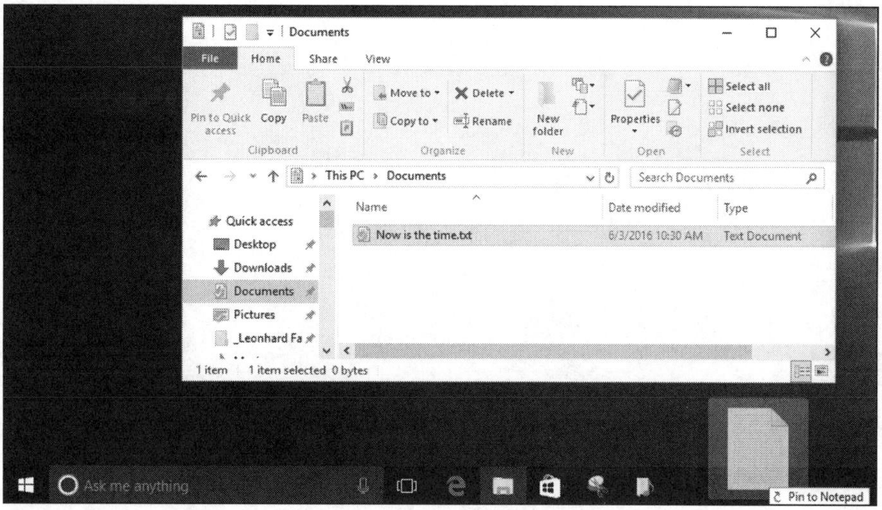

FIGURE 3-18:
Drag a file or
folder to pin it to
a taskbar icon.

>> Sometimes, you want to shut down all (or most) running programs, and you don't want Windows to do it for you. It's easy to see what's running by looking at the underline under the icon, if your eyesight and your monitor are good enough (refer to Figure 3-15). To close down all instances of a particular program, right-click its icon and choose Close Window or Close All Windows.

>> Sometimes, if a program is frozen and won't shut itself down, forcing the matter through the taskbar is the easiest way to dislodge it.

TIP

>> The terminology is a bit screwy here. Normally, you would choose Exit the Program, Choose File, Exit, Click the Red X, or some such. When you're working with the taskbar, you choose Close Window or Close All Windows from the choices that pop up when you right-click the icon on the taskbar. Different words, same meaning.

If you move your mouse to the lower-right corner and then click, Windows minimizes all open windows. Click again, and Windows brings back all minimized windows. You can also right-click and choose Peek at Desktop or Show Desktop.

TIP

Chapter 4

Working with Multiple Desktops

When talk turns to virtual desktops in Windows 10, most people are referring to Win10's capability to support and juggle multiple desktops. You can set up a desktop for your work, a desktop for fun things, a desktop for your favorite hobby or club, and Windows keeps them all separate. You can run programs on each desktop, run the same program on two or more desktops, and mix and match — and Windows keeps them from stepping all over each other.

In Figure 4-1, you can see three running desktops, and the way they appear in task view.

ASK
WOODY.COM

Apparently people have forgotten, but Windows XP had a similar capability, which could be brought to life by installing an app, er, a program distributed by Microsoft as one of the XP PowerToys.

Those of you who are sufficiently long in the tooth may recall that the XP PowerToys were basically a series of skunkworks programs that enhanced Windows XP, built by Microsoft employees, distributed by Microsoft, but never officially supported by Microsoft. XP Virtual Desktop Manager let you build and switch among four separate XP Desktops.

FIGURE 4-1:
These three
desktops run
independently.

The Windows 7 virtual desktop program I've used and recommend — Sysinternals Desktop — also comes from Microsoft and arrived with Mark Russinovich and the Sysinternals team, which Microsoft acquired in 2006. Like XP Virtual Desktop Manager, it enables you to set up to four desktops and switch among them by clicking a taskbar icon or by using a customizable key combination.

An entire industry of Windows virtual desktop add-ins exists — Dexpot, Finestra, mdesktop, Virtual Dimension, VirtuaWin, and others — many of which have fallen into disrepair. Virtual desktops are ancient in the Linux world, venerable on the Mac, and nothing new in Windows.

So what's new with Windows 10?

REMEMBER

The big change in Windows 10 comes from the fact that the multiple desktop feature is built into Windows itself. You don't need to install a separate program or run something strange in the background. Windows just does the deed.

Getting around Multiple Desktops

To see what's going on, try building a few desktops. Here's one way:

1. **Start Windows.**

2. **Crank up a few programs.**

Doesn't matter which ones. Get three or four going.

3. **Tap or click the Task View icon just to the right of Cortana (and shown in the margin).**

Windows lines up your running programs, darkens the main desktop, and puts a + (New Desktop) icon in the lower-right corner, as shown in Figure 4-2.

FIGURE 4-2: Task view lines up the currently running programs and adds a + icon for creating new desktops.

4. **Click or tap the + icon to add a new desktop.**

Windows creates a thumbnail for a second desktop and moves all the running programs to Desktop 1, as shown in Figure 4-3.

FIGURE 4-3: The first desktop gets all the running programs when a second desktop is added.

5. **Click the thumbnail marked Desktop 2.**

Windows shows you a clean, new desktop.

6. **Crank up a few more programs.**

They can be the same programs as the ones on Desktop 1 or new ones. Each desktop works independently.

7. **Click the Task View icon again.**

   Windows shows you the contents of Desktop 2 but also shows you thumbnails for Desktops 1 and 2, as shown in Figure 4-4.

   Note that the items shown in task view may vary depending on whether you're in tablet mode, or if you have the screen switched around into portrait.

FIGURE 4-4:
Now showing
Desktop 2.

8. **Tap or click the Desktop 1 thumbnail.**

   Desktop 1 reappears, with all its programs working.

   At the same time, all the programs on Desktop 2 stop. If you were playing music, the music stops. Watching a video? It freezes. Desktop 2 goes into suspended animation.

TIP

9. **Click the + icon again to add another desktop. And another.**

   You can also press Win+Ctrl+D to create a new desktop.

   In theory, there's no limit to the number of desktops you can run.

10. **To remove a desktop, hover your mouse cursor or tap and hold down the thumbnail, and choose the X icon at the top.**

    When you shut down a desktop, all its running apps get transferred to the next lower-numbered desktop.

Interacting between Desktops

Windows 10 has some built-in smarts that will help you take full advantage of multiple desktops. When you have a couple of desktops (or more) set up, as explained in the preceding section, try these calisthenics:

1. On the taskbar, tap or click the Task View icon to bring up task view.

If you have three desktops set up, task view might look like Figure 4-5.

FIGURE 4-5:
Task view with three desktops and the third desktop selected.

2. At the bottom, click Desktop 1. Then press Alt+Tab.

(You can change the behavior of Alt+Tab in the Settings app. I talk about that in the next section.)

This is the old Windows coolswitch, which has been around since Windows 95. Alt+Tab shows you all the running programs on a single desktop. In Figure 4-6, for example, I get three thumbnails, one for each program running on Desktop 3.

FIGURE 4-6:
Alt+Tab cycles among programs running on a single desktop.

3. Again, click one of the desktops at the bottom of the screen. Now press Windows key+Tab.

That pops you in and out of task view, just like clicking the icon in the taskbar next to Cortana.

4. To cycle among desktops, press Ctrl+Windows+left arrow or Ctrl+Windows+right arrow.

When you release the Windows key, Windows settles on the desktop that you've chosen.

This is a difficult way to switch among desktops because you can't see them in advance, nor can you tell how many desktops you have — you just move from desktop to desktop.

5. To shut down a desktop and move all the running programs from that desktop into the next desktop, press Windows+Ctrl+F4.

When you do so, Windows automatically shuffles you to the window that now contains all the programs that were running on the desktop you shut down.

6. To move a running program from one desktop to another:

a. Bring up task view (tap or click the icon next to Cortana, or press Windows Key+Tab).

b. Right-click (or click and hold down) the program you want to move.

c. Choose Move To, followed by the desktop name.

You can see this move in action in Figure 4-7.

FIGURE 4-7:
Move a program (or app) from one desktop to another.

7. **To quickly close a desktop: Bring up task view, hover your mouse cursor over the desktop you want to close, and click the X in the upper-right corner, as shown in Figure 4-8.**

All the running programs (apps) get shuffled to the next desktop.

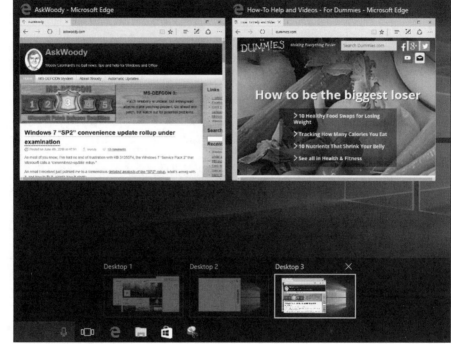

FIGURE 4-8:
The fast way to shut down desktops, without closing any programs: Click the X on the desktop name at the bottom.

Other Multiple Desktop Settings

The Windows Settings app lets you alter multiple desktop behaviors, just a little bit.

First, Windows shows you which programs are running on the current desktop by drawing a faint line under the taskbar icons of the running programs.

You can change that behavior, so Windows shows underlines for all programs that are running on any desktop. Here's how:

1. **Click or tap the Start icon and then the Settings icon.**

The Settings app appears.

Working with Multiple Desktops

2. Click or tap System ⇨ Multitasking.

You see the choices in Figure 4-9.

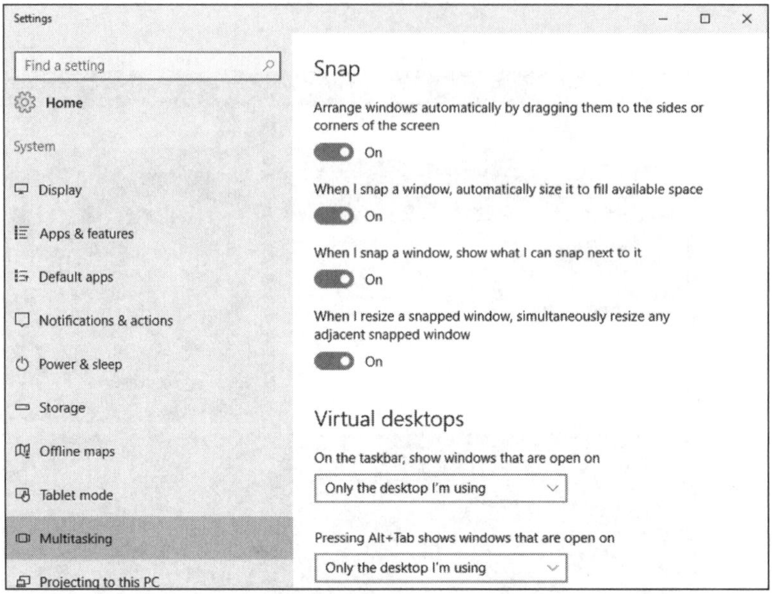

FIGURE 4-9:
You have multiple
desktop options.

3. In the top drop-down box, choose All Desktops.

Your taskbar changes immediately to show underscores for any program that's running on any desktop, as shown in Figure 4-10.

FIGURE 4-10:
Underlines
indicate which
programs are
running.

Similarly, you can switch the behavior of the Alt+Tab coolswitch. It can be set to only cycle among programs on the current desktop or to cycle among all running programs on all desktops.

Chapter 5

Internet Explorer, Chrome, and Firefox

For hundreds of millions of people, the web and Internet Explorer (IE) are synonyms. It's fair to say that IE has done more to extend the reach of PC users than any other product — enabling people from all walks of life, in all corners of the globe, to see what a fascinating world we live in.

At the same time, IE has become an object of attack by spammers, scammers, thieves, and other lowlifes. As the Internet's lowest (or is it greatest?) common denominator, IE draws lots of unwanted attention. That's changing though. Now, all the browsers get some of the flak. It's just that IE continues to get the worst of it.

IE usage rose rapidly from its release in 1995, taking half the browser market share by 1998. Usage of IE peaked in 2002–2003, with roughly 90 percent of all browser use worldwide. (See the sidebar "The history of Internet Explorer.")

ASK
WOODY.COM

By 2015, IE had clearly lost its decade-long supreme position in the web browser pecking order, with strong competition from Firefox and Chrome. By mid-2016, Chrome outflanked IE, and the trend is now clear: IE is a dead horse walking. Everybody's giving up on it — even Microsoft.

THE HISTORY OF INTERNET EXPLORER

More than any other product, Internet Explorer reflects the odd and tortured Microsoft approach to the web. After largely ignoring the Internet for many years, Microsoft released the first version of Internet Explorer in 1995, as an add-on to Windows. In 1996, Microsoft built Internet Explorer version 3 into Windows itself, violating antitrust laws and using monopolistic tactics to overwhelm Netscape Navigator.

Having illegally pummeled its competitor in the marketplace, Microsoft made almost no improvements to Internet Explorer between August 2001 and August 2006 — an eternity in Internet time. IE became the single largest conduit for malware in the history of computing, with major security patches (sometimes several) appearing almost every month.

And then there was Firefox. Dave Hyatt, Blake Ross (who was a sophomore at Stanford at the time), and hundreds of volunteers took on the IE behemoth, producing a fast, small, free alternative that quickly grabbed a significant share of the browser market. Microsoft responded by incorporating many Firefox features into Internet Explorer.

Although Google did provide most of the money that originally drove Firefox's development — Yahoo! pays a pretty penny to be the default search engine in Firefox now — the Googlies decided to make their own browser, with a different slant. First released in late 2008, Chrome has grown to the point that Chrome and Firefox often run neck-and-neck in web utilization statistics, with IE on a downward trend now below the 50-percent line.

With Windows 10's release, Microsoft isn't deprecating Internet Explorer as much as throwing it in a bottle of formaldehyde. You can still use IE all you want (it's under Start ➪ Windows Accessories), but Microsoft would much rather you use Edge. Which is good, because I would much rather you use Edge, too.

That's the story for desktop and laptop browsers. When you take mobile browsers (browsers used from smartphones and tablets) into account, mobile is taking over the world. In May 2015, Google reported that more than half of all Google searches were from mobile phones. Just phones. Clearly, the future of web browsing looks mobile, with IE (which doesn't run on mobile) rapidly fading into the sunset.

This chapter looks at desktop browsers: Internet Explorer, Firefox, and Google Chrome, each with its own strengths and weaknesses.

TIP

If you're looking for Edge, Microsoft's long-overdue replacement for Internet Explorer, you're in the wrong place. Edge is a Universal Windows Platform (UWP) app, one that lives on the new WinRT-based Universal/Modern/Metro side of the street. For that reason, I talk about it in Chapter 1 of the book that deals with the other side, Book 5.

This chapter looks at what's out there for the old-fashioned desktop, helps you choose one (or two or three) desktop browsers for your everyday use, shows you how to customize your chosen browser, and then offers all sorts of important advice about using the web.

Some of you may find that Edge isn't available on your Windows 10 machine. Some large companies want to "protect" the people on their networks by stifling Edge and offering only IE. Some companies don't have any choice — they've poured too much money into non-standard, creaky archaic IE programs, and they're unwilling or unable to rewrite them. Bah.

Which Browser Is Best?

I must hear the question, "Which browser is best?" a dozen times a week.

The short answer: It depends.

The long answer: It depends on lots of things. But one thing we know for sure. Microsoft itself doesn't think much of Internet Explorer. The old guy's been given the boot, tucked away in an obscure corner where you can conjure him up if you insist. Microsoft's money (and talent) is on Edge.

ASK WOODY.COM

I use Chrome for my day-to-day browser , but increasingly I find myself using the browsers on my Nexus phone and the family iPads. On those devices, I've installed Chrome and use it exclusively. My wife, though, uses the native Safari on her iPhone and iPad. Our Chromebook, which I love with a passion, runs only Chrome (of course).

TIP

I also hear, again and again, the question "How can I make my browser run faster?" The short answer: 99 percent of the time, you can't. The big problem isn't your browser — it's the speed of your Internet connection.

Considering security

Without a doubt, the number-one consideration for any browser user is security. The last thing you need is to get your PC infected with a drive-by attack, where merely looking at an infected web page takes over your computer.

Fortunately, for the first time in many years, if not ever, I feel confident in telling you that the desktop versions of all three major browsers — Internet Explorer, Firefox, and Chrome — are excellent choices. None has clear superiority over the others. All are (finally!) secure, as long as you follow a few simple rules.

The days of Microsoft taking all the heat for security holes has passed. Although it's true that there are more frontal assaults on Internet Explorer than on the other two, it's also true that Firefox- and Chrome-specific attacks exist.

In fact, browsers aren't the major source of attacks any more. Starting in 2007 or so, the bad guys turned their attention away from browsers and went to work on add-ons, specifically Flash and Acrobat PDF Reader, as well as browser toolbars. According to IBM's X-Force Team, the number of browser-attacking exploits has been declining steadily since 2007, with a concomitant rise in infections based on Flash, Reader, Java, toolbars, and other third-party add-ons. Edge limits all of them. Score one for the new kid on the block.

Old versions of Internet Explorer still have major security problems. Microsoft's been actively trying to kill IE 6 for years now. But as long as you stick to the latest browser version, keep your browsers reasonably well updated, and don't install any weird toolbars or other add-ons, your only major points of concern for any of the major browsers are Flash, Reader, and Java. I talk about all three in the following sections.

The place where the latest versions of IE fall down? The infernal parade of patches. Month after month, we're seeing dozens, if not hundreds, of patched parts of IE running out the Automatic Update chute. Inevitably one or more of the patch parts causes problems. IE may be the grand old gold standard, but it's on life support.

There's a good case to be made for running Edge, and I talk about that in Book 5, Chapter 1.

Both Chrome and Firefox have, in the Windows 8–era past, tried to make a browser that runs well in the new Universal Windows arena. To date, they haven't had much luck. That may change though, and if it does, it'd be well worth your while to try the Universal Windows version of Chrome and/or Firefox. I keep you up to date on www.AskWoody.com.

IE, Firefox, and Chrome aren't the only games in the Windows desktop app milieu. Some people swear by Safari (which is the Apple browser); others go for Opera. I don't like Safari (although it does sync bookmarks on Apple devices), but I do like Opera. I have my hands full just juggling the other three.

Looking at privacy

Privacy is one area that differentiates the Big Three. As best I can tell, nobody knows for sure how much data about your browsing proclivities is kept by the browser manufacturers, but this much seems likely:

>> If you turn on the Suggested Sites feature or SmartScreen Filter in Internet Explorer (see the section on Internet Explorer), IE sends your browsing history to Microsoft, where it is saved and analyzed. But then, you get that with a fully enabled Cortana, too.

>> Google keeps information about where you go with Chrome. Get over it.

>> Although Firefox is capable of keeping track of where you're going with your browser, Firefox is the least likely of the Big Three to keep or use the data. Why? Because, in direct contrast to both Microsoft and Google, Firefox doesn't have anything to sell you.

In general, the browser manufacturers can't track you directly, as an individual; they can track only your IP address (see the sidebar, "What's an IP address?").

But both Microsoft and Google mash together information that they get from multiple sources. As Microsoft puts it in the Internet Explorer Privacy Statement:

> In order to offer you a more consistent and personalized experience in your interactions with Microsoft, information collected through one Microsoft service may be combined with information obtained through other Microsoft services. We may also supplement the information we collect with information obtained from other companies.

Funny that the statement doesn't mention targeted advertising.

Google does the same thing: It actively collects information about you from every interaction you have with a Google product or location, including the search site and the browser. Google also gets info when you visit a page with a Google ad.

If privacy is very important to you, Firefox is your best choice. No question.

Internet Explorer, Chrome, and Firefox

WHAT'S AN IP ADDRESS?

When you're connected to the Internet interacting with a website, the website must be able to find you. Instead of using names (Billy Bob's broken-down ThinkPad), the Internet uses numbers, such as 207.46.232.182, something like a telephone number (that's one of Microsoft's addresses). When you go to a website, you leave behind your IP address. That's the only way the website has to get back to you. Nothing nefarious about it: That's the way the Internet works.

Although your IP address doesn't identify you, uniquely, the IP address for most computers with broadband connections rarely changes. Your IP address changes if you turn off your router and turn it back on again, but for most people, most of the time, the IP address stays constant.

The IP address actually identifies the physical box that's attached to the Internet. For homes and businesses with a network, the address is associated with the router, not individual computers on the Internet. If you're using a mobile (3G or 4G) connection, the IP address is associated with your mobile phone provider's equipment, not yours. In some developing countries, the whole country has a handful of IP addresses, and connections inside the country are handled as if they were on an internal network.

Picking a browser

With all the pros and cons, which browser should you choose?

For everyday browsing, I'd say stick with one of the desktop apps. Although each version of each browser is different, a few generalities about the different browsers seem to hold true:

>> **Internet Explorer** holds the title for most compatible with ancient websites. Unfortunately, sometimes that compatibility comes at a cost: You may have to install programs (such as ActiveX controls) that can have security holes. IE also has a few features that some people find useful, such as the capability to pin websites to the Windows taskbar.

>> **Firefox** has the most extensions, and some of them are quite worthwhile. Ghostery, for example, shows every tracking cookie on every web page; DownThemAll can download every link on a page and manage them all; IE Tab brings IE compatibility to most ancient web pages; NoScript blocks Flash and Java unless you unleash them on a specific site. Firefox is also the least likely to sprout privacy problems (see the preceding section).

» **Chrome** usually comes out on top in security tests. With built-in support for both PDF reading and Flash, and the Java programming language, Chrome can handle all three without relying on the Flash, Reader, or Java plug-ins, which are historically riddled with security holes. Chrome has also been a pioneer in new features and standards adoption and will take your settings along with you as you move from PC to PC.

Increasingly, Chrome is taking top prize for number and quality of extensions. Why? The folks at Chrome have devoted a ton of programming skill and talent to making Chrome extensions rock-solid. As the book went to press, there were strong rumors that Microsoft would announce full Chrome extension support in Edge (plus or minus a few minor changes). There are also rumors that Chrome will start running the full Android app menagerie on an upcoming version of Chrome. Think of that: Any Android app could run on Chrome and on Chromebooks. It's a brave new world, and Chrome is in the lead.

ASK
WOODY.COM

It isn't an either/or choice, actually. You can easily run Edge, Internet Explorer, Firefox, and Chrome side by side. Here's what I do:

» Most of the time, I run **Chrome.** Yes, I know that Google looks at everything I do while in the clutches of Chrome, but so be it. I particularly like the bookmarking interface — and the bookmarks travel with me, wherever I go, because I'm signed in. Chrome's capability to keep track of where I am and what I'm doing comes in handy when I switch from the desktop to my phone or an iPad: Chrome works the same way wherever I am, whatever I'm doing. And because I'm signed in, it's my number-one favorite digital assistant.

» I have a specific set of tabs open in **Firefox,** all day, every day. I keep two browsers open simultaneously to help me concentrate on Windows updating — that's in Firefox — and all of its nuances, while also working on everything else in Chrome. I like Firefox, with NoScript turned on and Ghostery sniffing out the frighteningly large number of cookies watching me. I don't block cookies with Ghostery, although I can. Mostly I want to see how much sites have sold out, reducing my privacy for their profits.

» I move to **Edge** on the rare occasion when I want a third browser window open, or when I'm testing something. Edge has nice rendering — pages show up better in Edge — and it's fast. But it still has a few years to go before it's ready to bat with the big boys.

» And **Internet Explorer** is always ready, standing by in case I hit an older web page that doesn't work right in Edge, Firefox, or Chrome. Yes, there are plenty of them — I won't mention my bank by name, and Microsoft.com is one of the worst offenders. Instead of switching Firefox over to the IE Tab add-on, I just jump the monkey and go to IE.

WHAT'S DO NOT TRACK?

Microsoft made a huge step in the direction of helping to protect consumer privacy back when Windows 8 hit. Yes, *that* Microsoft. It turned on Do Not Track by default during Windows 8 setup, in both the desktop and tiled versions of Internet Explorer 11.

Unfortunately, Microsoft was backed into a corner when the folks who promulgated DNT specifically said that a browser can't turn it on by default. Thus, in Windows 10, both IE and Edge don't have DNT enabled by default.

What's DNT? Good question.

Whenever you go to a website, your browser leaves certain fingerprints at each site you visit: the name of your browser, your operating system, your IP address, time zone, screen size, whether cookies are enabled, the address of the last website you visited, that kind of thing. I'm not talking about cookies. I'm talking about data that's inside the header at the beginning of the interaction with every web page. Even if you go incognito (in Chrome), private (in Firefox), or InPrivate (in Internet Explorer or Edge), your browser still sends all that information to every site, every time you visit.

The Do Not Track proposal — and it's only a proposal at this point — would assign one more bit in the header that says, "The person using this browser requests that you not track anything he's doing." DNT was originally developed by Firefox. You can turn on DNT in any recent version of Firefox by clicking the Firefox button, Options, Privacy, and selecting the Tell Web Sites I Do Not Want to Be Tracked check box.

As with everything Internet-related, DNT isn't cut and dried. There are lots and lots of nuances. First and foremost, it's entirely voluntary: Websites can ignore the DNT bit if the site's programmers want to. Second, the precise definition of *track* can get a little squishy. Third, there's no possible way to enforce the DNT settings — no way to tell which of the dozens of billions of websites now readily accessible even claim to have a DNT policy, much less implement it. The advertising industry and the privacy partisans have yet to agree on anything, much less a DNT proposal. Still, it's a start in the right direction.

Setting a browser as your default

When you get Windows, Edge is set up as the default browser: Click a web link in a document, for example, and Edge jumps up to load the web page.

Both Firefox and Chrome offer to become your default web browser, as soon as you install them. Internet Explorer has the option, but it isn't so in your face. They also have a check box that basically tells them to quit asking. I always select that box.

It's easy to change your default browser. Here's how:

1. **Right-click the Start icon, and choose Control Panel.**

2. **Click the Programs link. Under Default Programs, click the Set Your Default Programs link.**

You see the Set Your Default Programs dialog box shown in Figure 5-1.

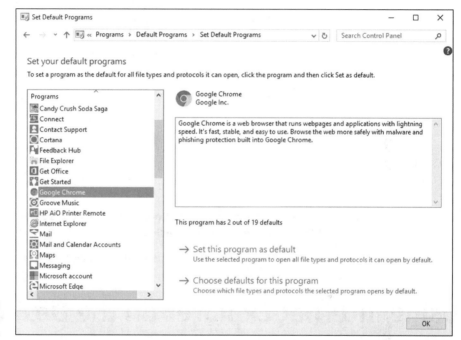

FIGURE 5-1:
Set your default
browser here.

3. **To see what is happening, on the left, select the browser you want to turn into your default. Then select the Choose Defaults for This Program link.**

WARNING

This tells Windows to associate with the browser all the filename extensions that the browser can handle. You can see a detailed list in Figure 5-2.

Using this example, after you set Chrome as the default, double-clicking an HTML file will open the file with Chrome.

4. **You can set a program to handle individual file types by using the details in Figure 5-2, but if you just want to switch all the file types to use a particular program (as you would, for example, if you wanted to set Chrome as your default browser), click Cancel.**

The Set Your Default Programs dialog box re-appears (refer to Figure 5-1).

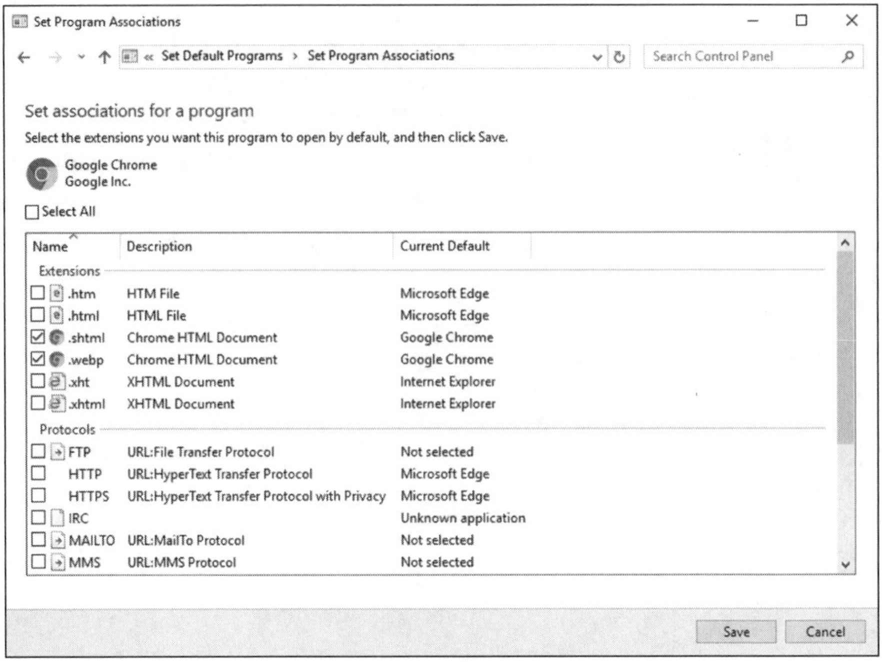

FIGURE 5-2:
Chrome can
handle these
kinds of files and
protocols.

5. **Click your preferred program (Google Chrome in this case), and then click Set This Program as Default. Click OK.**

Your chosen program (in this case your browser) becomes the default.

Using Internet Explorer on the Desktop

Internet Explorer 11 on the Windows 10 desktop (see Figure 5-3) is similar to — almost indistinguishable from — Internet Explorer 11 on Windows 7 or 8. It has the old, familiar interface. It runs all the add-ons you've come to know and love and distrust. Internet Explorer 11 gives you just about everything a modern browser can give you — except an extensive library of customized add-ons — but it's big, fat, slow, and curiously buggy. Any way you look at it, Microsoft isn't giving IE much love these days. It's definitely on the way out. Which isn't necessarily a bad thing, for you and me.

Navigating in IE

One great thing about Internet Explorer is that you can be an absolute no-clue beginner, and with just a few hints about tools and so on, you can find your way around the web like a pro. A big part of the reason why: Hundreds of millions of people, if not more than a billion, have already used IE. For many, *IE* is synonymous with *web.* And that's kind of sad.

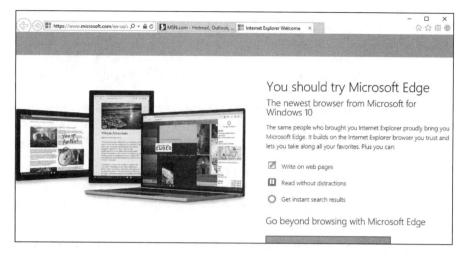

FIGURE 5-3:
Sign of the times: Internet Explorer 11's new welcome page invites you to switch to Edge.

Figure 5-4 gives you a diagram of the basic layout of the Internet Explorer window. You get forward and back buttons, an address bar with search (magnifying glass) and refresh (circle) icons, and icons for home page(s), favorites/history (star), settings (gear), and a "let us know what you think" (happy face).

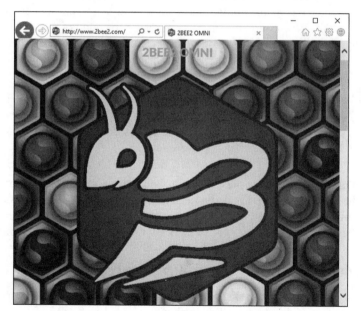

FIGURE 5-4:
The IE window includes everything you need to work on the web.

Don't work too hard

A handful of Internet Explorer tricks can make all the difference in your productivity and sanity. Every IE user should know these shortcuts:

>> **You rarely need to type *www* in the address bar at the beginning of an address and you never need to type *http://.*** People who build websites these days are almost always savvy enough to let you drop the use of the *www* at the beginning of the website's name. Unless the site you're headed to was last updated in the late 17th century, you can probably get there by simply typing the name of the site, as long as you include the part at the end. So you can type *http://www.dummies.com* if you want to, but typing *dummies.com* works just as well.

REMEMBER

>> **IE automatically sticks *http://www.* onto the front of an address you type and *.com* on the end if you press Ctrl+Enter.** So if you want to go to the site http://www.dummies.com, you need to type only *dummies* in the address bar and press Ctrl+Enter.

>> **With a few exceptions, address capitalization doesn't matter.** Typing either *AskWoody.com* or *askwoody.com* gets you to my website—as does *asKwoodY.cOm*. On the other hand, hyphens (-) and underscores (_) aren't interchangeable: some-site.com and some_site.com would be two different sites if they were the real deals. Similarly, the number 0 isn't the same as the letter O, the number 1 isn't a letter l, and radishes aren't the same as turnips. Or so my niece tells me.

ASK WOODY.COM

The exceptions? Web addresses from one of the thousands of websites that now have shortened URLs. Go to bit.ly, for example, or goo.gl, feed it an URL that's a gazillion letters long, click a button, and you get back something that looks like this: goo.gl/XY2Am. In those kinds of addresses — shortened ones — capitalization *does* matter.

TIP

While we're on the topic of working too hard, keeping track of passwords rates as the single biggest pain in the neck in any browser. You have passwords for, what, a hundred different sites? If you haven't yet discovered LastPass (or Roboform or 1Password or KeePass), get to Book 10, Chapter 5, and check it out.

Moving around the main desktop window

As you can see, IE packs lots of possibilities into that small space. The items you use most often are described in this list:

>> **Backward** and **forward arrows:** Go to the previously displayed page; hold down to see a list of all previous pages.

- **Address bar:** This enables you to type the web address of a page that you want to move to directly. You can also type search terms here; click the spyglass or press Enter, and IE looks them up using your default search engine.

- **Refresh:** If you think the page has changed, tap or click this circle arrow icon to have IE retrieve it for you again.

- **Tab:** You can have many pages open at a time, one on each tab. To create a new tab, click the small, gray blank tab on the right.

- **Home page:** This replaces the current tab with the tab(s) on your home page(s).

- **Favorites icon:** This lets you set, go to, and organize favorite websites, as well as look at your browsing history.

- **Settings:** This eight-spoke wheel takes you under the covers to change the way IE behaves. Or misbehaves.

TIP

If you want to see the old-fashioned toolbar menus (File, Edit, View, and all the others) in Internet Explorer, press Alt. Yep, that's how you get to IE's inner workings.

Tinkering with tabs

ASK WOODY.COM

Tabs offer you a chance to bring up multiple web pages without opening multiple copies of IE. They're a major navigational aid because it's easy to switch among tabs. If you've never used browser tabs, you may wonder what all the fuss is about. It doesn't seem like there's much difference between opening another window and adding a tab (see Figure 5-5). But after you get the hang of it, tabs can help you organize pages and quickly jump to the one you want.

You can add a new tab to IE in any of these four ways:

- Click the gray box to the right of the rightmost tab. That starts a blank new tab, and away you go.

- Ctrl+click a link to open the linked page in a new tab.

- Press Ctrl+T to start a new tab. When the tab is open, you get to navigate manually, just as you would in any other browser window.

- Right-click a link, and choose Open in New Tab.

In addition, the web page you're looking at may specify that any links on the page are to open in a new tab, instead of overwriting the current one.

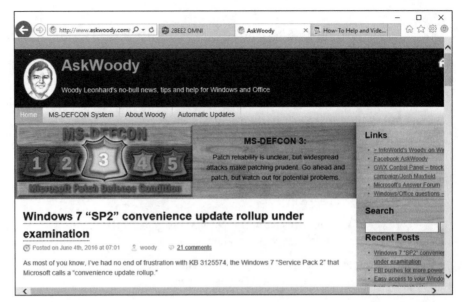

FIGURE 5-5:
If you've never
used tabs, you're
in for a treat.

ASK
WOODY.COM

Why do I like tabs? I can set up a single window with a bunch of related tabs and then bookmark the whole shebang. That makes it one-click easy to open all my favorite news sites, research sites, or financial sites. While my browser's out loading pages, I can go do something else and return to the tabbed window when everything's loaded and ready to go.

TIP

You can reorganize the order of tabs by simply clicking a tab and dragging it to a different location.

Using the address bar

No doubt you're familiar with basic browser functions, or you can guess when you know what the controls mean. But you may not know about some of these finer points:

>> When you type on the address bar, IE looks at what you're typing and tries to match it with the list of sites it has in your history list and in your favorites. Sometimes, you can get the right address (URL) by typing something related to the site. Watch as you type and see what IE comes up with.

TIP

If you turn on Bing Suggestions (sometimes called Suggested Sites), IE sends all your keystrokes to Mother Microsoft and has Bing try to guess what you're looking for. Depending on how you feel about privacy, that may or may not be a good idea. See the section "Turning on key features," later in this chapter.

>> Click a link, and the web page decides whether you move to the new page in the current browser tab or a new tab appears with the clicked page loaded. Many people don't realize that the web page makes the decision about following the link in the same tab or creating a new one. You can override the web page's setting.

- Shift+click, and a new browser window always opens with the clicked page loaded.

- Ctrl+click, and the clicked page appears on a new tab in the current browser window. Similarly, if you type in the search bar and press Ctrl+Enter, the results appear in a new tab.

>> Even if the web page hijacks your backward and forward arrows, you can always move backward (or forward) by clicking and holding down the directional arrow, and choosing the page you want.

TIP

You can bring up a history of all the pages you visited in the past few weeks by pressing Ctrl+H, as shown in Figure 5-6.

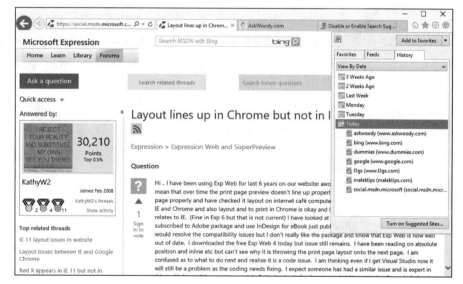

FIGURE 5-6:
Bring up the browsing history with Ctrl+H.

To search for a particular word or phrase on a page, press Ctrl+F. Force your browser to refresh a web page (retrieve the latest version, even if a version is stored locally) by pressing F5. If you need to make sure that you have the latest version, even if the timestamps may be screwed up, press Ctrl+F5.

Internet Explorer, Chrome, and Firefox

Saving space, losing time

Increasing or decreasing the number of days of browsing history that IE stores doesn't have much effect on the amount of data stored on the hard drive: Even a hyperactive surfer will have a hard time cranking up a History folder that's much larger than 1MB. By contrast, temporary Internet files on your computer can take up 10, 50, or even 100 times that much space.

Those temporary Internet files exist only to speed your Internet access: When IE hits a web page that it has seen before, if a copy of the page's contents appears in the Temporary Internet Files folder, IE grabs the stuff on the hard drive rather than wait for a download. That can make a huge difference in IE's responsiveness, particularly if you have a slow Internet connection, but the speed comes at a price: 250MB, if you haven't changed it.

To clear out the IE temporary Internet files, follow these simple steps:

1. **Start Internet Explorer.**

2. **Click the Settings icon and choose Internet Options.**

The Settings icon is in the upper right. The Internet Options dialog box appears.

3. **On the General tab, under Browsing History, click the Delete button.**

You see the Delete Browsing History dialog box shown in Figure 5-7.

Delete Browsing History   ✕

☑ **Preserve Favorites website data**
  Keep cookies and temporary Internet files that enable your favorite websites to retain preferences and display faster.

☑ **Temporary Internet files and website files**
  Copies of webpages, images, and media that are saved for faster viewing.

☑ **Cookies and website data**
  Files or databases stored on your computer by websites to save preferences or improve website performance.

☑ **History**
  List of websites you have visited.

☐ **Download History**
  List of files you have downloaded.

☐ **Form data**
  Saved information that you have typed into forms.

☐ **Passwords**
  Saved passwords that are automatically filled in when you sign in to a website you've previously visited.

☐ **Tracking Protection, ActiveX Filtering and Do Not Track**
  A list of websites excluded from filtering, data used by Tracking Protection to detect where sites might automatically be sharing details about your visit, and exceptions to Do Not Track requests.

About deleting browsing history   Delete   Cancel

FIGURE 5-7: You have full control over what kinds of browsing history gets deleted.

4. **Choose the kinds of data you want to delete, and click Delete; then click OK to close the Internet Options dialog box.**

You won't hurt anything, but revisited web pages take longer to appear. For advice about cookies, see the next section.

Dealing with cookies

A *cookie,* as you probably know, is a text file that a website stores on your computer. The website can put information inside its own cookie (say, the time and date of your last visit or the page you were last viewing or your account number). At least in theory, a website can look at and change only its own cookies: The cookie provides a means for an individual website to store information on your computer and to retrieve it later, using your browser.

In general, that's A Good Thing. Cookies can minimize the amount of futzing around that you need to do on a site. Most shopping cart/checkout sites need cookies.

Of course, nothing ever goes precisely as planned. Bugs have appeared in the way Internet Explorer, in particular, handles cookies and, historically, it's been possible for rogue websites to retrieve information from cookies other than their own.

ASK
WOODY.COM

Because of ongoing problems, sound and fury frequently raised by people who don't understand, and concomitant legislation in many countries, first-party cookies these days rarely include any interesting information. Mostly, they store innocuous settings and perhaps a randomly generated number that's used to track a customer in the company's database. To a bad guy, the data stored in most cookies varies between banal and useless.

What's a third-party cookie?

By contrast, *third-party cookies* (or *tracking cookies*) aren't as bland. They have significant commercial value because they can be used to keep track of your web surfing. Here's how: Suppose ZDNet (www.zdnet.com), which is owned by CBS, sells an ad to DoubleClick. When you venture to any ZDNet page (they all have tiny, one-pixel ads from DoubleClick), both ZDNet/CBS and DoubleClick can stick cookies on your computer. ZDNet can retrieve only its cookie, and DoubleClick can retrieve only its cookie. Cool. DoubleClick may keep information about you visiting a ZDNet site that talks about, oh, an Android phone.

Now suppose that DealTime (www.dealtime.com) sells an ad to DoubleClick. You go to any page on DealTime (they also have tiny 1-pixel DoubleClick ads on every page), and both DealTime and DoubleClick can look at their own cookies. DealTime may be smart enough to ask DoubleClick whether you've been looking at

Android phones and then offer you a bargain tailored to your recent surfing. Or an insurance company may discover that you've been looking at information pages about the heartbreak of psoriasis. Or a car company may find out you're very interested in its latest Stutzmobile.

Multiply that little example by 10, 100, or 100,000, and you begin to see how third-party cookies can be used to collect a whole lot of information about you and your surfing habits. There's nothing illegal or immoral about it. But some people (present company certainly included) find it disconcerting. Oh, you know that Google owns DoubleClick, yes?

ASK
WOODY.COM

I don't get too worked up about cookies these days. If you've ever worked with them programmatically, you're probably at the yawning stage too. But the potential is there for them to become pernicious.

Deleting cookies

Cookies don't have anything to do with spam — you receive the same junk email even if you tell your computer to reject every cookie that darkens your door. Cookies don't spy on your PC, go sniffing for bank accounts, or keep a log of those . . . ahem . . . artistic websites you visit. They do serve a useful purpose, but like so many other concepts in the computer industry, cookies are exploited by a few companies in questionable ways. I talk about cookies extensively in Book 9, Chapter 1. If you're worried about cookies and want to know what's really happening, that's a great place to start.

To delete all cookies in Internet Explorer, follow the instructions in the earlier section "Saving space, losing time" to bring up the Delete Browsing History dialog box (refer to Figure 5-7). Make sure you select Cookies and Website Data, and click Delete. IE deletes all your cookies.

ASK
WOODY.COM

Internet Explorer has a mechanism for blocking third-party cookies, but I don't think it works very well. It's based on an old standard known as P3P, which is actually used by about a dozen websites based in Lower Slobovokia — and that's about it. Even some of Microsoft's own sites don't use P3P. I talk about the problems with IE's third-party cookie blocking in one of my *Info-World* Tech Watch articles, at `www.infoworld.com/t/internet-privacy/` `googles-cookie-runaround-in-ie-not-big-deal-186889`.

Changing the home page

Every time you start the desktop version of IE, it whirrs, and after a relatively brief moment (how brief depends primarily on the speed of your Internet connection), a web page appears. The information that page contains depends on whether your computer is set up to begin with a specific page known as a *home page*.

Microsoft sets up www.msn.com as the IE home page (see Figure 5-8) by default —
a page best known for its, uh, quirky choice of news items and phenomenally high
density of ads, including Microsoft's own ads. Many PC manufacturers set the
Internet Explorer home page to display something related to their systems.

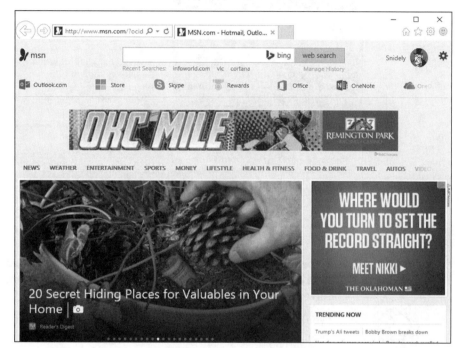

FIGURE 5-8:
If msn.com is
your favorite
page on the web,
you may want to
consider a pre-
frontal lobotomy.

If the ditzy, ad-laden MSN home page leaves you wondering whether P.T. Barnum
still designs web pages (there's one born every minute), or if your PC manufacturer's idea of a good home page doesn't quite jibe with your tastes, you can easily
change the home page. Here's how:

1. **Start IE.**

2. **Navigate to the page or pages you want to use for a home page.**

   You can bring up as many pages as you like on separate tabs. All the tabs
   will become your home page. See the previous section, "Tinkering with Tabs,"
   if you're not sure how to use tabs.

3. **Tap or click the Setting icon, choose Internet Options, and click the
   General tab.**

   You see the Home Page settings shown in Figure 5-9.

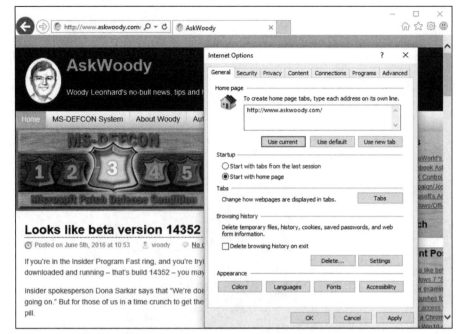

FIGURE 5-9:
Set the home page(s) here.

4. **At the top, make sure you have the list of all the tabs you would like to open as your home page, and then tap or click the button marked Use Current.**

If you choose Use New Tab, IE starts with no new page at all. That can be considerably faster than starting with a real home page.

TIP

5. **Click OK.**

Every time IE runs, it brings up the tabs you selected.

Turning on key features

Microsoft has a long list of improvements to its latest version of Internet Explorer. Most of those improvements operate behind the scenes; you'll know that they're there only when you don't get infected, if you know what I mean.

The last few IE versions have brought along a few worthwhile improvements, which you may not have seen:

» **You can pin a specific page to the desktop taskbar.** To pin a site to the taskbar, click the favicon, to the left of the page's address, or click the entire tab, and drag it down to the taskbar.

Microsoft says that a website accessed from the taskbar this way "takes on the branding of the site." What Microsoft means is that the background and border colors of the browser take on the main color of the site. Whooo-boy.

» **IE analyzes add-ons and tells you how much they're dragging your system down,** each time you launch IE. In general, you see the analysis only when your add-ons are causing big problems. There's a detailed explanation on the IE Blog at `http://blogs.msdn.com/b/ie/archive/2011/03/23/updates-to-add-on-performance-advisor.aspx`.

» *Suggested Sites* **(also called Bing Suggestions) is a feature added in IE 8 that keeps track of keys as you type them,** sending your keystrokes to Microsoft (Bing), generating potential matches and suggestions on the fly. Matches are based primarily on your browsing history. To turn on Suggested Sites, click the star Favorites (star) icon, and at the bottom of the box, select Turn on Suggested Sites.

TIP

As you may imagine, there's a great deal of controversy about the privacy aspects of Suggested Sites: Microsoft records every keystroke that you type into IE and watches your browsing history. Note that Suggested Sites is not turned on by default: You must enable it. (Check by tapping or clicking the gear icon in the upper right, choose Internet Options, then on the Advanced tab, look for Enable Suggested Sites.) Microsoft has a detailed report on its side of the story on the IE Blog at `http://blogs.msdn.com/b/ie/archive/2009/02/05/suggested-sites-privacy.aspx`.

» *SmartScreen Filter* **— the collaborative Internet Explorer Phishing Filter — keeps up-to-the-minute blacklists** of websites that have been identified by other IE users as possible phishing sites. Before you go to a website, SmartScreen Filter compares the site's address to its blacklist and warns you if the site has been identified as an unsafe site. It also looks on the page for telltale unsafe behavior and warns you if the site looks fishy. It also checks files before you download them to see if they're on Microsoft's whitelist, warning you that the file is not commonly downloaded if it's a relative newcomer.

TECHNICAL
STUFF

Unlike Suggested Sites, which sends all your information to Microsoft, the SmartScreen Filter maintains a small list of bad sites inside your computer that's updated frequently. That's a very effective trick first employed by Firefox.

To turn off SmartScreen Filter (for whatever reason), click the Tools icon (the one that looks like a gear), choose Safety, and then Turn off SmartScreen Filter. If you hit a dicey site — perhaps you were sent there by an apparent phishing email message — you can report the site by clicking the gear icon and choosing Report Unsafe Website.

>> *InPrivate Browsing* **lets you surf anywhere on the web without leaving any records on your PC of where you dallied.** It doesn't matter whether it's a racy page, the political headquarters of a candidate you detest, or a squealing fan site for a sappy soap opera, InPrivate Browsing makes sure that no details are left on your machine.

This kind of cloaking keeps only your PC clean. The sites you travel to can keep track of your Internet address (your IP address; see the earlier section "Looking at privacy," in this chapter, for details). Depending on how you connect to the Internet, your IP address can generally be traced to the router you're using to connect to the Internet. *Caveat surfor.*

REMEMBER

Searching with alacrity . . . and Google

It shouldn't surprise you that Internet Explorer ships with Microsoft's Bing as its default search engine. If you like Bing, my hat's off to you. But if you want to change to Google (or DuckDuckGo, www.duckduckgo.com, which doesn't keep records of your searches; Dogpile, www.dogpile.com; Hotbot, www.hotbot.com; or Wolfram Alpha, www.wolframalpha.com, all of which have their high points), it's remarkably difficult.

Unless Microsoft changes IE 11 (or a judge forces the company to change, to provide better access to alternative search engines), here's the official way to move from Bing to Google in IE 11. Note that this method changed after the original Windows 10 IE 11 shipped:

1. **Start IE.**

2. **Click the Settings icon. Then click Choose Manage Add-ons.**

   IE takes you to the Manage Add-Ons dialog box, as in Figure 5-10.

3. **On the left, choose Search Providers. At the bottom, click the Find More Search Providers link.**

   IE takes you to the Internet Explorer Gallery web page.

4. **When you find Google Search, click Add.**

   IE responds with the Add Search Provider dialog box.

5. **Click Add.**

6. **X out of the Internet Explorer Gallery page.**

7. **X out of the Manage Add-Ons dialog.**

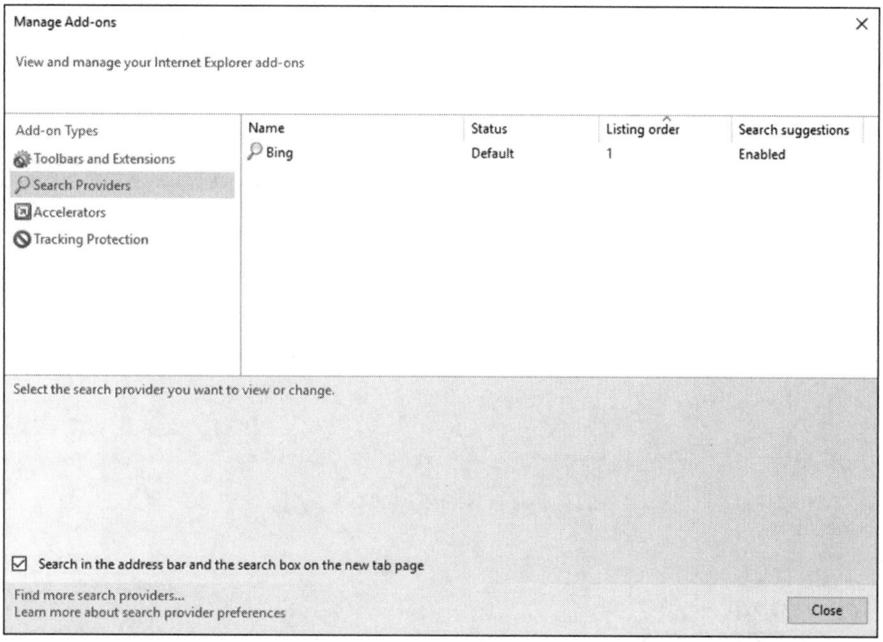

Manage Add-ons				×
View and manage your Internet Explorer add-ons				

Add-on Types	Name	Status	Listing order	Search suggestions
Toolbars and Extensions	Bing	Default	1	Enabled
Search Providers				
Accelerators				
Tracking Protection				

Select the search provider you want to view or change.

☑ Search in the address bar and the search box on the new tab page

Find more search providers...
Learn more about search provider preferences

Close

FIGURE 5-10:
This is where you add a new search provider.

You end up with a new Manage Add-Ons dialog box that looks like Figure 5-11.

8. **Once again, click the Settings icon and then Manage Add-Ons. On the left, choose Search Providers.**

You end up with a new Manage Add-Ons dialog box that looks like Figure 5-11.

9. **Click to select Google. At the bottom, click Set as Default.**

IE doesn't say a thing, but it changes your default search provider to Google.

How can you tell without running a search that Google is the default? Click the down arrow next to the magnifying glass icon again, and at the bottom, the tiny Google icon appears to the left of the Bing icon. That's how you know Google is the default search engine.

From that point on, you can type your search terms in the address bar and press Enter, or tap or click the magnifying glass icon, and IE sends the search terms to Google.

TIP

The *easiest* way to change IE to use Google as its default search provider? Let Google do the hard work. Go to www.google.com/homepage/search and click the button marked Make Google My Default Search Engine.

I have a section later in this chapter that gives some pointers about searching on the web.

ASK
WOODY.COM

Internet Explorer, Chrome, and Firefox

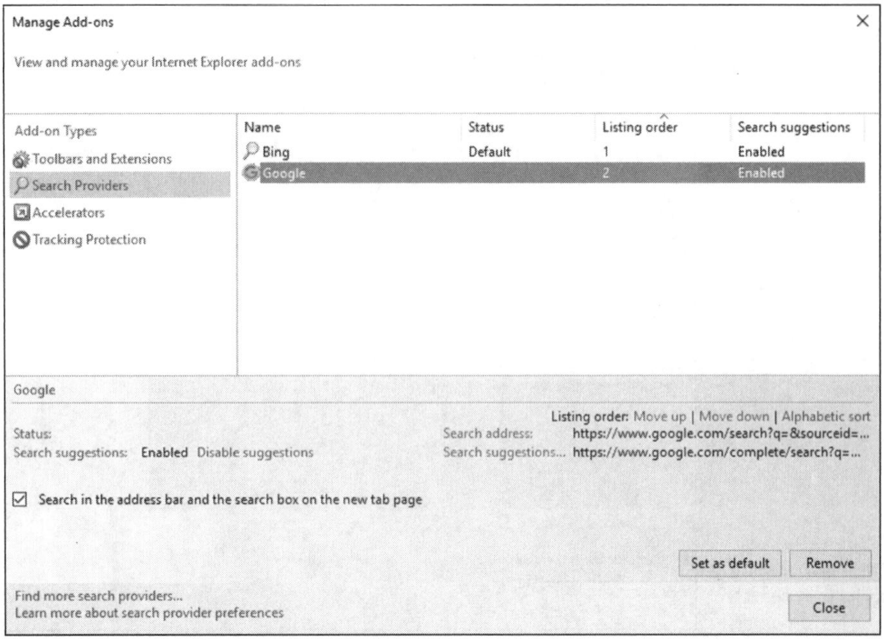

Manage Add-ons   ×

View and manage your Internet Explorer add-ons

Add-on Types	Name	Status	Listing order	Search suggestions
⚙ Toolbars and Extensions	🔎 Bing	Default	1	Enabled
🔎 Search Providers	G Google		2	Enabled
🅰 Accelerators				
🚫 Tracking Protection				

Google

Status: Listing order: Move up | Move down | Alphabetic sort
Search suggestions: **Enabled** Disable suggestions   Search address: https://www.google.com/search?q=&sourceid=...
   Search suggestions... https://www.google.com/complete/search?q=...

☑ Search in the address bar and the search box on the new tab page

Set as default   Remove

Find more search providers...
Learn more about search provider preferences   Close

FIGURE 5-11:
This is the Microsoft way to make Google your default search provider.

Customizing Firefox

Hey, you can use Internet Explorer if you want to. Without doubt, IE has a few features that other browsers can't match — dragging and dropping websites on the taskbar, Web Slices, InPrivate Filtering, and Accelerators come to mind. It also supports ActiveX controls and fits right in with Silverlight. If those ring your chimes, you need to play the IE game.

ASK WOODY.COM

I use Chrome and Firefox. I've recommended Firefox in my books for years and have recently switched to primarily using Chrome. Debating the relative merits of web browsers soon degenerates to a fight over the number of angels that can stand on the head of a pin. Suffice it to say that I feel Firefox has more options, although both Firefox and Chrome have started grabbing system resources like they own the place. I also like the fact that Firefox has no vested interest in keeping track of what I'm doing.

REMEMBER

I don't mean to imply that Firefox is perfect. It isn't. The Firefox team releases security patches too, just like IE and Chrome teams, and you need to make sure you keep Firefox updated. But I think you'll enjoy using Firefox more than Internet Explorer. I also would bet that you hit far fewer in-the-wild security problems with the Fox.

Installing Firefox

Installing Firefox can't be simpler. You don't need to disable Internet Explorer, pat your head and rub your belly, or jump through any other hoops (although clicking your heels and repeating "There's no place like home" may help). Just follow these steps:

1. **Using any convenient browser (even Edge or IE), go to** www.firefox.com **and follow the instructions to download and run the installer for the latest version of Firefox.**

In Figure 5-12, I pull up Firefox by using Edge.

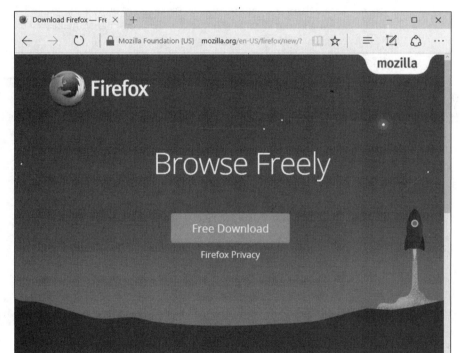

FIGURE 5-12:
You can install
Firefox from
Edge or any other
browser.

2. **Do the following:**

a. *Click the big, green Free Download button.*

b. *Chances are good that you'll need to click Save or Run or both to get the installer going.*

c. *Give the Windows User Account Control message box a Yes.*

d. *On the installer's splash screen, click Install.*

The Setup Wizard finishes.

3. **Respond to the wizard's question about importing bookmarks from IE, Chrome, or Edge. Then click Next.**

I generally choose Neither because I prefer to build my favorites in each browser separately, but your opinion may vary. Choose one or the other or neither or both.

The Firefox setup page appears (Figure 5-13). Firefox requires you to create a Firefox account. One of the nicest features in most modern browsers is their capability to sync bookmarks, history, and other settings. With Firefox, you can sync across Windows, Android, or iOS versions of the browser. All it takes is a (gulp) Firefox account.

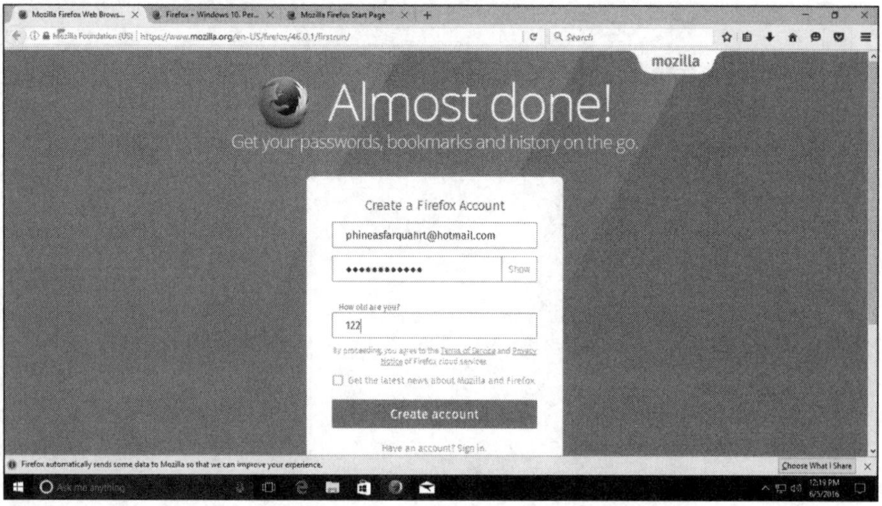

FIGURE 5-13: Firefox is up and running.

4. To get a Firefox account:

a. *Log in with a valid email address (it can be a throwaway free address, as long as you can retrieve mail from that address).*

b. *Provide a password (which does not need to be the same as your email password).*

c. *Type an age (creativity counts).*

d. *Select what you want to sync.*

Any time you want to sync your settings with another copy of Firefox, follow the same procedure and sign in with the same Firefox Account. You can use multiple Firefox accounts, if you want to sync groups of machines in different ways.

You may be asked whether you want to make Firefox your default browser. I click Not Now, because I'd rather make Chrome my default browser.

All the tricks I mention in the previous IE section called "Don't work too hard," also work in Firefox. You never need to type *http://*, almost never need to type *www*, and typing something like *dummies* followed by a Ctrl+Enter puts you spot-on for www.dummies.com.

Setting a home page in Firefox is similar to setting one in IE. To get to the right place, click the Firefox hamburger (three lines) menu, in the upper-right corner, to bring up the Settings menu shown in Figure 5-14. Choose Options. Home page settings are on the General tab.

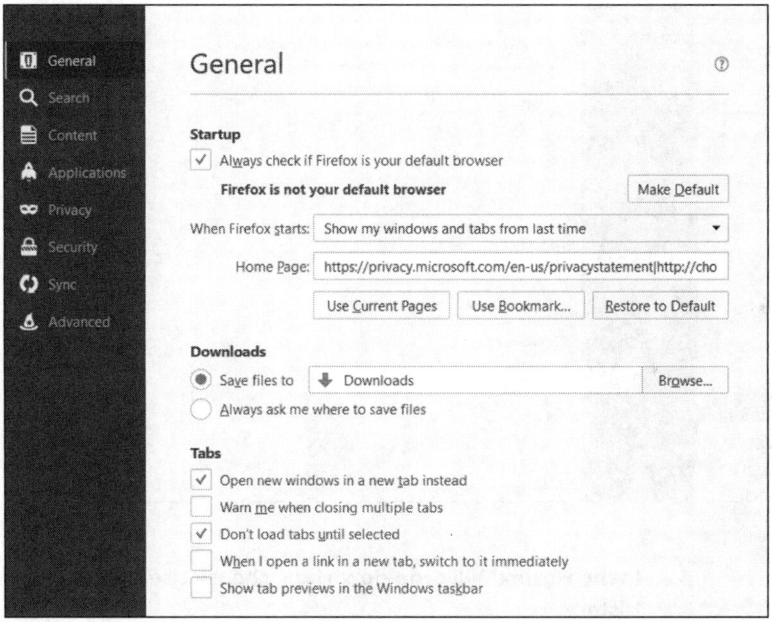

General

Startup

☑ Always check if Firefox is your default browser

Firefox is not your default browser   Make Default

When Firefox starts: Show my windows and tabs from last time ▼

Home Page: https://privacy.microsoft.com/en-us/privacystatement|http://cho

Use Current Pages   Use Bookmark...   Restore to Default

Downloads

◉ Save files to ⬇ Downloads   Browse...

○ Always ask me where to save files

Tabs

☑ Open new windows in a new tab instead

☐ Warn me when closing multiple tabs

☑ Don't load tabs until selected

☐ When I open a link in a new tab, switch to it immediately

☐ Show tab previews in the Windows taskbar

FIGURE 5-14:
The Firefox settings (hamburger) menu.

Internet Explorer, Chrome, and Firefox

Browsing privately in Firefox

Firefox has a private browsing feature similar to IE's InPrivate browsing, which I describe in the section "Turning on key features" in the IE part of this chapter. Firefox's version is called, er, private browsing. (Hey, Firefox invented it!)

To start a private browsing session, click the hamburger icon in the upper right and choose New Private Windows.

Some people prefer to always work in private browsing mode. There's much to be said for that approach, although you won't get the advantages of having cookies hanging around. Staying in private browsing mode is easy to do in Firefox. Here's how:

1. **Start Firefox. Click the hamburger icon in the upper right, and choose Options. On the left, click Privacy.**

   You see the Options dialog box shown in Figure 5-15.

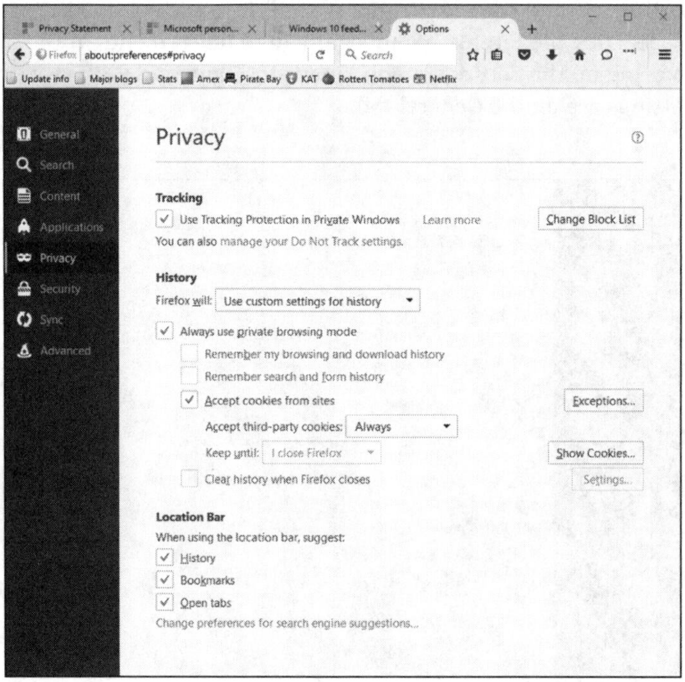

FIGURE 5-15:
It's easy to have Firefox always start in private browsing mode.

2. **In the Firefox Will drop-down box, choose Use Custom Settings for History.**

3. **Select the Always Use Private Browsing Mode option.**

4. **If you want to turn on Do Not Track (see the sidebar, "What is Do Not Track?" earlier in this chapter), select the Tell Websites That I Do Not Want to Be Tracked check box.**

   Admittedly, DNT doesn't do much, but it doesn't hurt and may block a few sites.

5. **Click OK.**

The next time you start Firefox, it'll be in private browsing mode. If you ever want to drop back into regular mode, click the hamburger icon and follow the above steps, choosing Firefox Will: Remember History.

Bookmarking with the Fox

Firefox handles bookmarks differently from Internet Explorer. (In IE, they're called favorites. Same thing.)

The easiest way to understand Firefox bookmarks? Start with the Unsorted Bookmarks folder. Go to the site you want to bookmark, and tap or click the Bookmark icon (the big star) to the right of the address bar. This step bookmarks the page and puts the bookmark in a type of "all others" folder named Unsorted Bookmarks.

Now follow these steps to assign a tag to your bookmark and then stick your bookmark in a place where you can find it later:

1. **Click the clipboard to the right of the Bookmark (star) icon and then click Show All Bookmarks.**

2. **Go down to Unsorted Bookmarks, which is on the left. Then on the right, look for the bookmark you want to change.**

   Firefox shows you all the bookmarks that aren't yet assigned to a folder, as in Figure 5-16.

3. **In the Tags area (the middle column), type any tags you want to associate with the bookmark.**

   Tags help you find things on the address bar. For example, if you assign a Stuxnet tag to the bookmark, typing **stux** in the address bar brings up this particular bookmark.

REMEMBER

4. **Right-click any empty spot at the top of the Firefox window and select Bookmarks Toolbar.**

   You see the bookmarks toolbar, below the address bar.

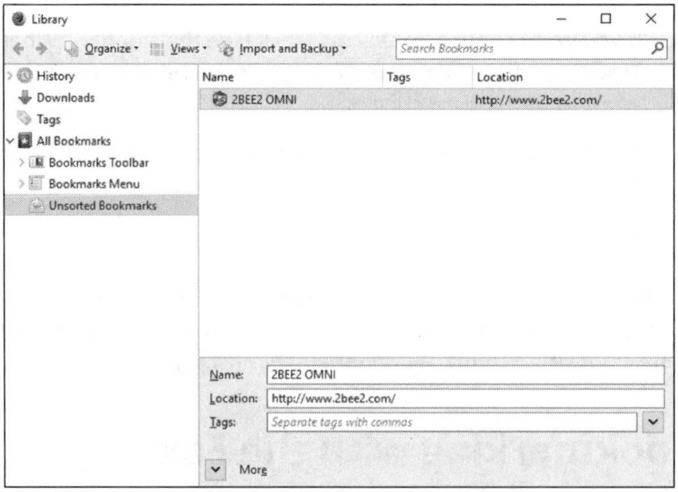

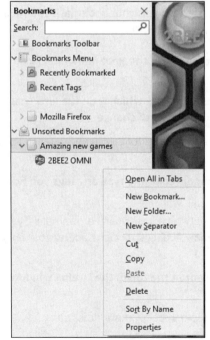

FIGURE 5-16:
Edit your raw,
unsorted
bookmark.

5. **Click the clipboard icon to the right of the star and choose View Bookmarks Sidebar.**

   The bookmarks sidebar, shown in Figure 5-17, has all the tools you need to manage bookmarks. You can click and drag folders, for example.

FIGURE 5-17:
Add new folders
here.

6. **To create a new Bookmarks folder, right-click inside the bookmarks sidebar and choose New Folder.**

   If you create a new folder, you can leave it in the Unsorted Bookmarks folder, but if you want to make it more readily accessible from the bookmarks toolbar, click and drag the new folder in the bookmarks sidebar so the folder appears under the Bookmarks Sidebar folder.

In Figure 5-18, I put the News folder under the Bookmarks Toolbar folder, and it appears on the bookmarks toolbar.

The bookmarks toolbar is convenient, but it takes up precious space on the screen. Many people prefer to work with the Bookmark icon, on the far right. Optionally, you can usually click and drag bookmarks into different (existing) folders.

After the folder has been created (and, optionally, located on the Bookmarks menu or the bookmarks toolbar), you can place any bookmark in the folder by double-clicking the bookmark star.

Changing the default search engine

Firefox puts its searches through Yahoo! Search. What is Yahoo! Search, you ask? Good question. As the book went to press, Yahoo! Search (as, indeed, all of Yahoo!) is in a state of rapid flux. Back in more deterministic times, Yahoo! Search was just a front for Microsoft's Bing; a search made through Yahoo! Search drew its answers from Bing, and Yahoo! paid Microsoft big time, pulling through Microsoft's advertising and spitting it out in Firefox. In late 2015, Yahoo! renegotiated its agreement with Microsoft, and as of this writing, up to 49 percent of all responses come from Google, including Google ads. What will the future bing, er, bring, especially with Yahoo! in its currently precarious financial position? Who knows. Stay tuned.

It's hard to change the default search engine in most browsers. Not so in Firefox. Here's how you do it:

1. **In the Firefox search bar (the one with the dimmed *Search*), click or tap the magnifying glass.**

   You see the Search With choices shown in Figure 5-19.

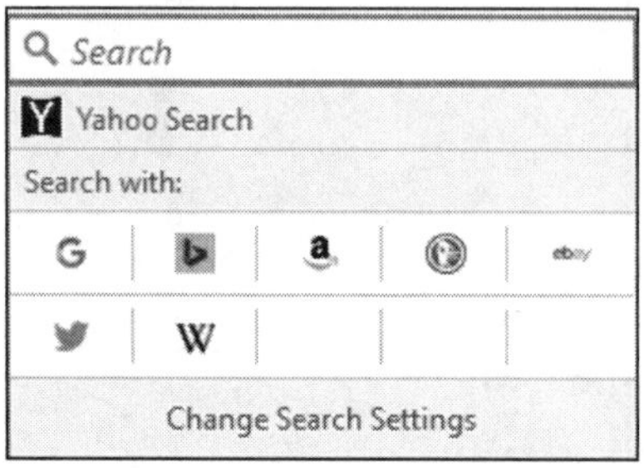

FIGURE 5-19:
Firefox makes it
easy to switch
search engines.

2. **At the bottom, click Change Search Settings.**

3. **From the offered drop-down list, simply pick your preferred search engine.**

   Remember that DuckDuckGo — the icon with a duck on it — doesn't track your searches and doesn't sell your data to advertisers.

That's all it takes. Whichever search engine you choose becomes your default, and it'll stay that way until you change it.

Firefox's competitors could learn a thing or three.

Adding Firefox's best add-ons

One of the best reasons for choosing Firefox over IE and Chrome is the incredible abundance of add-ons. If you can think of something to do with a browser, chances are good there's already an add-on that'll do it.

An enormous cottage industry has grown up around Firefox. The Firefox people made it relatively easy to extend the browser itself. As a result, tens of thousands of add-ons cover an enormous range of capabilities.

To search for add-ons, click the hamburger icon in the upper right and choose Get Add-Ons (see Figure 5-20). You can search for the add-ons recommended by Firefox itself or look for the most frequently downloaded add-ons.

FIGURE 5-20: Firefox makes it easy to extend the browser with add-ons made by other groups.

Here are some of my favorites. I always install the first four on any Firefox system I come into contact with:

ASK
WOODY.COM

>> **NoScript** lets you shut down all active content — Java, JavaScript, Flash, and more — either individually or for a site as a whole. Some sites don't work with JavaScript turned off, but NoScript gives you a fighting chance to pick and choose the scripts you want. Between JavaScript and Flash blocking, NoScript significantly reduces your exposure to online malware.

>> **Ghostery** keeps an eye on sites that are watching you. It tells you when sites contain web beacons or third-party cookies that can be used to track your surfing habits. I don't use Ghostery to stop cookies, but I do use it to watch who's watching me.

>> **Adblock Plus** blocks ads. (What did you expect?) It blocks lots of ads — so much so that you may want to pull it back a bit. That's easy too. See a demo at adblockplus.org/en.

REMEMBER

>> **DownThemAll** scrapes all downloadable files on a web page and presents them so you can choose which files to download. Click Start, and they all come loading down.

>> **Greasemonkey** adds a customizable scripting language to Firefox. After you install Greasemonkey, you can download scripts from `https://greasyfork.org/en` that perform an enormous variety of tasks, from tweet assistance to downloading Flickr files.

>> **IETab +** embeds Internet Explorer inside Firefox. If you hit a site that absolutely won't work with Firefox, right-click the link, choose Tools and then choose Open This Link in IETab, and Internet Explorer takes over a tab inside Firefox.

>> **eBay Sidebar** watches your trades while you're doing something else. It's from eBay.

>> **Video DownloadHelper** makes it easy to download videos from the web. **Easy YouTube Video Downloader** does the same thing, but it's specialized for YouTube.

>> **Linky** lets you open all links or images on a page, all at once, either on separate tabs or in separate windows. It's a helpful adjunct to Google image search.

To install the latest edition of any of these add-ons, go to Add-Ons Manager (click the hamburger icon, then Get Add-Ons) search for the add-on's name. Each add-on's page has download and installation instructions — usually just a click or two and a possible restart of Firefox.

Optimizing Google Chrome

Google Chrome has several advantages over IE and Firefox. Foremost among them: world-class sandboxing of Flash, Java, and PDF support, which greatly reduces the chances of getting stung by the largest source of infections these days. IE and Firefox have both added similar protection, but Chrome was first and, I think, best.

As for Edge. . . it looks like Edge's going to beat Chrome at the sandboxing game, but it's still too early to tell. The bad guys are smart and getting smarter. Edge's still the new kid on the block. Time will tell.

That said, the biggest disadvantage is Google's (readily admitted!) tendency to keep track of where you've been, as an adjunct to its advertising program. If you install Chrome, sign in with your Google account, and start browsing, Google knows all, sees all, saves all — unless you turn on Incognito (private) browsing.

The second major disadvantage? Chrome's a resource hog. If you only open, oh, 10 tabs, Chrome's great. But if you open 20 or 30 at a time — I'll confess I'm among the guilty — Chrome can bog things down significantly.

Installing Chrome

Installing Google Chrome is like falling off a log:

1. **With any browser, go to** www.chrome.google.com.

You probably see a big blue button that says Download Now.

2. **Click the button to download.**

You see a user agreement. Read all 214,197 pages of it.

3. **Deselect the check box marked Set Google Chrome as My Default Browser, and click Accept and Install.**

4. **Click Run, or Save and then Run, depending on what browser you're using to download Chrome.**

The installer takes a minute or two, and then asks you to choose a default browser.

5. **Choose your default browser.**

I say yes to Chrome, but then I'm biased. The installer goes straight to work, as shown in Figure 5-21.

6. **If you want your Chrome settings to follow you onto any computer, tablet, or phone:**

a. *Sign in with a Google ID, such as a Gmail address.*

b. *Click the hamburger icon and choose Settings.*

c. *Sign in at the top.*

Syncing across many kinds of devices is one of the best parts about Chrome. But I'm ever mindful of the fact that Google keeps tabs on everywhere I go and uses the accumulated information to dish up ads designed to convince me to click.

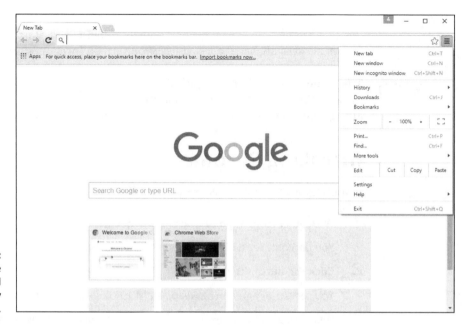

FIGURE 5-21:
Google Chrome
has all the usual
controls, easily
available.

Navigating in Chrome

Navigation in Chrome is very similar to that in Firefox, except there's no search bar. Chrome doesn't need one: You just type in the address bar. (Google calls it an *omnibar*, which is cool because they came up with the idea.)

All the tricks I mention in the earlier IE section called "Don't work too hard" also perform in Chrome. You never need to type *http://*, almost never need to type *www*, and typing something like *dummies* followed by a Ctrl+Enter puts you directly into www.dummies.com.

The default home page in Chrome is a little different from both IE and Firefox. Chrome displays its New Tab page, which has an icon for Google Apps (the tic-tac-toe icon in the upper right). Click the icon and you see thumbnails for the Chrome Web Store and other pages that you've frequently visited (see Figure 5-22). The New Tab page adds more entries as you use the browser. The Apps button brings up Google Docs, Gmail, Google Drive, YouTube, Google Sheets, Slides, and more.

 If you want to change the home page in Chrome, navigate to the page(s) you want to use. Click the hamburger icon in the upper right (and shown in the margin), and choose Settings. A new tab opens with various Chrome settings. Under the heading On Startup, select the Open a Specific Page or Set of Pages option, and then tap or click the Set Pages link. In the lower left, tap or click Use Current Pages. You see a list like the one in Figure 5-23. Verify that you have the right pages, and tap or click OK.

FIGURE 5-22:
The New Tab
page in Chrome
includes an Apps
button.

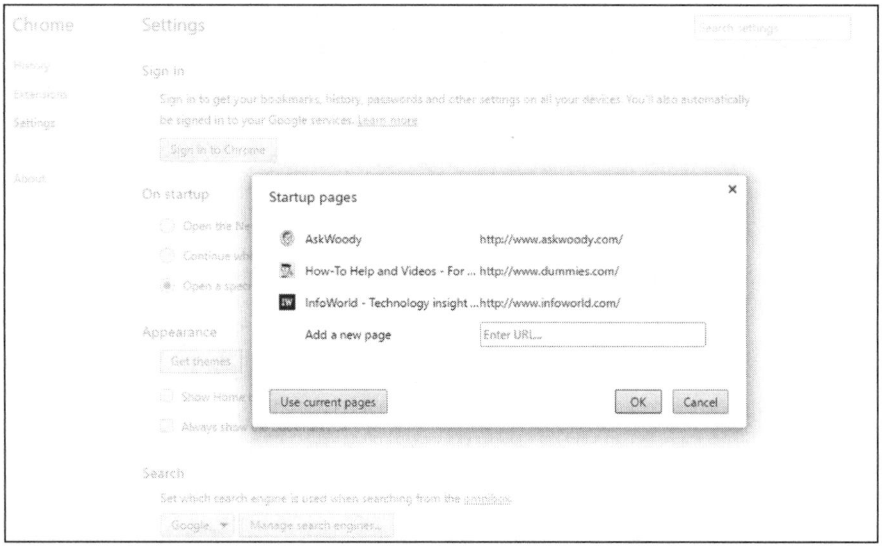

FIGURE 5-23:
It's easy to set the
home page(s) for
Chrome.

Internet Explorer,
Chrome, and Firefox

Like IE, Firefox, and Edge, if you signed in to Chrome using a Google ID (such as a Gmail email address), changing the home page(s) here will change your Chrome home pages on all the computers — whether they're on PCs, tablets, smartphones — anywhere you go. Your add-ons and favorites travel with you, too.

The following Chrome features are helpful as you move around the web using Chrome:

>> **The default search engine:** The default search engine setting is on the same settings tab shown in Figure 5-23. Bing is one of the listed options, but you can add just about any search engine. Compare and contrast that with IE's default search engine hunting game.

>> **Private browsing:** Chrome's version of InPrivate Browsing is called Incognito. To start a new Incognito window, click the hamburger icon and choose New Incognito Window.

ASK
WOODY.COM

>> **Bookmarks:** I find Chrome's bookmarks capability much easier to use than Firefox's. To see why, go to a web page that you'd like to bookmark, and click the bookmark star icon, on the right. If you want to rearrange your bookmark folders, click the Edit button, and you can work with a full, hierarchical organization of folders, as in Figure 5-24.

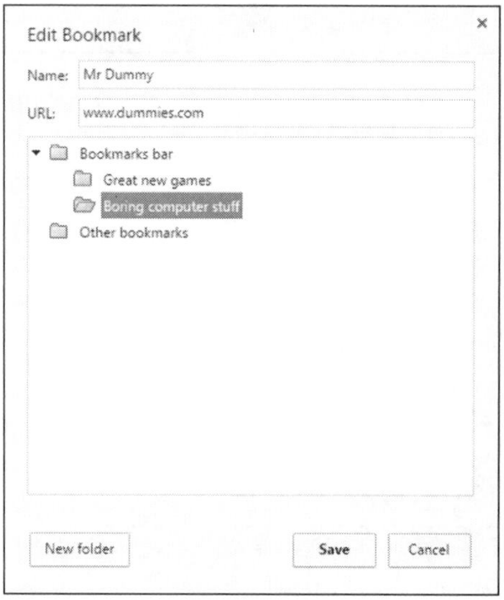

FIGURE 5-24:
Chrome book-marks are simple and easy to organize.

Edit Bookmark	×

Name: Mr Dummy

URL: www.dummies.com

▼ 📁 Bookmarks bar
    📁 Great new games
    📂 Boring computer stuff
  📁 Other bookmarks

New folder   Save   Cancel

ASK
WOODY.COM

Chrome Extensions, once a small subset of all great add-ons, now rate as absolutely first-class. Click the hamburger icon in the upper right, and choose More Tools, Extensions. If you're looking for great extensions, try Taco (for customizing the New Tab page) and Noisli (for distraction-busting ambient sounds), or look at my latest list at www.infoworld.com/article/2606761/web-browsers/150797-12-Chrome-extensions-power-users-will-love.html. TooManyTabs and the newer OneTab let you consolidate your tabs, reducing the amount of screen real estate consumed and also cutting back on Chrome's infamous memory hogging. I use LastPass for Chrome all the time.

Searching on the Web

Internet searching can be a lonely business. You're out there, on the Internet range, with nothing but gleaming banner ads and text links to guide you. What happens when you want to find information on a specific subject, but you're not sure where to start? What if Google leads you on a wild goose chase? What if the Microsoft Bing decision engine takes the wrong turn?

Google's good. It's the search engine I use every day. But there are some decent alternatives, several of which can help in specific situations. For example:

>> Microsoft's **Bing** (www.bing.com) isn't all that bad, and it's getting better. It remains to be seen if Bing can come up with any really compelling reasons to switch from Google. Microsoft's dumping a ton of money into search — more than a billion dollars a year, at last count — and I'm not sure it's come up with anything that puts Bing clearly in the lead.

>> **DuckDuckGo** (www.duckduckgo.com) is an up-and-comer that I find fascinating. It relies heavily on information from crowd-sourced sources, including Wikipedia. At this point, the results DuckDuckGo delivers aren't as close to what I want as Google's, but they're getting better. One big point in this search engine's favor: Like Firefox, DuckDuckGo doesn't track what you do.

>> **Dogpile** (www.dogpile.com), an old favorite, aggregates search results from Google, Bing, Yahoo!, and other engines and smashes them all together in a remarkably quick way. If I can't find what I need on Google, I frequently turn to Dogpile.

>> **Wolfram Alpha** (www.wolframalpha.com) isn't exactly a search engine. It's a mathematical deduction engine that works with text input. So, for example, it can compare methanol, ethanol, and isopropanol. Or it can describe to you details of all the hurricanes in 1991. Or it can analyze the motion of a double pendulum.

But I find myself going back to Google.

Google has gone from one of the most admired companies on the web to one of the most criticized — on topics ranging from copyright infringement to pornography to privacy and censorship — and the PageRank system has been demonized in terms rarely heard since the Spanish Inquisition. Few people now believe that PageRank objectively rates the importance of a web page; millions of dollars and thousands of person-months have been spent trying to jigger the results. Like it or not, Google just works. The Google spiders (the programs that search for information), which crawl all over the web, night and day, looking for pages, have indexed billions of pages, feeding hundreds of millions of searches a day. Other search engines have spiders too, but Google's outspiders them all.

Internet Explorer, Chrome, and Firefox

As this book went to press, Google (and its parent company, Alphabet) was worth about $500 billion, the verb *google* had been embraced by prestigious dictionaries, the company was taking on Microsoft *mano a mano* in many areas, and many other search engines offered decent alternatives to the once almighty Google. "OK, Google" has entered my lexicon for querying my phone about anything under the sun. Self-driving cars, robots, fiber optic cable, Internet from hot air balloons, play Go — even a run at "curing" death — are now part of the Google fold. Everything's changing rapidly, and that's good news for us consumers.

In this section, I show you several kinds of searches you can perform with Google (and the other search engines). No matter what you're looking for, a search engine can find it!

Finding what you're looking for

Google has turned into the 800-pound gorilla of the searching world. I know people who can't even find AOL unless they go through Google. True fact.

The more you know about Google, the better it can serve you. Getting to know Google inside and out has the potential to save you more time than just about anything in Windows proper. If you can learn to search for answers quickly and thoroughly — and cut through the garbage on the web just as quickly and thoroughly — you can't help but save time in everything you do.

You can save yourself lots of time and frustration if you plot out your search before your fingers hit the keyboard.

Obviously, you should choose your search terms precisely. Pick words that will appear on any page that matches what you're looking for: Don't use *Compaq* when you want *Compaq S710*.

Beyond the obvious, the Google search engine has certain peculiarities you can exploit. These peculiarities hold true whether you're using Google in your browser's search bar or you venture directly to www.google.com:

>> **Capitalization doesn't matter.** Search for *diving phuket* or *diving Phuket* — either search returns the same results.

>> **The first words you use have more weight than the latter words.** If you look for *phuket diving,* you see a different list than the one for *diving phuket.* The former list emphasizes websites about Phuket that include a mention of diving; the latter includes diving pages that mention Phuket.

>> **Google first shows you only those pages that include all the search terms.** The simplest way to narrow a search that returns too many results is to add more specific words to the end of your search term. For example, if *phuket diving* returns too many pages, try *phuket diving beginners.* In programmer's parlance, the terms are ANDed together.

>> **If you type more than ten words, Google ignores the ones after the tenth.**

>> **You can use OR** to tell Google that you want the search to include two or more terms — but you have to capitalize OR. For example, *phuket OR samui OR similans diving* returns diving pages that focus on Phuket, Samui, or the Similans.

>> **If you want to limit the search to a specific phrase, use quotes.** For example, *diving phuket "day trip"* is more limiting than *diving phuket day trip* because in the former, the precise phrase *day trip* has to appear on the page.

>> **Exclude pages from the results by putting a space and then a hyphen in front of the words you don't want.** For example, if you want to find pages about diving in Phuket but you don't want to associate with lowly snorkelers, try *diving phuket -snorkeling.*

REMEMBER

>> **You can combine search tricks.** If you're looking for overnight diving, try *diving phuket -"day trip"* to find the best results.

>> **Google supports wildcard searches** in quite a limited way: The asterisk (*) stands for a single word. If you're accustomed to searches in, say, Word or Windows, the * generally indicates a sequence of characters, but in Google it stands for only an entire word. You may search for *div** and expect to find both diver and diving, but Google won't match on either. Conversely, if you search for, oh, *email * * wellsfargo.com,* you find lots of email addresses. (The second * matches the at sign [@] in an address. Try it.)

TIP

If you use Google to search for answers to computer questions, take advantage of any precise numbers or messages you can find. For example, Googling *computer won't start* doesn't get you anywhere; but *two beeps on startup* may. *Can't install* won't get you anywhere. *Install error 800F9004* turns up wonders. If you're trying to track down a Windows error message, use Google to look for the precise message. Write it down, if you have to.

Using Advanced Search

Didn't find the results you need? Use Google Advanced Search. There's a trick.

If you need to narrow your searches — in other words, if you want Google to do the sifting rather than do it yourself — you should get acquainted with Google's Advanced Search capabilities. Here's a whirlwind tour:

1. **Run your search; if it doesn't have what you want, click the gear icon and choose Advanced Search.**

   REMEMBER

   The Google gear icon is located in the upper-right corner *of the search results page* — it's not part of your browser, it's actually on the search results page.

   Google brings up its Advanced Search page (see Figure 5-25).

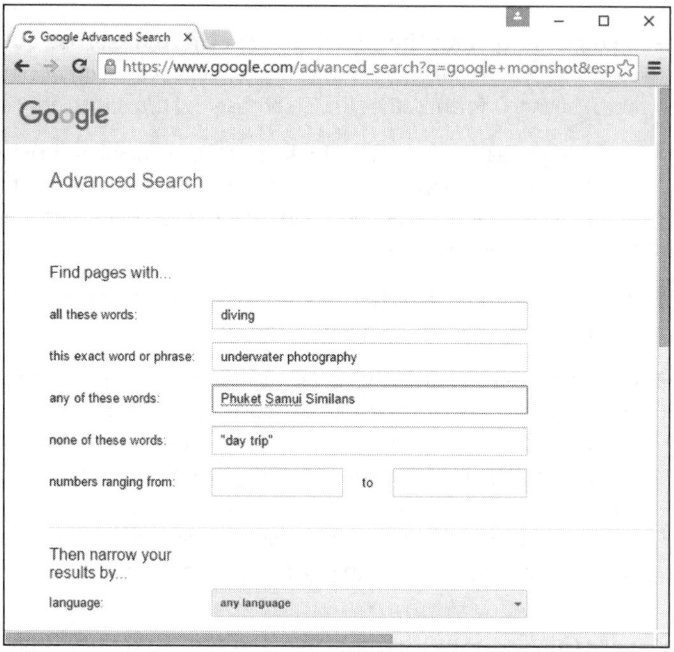

FIGURE 5-25:
Advanced Search lets you narrow your Google search quickly and easily.

2. **Fill in the top part of the page with your search terms.**

   In Figure 5-25, I ask for sites that include the word *diving* and the exact phrase *underwater photography*. I also want to exclude the phrase *day trip* and return pages pertaining only to Phuket, Samui, or the Similans.

   REMEMBER

   Anything you can do in the top part of this page can also be done by using the shorthand tricks mentioned in the preceding section. If you find yourself using the top part of the page frequently, save yourself some time and brush up on the tricks (such as typing **OR**, **-**, **""**) that I mention in the earlier section, "Finding what you're looking for."

3. **In the bottom part of the Advanced Search page, further refine your search by matching on the identified source language of the page (not always accurate); a specific filename extension (such as .pdf or .doc); or the domain name, such as** `www.dummies.com`.

You can also click the link at the bottom to limit the search to pages stamped with specific dates (notoriously unreliable), pages with specific licensing allowances (not widely implemented), and ranges of numbers.

4. **Press Enter.**

The results of your advanced search appear in a standard Google search results window (see Figure 5-26).

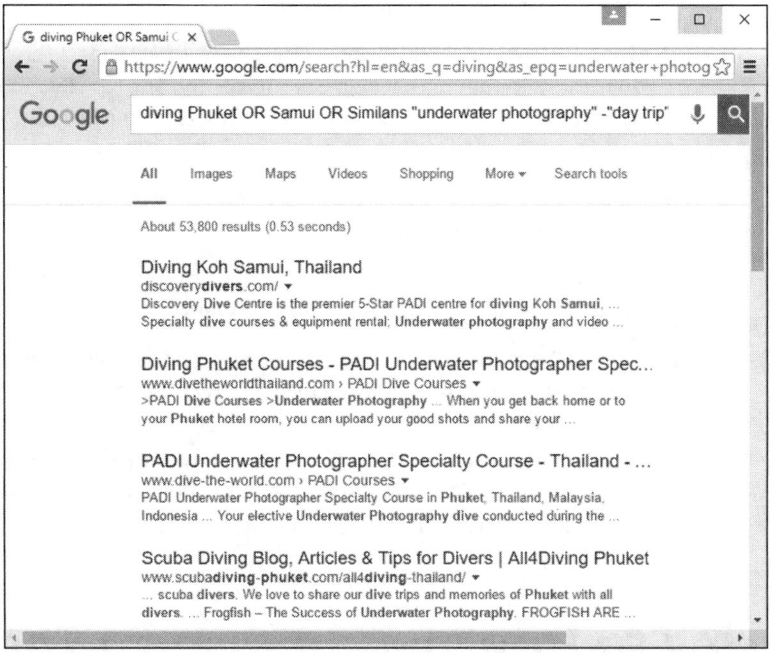

FIGURE 5-26:
Running the stringent search specified in Figure 5-25 turns up 53,800 hits.

You can find more details about Google Advanced Search on the Google Advanced Search page, `www.google.com/help/refinesearch.html`.

Pulling out Google parlor tricks

Google has many tricks up its sleeve, some of which you may find useful — even if it's just to win a bet at a party. For example:

>> To find the status of your UPS, FedEx, or USPS delivery, just type the package number (digits only) in the Google search box.

>> The search box is a stock ticker. Type a symbol such as **MSFT**, **GOOG**, or **AAPL**.

>> To use Google as a calculator, just type the equation in the Google search box. For example, to find the answer to 1,234 × 5,678, type **1234*5678** in the search box and press Enter. Or to find the answer to 3 divided by pi, type **3/pi**. No, Google doesn't solve partial differentials or simultaneous equations — yet. For that, check out Wolfram Alpha.

>> Google has a built-in units converter. The word *in* triggers the converter. Try **10 meters in feet** or **350 degrees F in centigrade** (or **350 f in c**) or **20 dollars in baht** or (believe me, this is impressive) **1.29 euros per liter in dollars per gallon**.

>> To find a list of alternative (and frequently interesting) definitions for a word, type **define**, as in **define booty**.

>> You can see movie reviews and local showtimes by typing **movie** and then the name of the movie, such as **movie star wars 7**.

>> Try quick questions for quick facts. For example, try **height of mt everest** or **length of mississippi river** or **currency in singapore**.

If you click the microphone icon in the search bar, or if you're using a smartphone and start by saying "OK Google," all these tricks work under voice command, as well. "OK, Google" (pause) "when was the end of the Cretaceous period?"

Referring to Internet Reference Tools

I get questions all the time from people who want to know about specific tools for the Internet. Here are my choices for the tools that everyone needs.

Internet speed test

Everybody, but everybody, needs (or wants) to measure her Internet speed from time to time. The sites I use these days for testing is www.dslreports.com/speedtest and www.testmy.net.

A million different speed tests are available on the Internet, and 2 million different opinions about various tools' accuracy, reliability, replicability, and other measurements. I used to run speed tests at Speakeasy, but then found that my ISP was caching the data — in fact, caching all the data from a OOKLA-based test — so the results I saw were just local; they didn't reflect long-distance speeds. So I moved to DSLReports, with its tests that can't be cached, and haven't looked back.

I later added `www.testmy.net` because the reports appear valid — and the site has automatic testing, so I can run tests every hour for days on end.

DNSStuff

Ever wonder whether the website BillyJoeBobsPhishery.com belongs to BillyJoeBob? Head over to `www.dnsstuff.com` (see Figure 5-27) and find out.

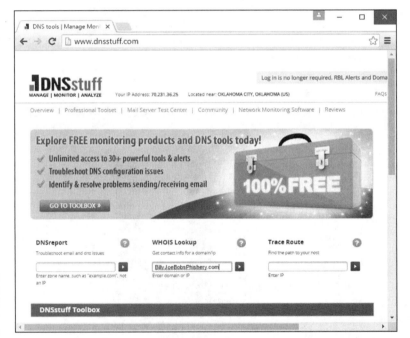

FIGURE 5-27:
DNSStuff offers
a wide array of
web- and Net-
related tools.

You give DNSStuff a domain name, and the site divulges all the public records about the site, commonly known as a whois: who owns the site (or at least who registered it), where the rascals are located, and whom to contact — although you must register a valid email address to get all the info.

DNSStuff also tells you the official abuse contact for a particular site (useful if you want to lodge a complaint about junk mail or scams), whether a specific site is listed on one of the major spam databases, and much more.

3d Traceroute

So where's the hang-up? When the Internet slows down, you probably want to know where it's getting bogged down. Not that it will do you much good, but you may be able to complain to your ISP.

My favorite tool for tracing Internet packets is the free product 3d Traceroute from German Holger Lembke in Braunschweig. You can download it at this website: `http://d3tr.de`. 3d Traceroute has no installer — it just runs. I like that.

When you run 3d Traceroute, you feed it a target location — a web address to use as a destination for your packets. As soon as you enter a target, 3d Traceroute runs out to the target and keeps track of all the hops — the discrete jumps from location to location — along the way. It measures the speed of each hop (see Figure 5-28).

Hop	IP	Hostname	last [ms]	min [ms]	max [ms]	ava. [ms]	var. [ms]	total Loss	perc. Loss	Latitude	Longitude	RTTL	ASN
1	192.168.1.254	homeportal	0	0	1	0	0					64	
2	23.114.160.1	23-114-160-1.lightspeed.nsvltn.sbcglobal.net	2	2	4		1					63	AS8075
3	99.174.25.172	99.174.25.172	3	3	6	4	1					62	
4	99.131.205.78	99.131.205.78	3	3	9		2					61	
5	99.131.205.123	99.131.205.123	3	3	6		1					60	
6	12.83.112.17	12.83.112.17	6	3	6		1						AS7018
7	12.122.141.105	ggr1.attga.ip.att.net	11	10	11	11	0						AS7018
8	206.121.10.34	206.121.10.34	11	10	11	11	1					55	
9	104.44.224.190	ae9-0.atb-96cbe-1b.ntwk.msn.net	11	10	11	10	0					54	AS8075
10	104.44.8.102	104.44.8.102	111	106	111	106	1						AS8075
11	104.44.4.49	be-3-0.ibr01.bn1.ntwk.msn.net	108	107	110	108	1						AS8075
12	104.44.4.63	be-1-0.ibr02.bn1.ntwk.msn.net	109	107	109	108	1						AS8075
13	104.44.4.26	be-3-0.ibr02.was05.ntwk.msn.net	107	106	109	107	1						AS8075
14	104.44.4.29	be-4-0.ibr02.nyc04.ntwk.msn.net	109	107	109	108	1						AS8075
15	104.44.5.29	104.44.5.29	100	100	120	102	6					48	AS8075
16	104.44.225.175	ae22-0.lts-96cbe-1b.ntwk.msn.net	101	100	102	101	1					47	AS8075
17	104.44.9.150	be-62-0.ibr01.lts.ntwk.msn.net	108	107	109	108	1						AS8075
18	104.44.4.232	be-5-0.ibr01.amb.ntwk.msn.net	107	106	108	107	1						AS8075
19	104.44.4.212	be-1-0.ibr02.amb.ntwk.msn.net	108	106	109	107	1						AS8075
20	104.44.9.239	104.44.9.239	106	106	107	106	0					43	AS8075
21													

FIGURE 5-28: Why is the Internet so slow? 3d Traceroute pinpoints pileups.

If you look at the ASN column, on the far-right end in Figure 5-28, you can see a list of AS numbers. Each number uniquely identifies a network operator. You can search for the AS number at `www.google.com` and see where your packets hit a roadblock.

Down for everyone or just me?

So you try and try and can't get through to Wikipedia, or Outlook has the hiccups: The browser keeps coming back and says it's timed out, or it just sits there and does nothing.

It's time to haul out the big guns. Hop over to www.downforeveryoneorjustme.com (no, I don't make this stuff up), and type the address of the site that isn't responding. The computer on the other end checks to see whether the site you requested is still alive. Cool.

The Wayback Machine

He said, she said. We said, they said. Web pages come and go, but sometimes you just have to see what a page looked like last week or last year. No problem, Sherman: Just set the Wayback Machine for November 29, 1975. (That's the day Bill Gates first used the name Micro Soft.)

If you're a Mr. Peabody look-alike and you want to know what a specific web page really said in the foggy past, head to the Internet Archive at www.archive.org, where the Wayback (or is it WABAC?) Machine has more than 85 billion web pages archived and indexed for your entertainment (see Figure 5-29).

FIGURE 5-29: Everything old is new again with the Archive.org Wayback Machine. This is what windows.com looked like almost 20 years ago on October 11, 1997.

Chapter 6

Hey, Cortana!

"Hey, Cortana!"

"Yes, Boss."

"Get me a double skinny latte."

"I'll bring it to you. Okay to charge your Amex four dollars and thirty seven cents?"

Cortana isn't quite there yet. That was in my dream last night. In fact, if you try to order a double skinny latte in Windows 10, you get the response in Figure 6-1.

Cortana's good, but she isn't *that* good.

Launched on Windows Phone, Cortana is Microsoft's digital-assistant answer to Apple's Siri and Google's OK Google.

Cortana, however, is a bit more refined: She (and I'll relentlessly refer to her as *she*; please forgive the anthropomorphism!) is tied into all Windows 10 searches. That's both good and bad, as I discuss later in this chapter.

She's also lots of fun.

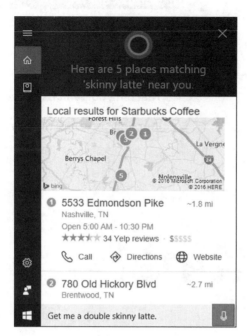

FIGURE 6-1:
Baristas don't have to worry about their jobs. Yet.

The Cortana Backstory

There aren't many parts of Windows 10 that have a backstory, so indulge me for a minute here.

Cortana is a fully developed artificial intelligence character from the video game series Halo. She lives (or whatever AIs do) 500 years in the future. In the Halo series, she morphs/melds into Master Chief Petty Officer John-117 and, in that position, tries to keep Halo installations from popping up all over the galaxy. Halo installations, of course, destroy all sentient life.

Cortana actually chose John-117, not the other way around. She was supposed to be the resident AI on a ship, temporarily, but plans changed and she ended up the permanent AI, apparently because of the deviousness of a Colonel Ackerson. It's not nice to fool Cortana, so she hacked into Ackerson's system and black-mailed him.

If that sounds a little bit like the kind of life you lead, well, you're ready for Cortana.

Make Cortana Respond to "Hey, Cortana"

If you've never used Cortana before, she won't respond to "Hey, Cortana!" in spite of all the demos you've seen. Instead, you need to click in the Ask Me Anything search box to the right of the Start icon. Cortana responds with a notice that she can do much more, shown in Figure 6-2. Hard to tell if that's a brag or a fact.

1. **Click the Cortana Can Do Much More link.**

   After a couple of screens of unabashed braggadocio, delivered in a most tasteful way, Cortana asks if she can look at your location, contacts, email, browser history, search history, calendar and other info, as in Figure 6-3.

2. **If you're ready to let Cortana into your life, scroll down and click Sure.**

   You can read the privacy statement, if you really want to wade through 147 pages of dense legalese.

   Cortana asks if she can use your account to personalize your experience.

Hey, Cortana!

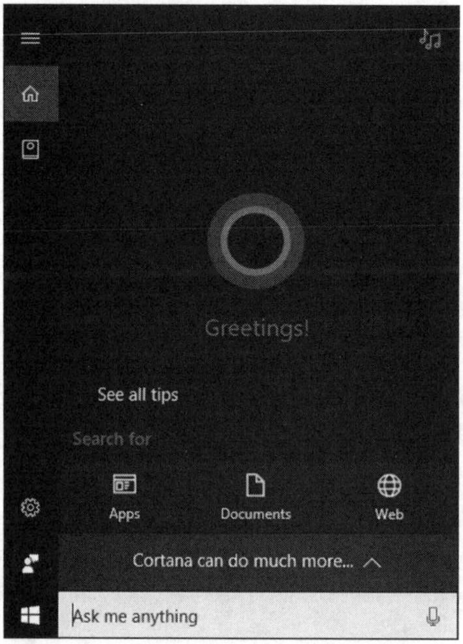

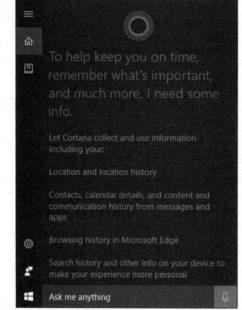

FIGURE 6-2:
Start by letting
Cortana in
the door.

FIGURE 6-3:
Time to fish
or cut bait.

3. **If you're willing to open up everything to Cortana's perusal (and filing), click Sign In.**

Cortana picks up your location and any other information you have stored with your Microsoft account, and shows you the latest local weather and news.

4. **Scroll down to the bottom of the Cortana news list. Where you see the question "Want traffic updates? I need your home address." Click Enter Address, and tell Cortana where to find you, if you feel so inclined.**

Cortana asks if you want to talk like real pals, so she can respond when you say, "Hey, Cortana!" She also wants to watch your typing history and your speech and handwriting.

5. **If you'd like to let a 500-year-in-the-future AI listen to everything you say, attempting to parse the words "Hey, Cortana!" click Sure.**

6. **When Cortana shows you a nonsense question, click the notebook icon (on the left bar of the Cortana pop-up), and then click About Me.**

A bunch of customizing options appear, as in Figure 6-4.

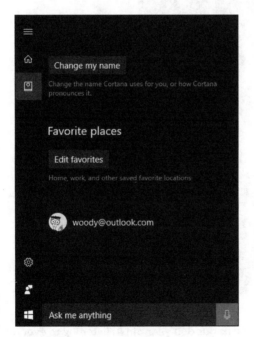

FIGURE 6-4:
Start the
customizing.

7. Make the following customizations:

a. *Click Change My Name.*

b. *Type the name you want Cortana to use for you.* I'll be first to pay obeisance to our AI overlords when the time comes, but for now I'll just have her call me Boss.

c. *Click Enter.*

d. *Click the Hear How I'll Say It link.* Cortana then tries to pronounce your name.

e. *If her pronunciation sounds good, click Sounds Good.*

f. *Make other customizations by clicking Edit Favorites and then Locate Family.*

g. *When you get tired of customizing, click the Settings (wheel) icon on the bottom left.*

Cortana lists another bunch of customizing options, shown in Figure 6-5.

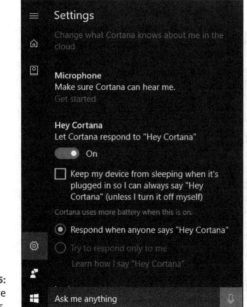

8. If you don't mind a minus-500-year-old AI listening to everything in your office:

a. *Slide the Hey Cortana entry to Yes.* Cortana warns you that, if you want her to listen all the time, the computer can't go to sleep.

b. *Click Yes.*

9. **Say "Hey, Cortana!"**

If that doesn't rouse the old biddy, click inside the Ask Me Anything search box and then ask your question. I tried, "What is the sound of one hand clapping?" All I got was a Bing search.

After the first time or two, Cortana gets the idea that she's supposed to be listening for the sound of your voice.

10. **Practice asking all sorts of questions. Test a bit.**

You'll find that you need to pause slightly after saying "Hey, Cortana." For example, if I say "Hey, Cortana" (pause a second) "How is the weather," I get a response like the one in Figure 6-6.

FIGURE 6-6: Cortana's great at telling you the MSN weather forecast.

Setting up Cortana

Cortana's still a fledgling. As time goes by, we're assured, she'll get better and better at bringing up information that interests you, collating things like your flight schedules, warning about appointments, and on and on.

That said, there's much you can do with and to Cortana right now. If you open up the Ask Me Anything search bar (click in the bar or say "Hey, Cortana," if she's listening), you get four settings under the hamburger icon. See the left side of Figure 6-4. Here are the icons and what they do:

 » **Home:** This is where you start if you don't ask a question, brings up a list of cards that are supposed to reflect your interests. At this point, that usually means local news, as in Figure 6-7.

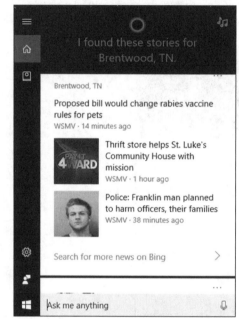

FIGURE 6-7: The home page has cards of items that interest you. Sorta.

» **Notebook:** This icon displays the Notebook (see Figure 6-8). You use the Notebook to make choices and recommendations, to help guide Cortana in her pursuit of personal assistanceship. Or something like that.

For example, the About Me entry at the top of the Notebook list brings up a pane that lets you change your name and the way Cortana pronounces your name. You can also add favorite places, including home and work locations. Favorites is an odd one because it ties into the Universal Windows Map app. In Figure 6-9, I added Homer, Alaska, to my list of favorites and set it as my work location.

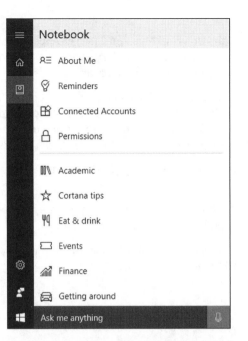

FIGURE 6-8:
The Notebook
contains all sorts
of settings.

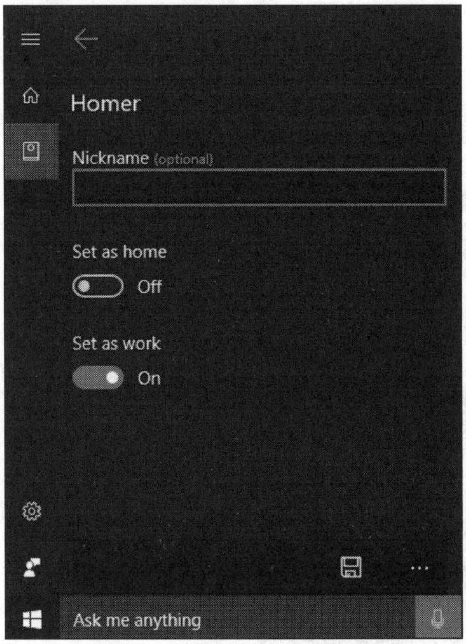

FIGURE 6-9:
Get to Homer the
hard way. Alaska
Highway,
here I come!

If I then cranked up the Universal Map app (Start, All Apps, Maps), Homer is listed as my work location, and Maps dutifully gives me full driving directions — for 70 hours and 4,000 miles. Now *that's* a commute.

ASK WOODY.COM

Follow through the Notebook sections and you can tell Cortana about your food preferences, which stocks you own, what kind of movies you like, your music preferences, weather locations, news, sports and travel preferences, and the color of your favorite vegetable. (Okay, I fibbed a bit.) It's loaded.

The Notebook also contains the settings for all of Cortana, which I discuss at the end of this chapter.

>> **Settings:** The gear icon displays settings ato turn off the microphone and to allow Cortana to respond when you say "Hey Cortana."

>> **Feedback:** The last icon, which looks like a dummy staring at a projector screen, lets you make suggestions for Cortana.

Using Cortana Settings

The most important part of Cortana comes when you click the Settings icon. You see the main settings in Figure 6-5. Scroll down a bit and you'll see the privacy stuff, as shown in Figure 6-10.

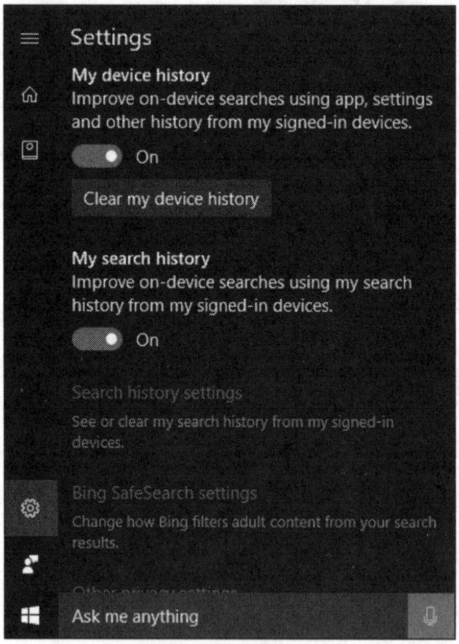

Settings

My device history
Improve on-device searches using app, settings and other history from my signed-in devices.

On

Clear my device history

My search history
Improve on-device searches using my search history from my signed-in devices.

On

Search history settings

See or clear my search history from my signed-in devices.

Bing SafeSearch settings

Change how Bing filters adult content from your search results.

Other privacy settings

Ask me anything

FIGURE 6-10: Cortana's settings lead to interesting places.